POLITICAL THEORY AND THE ENVIRONMENT

A Reassessment

Of Related Interest

ECOLOGY AND DEMOCRACY
edited by Freya Mathews

ECOLOGICAL MODERNISATION AROUND THE WORLD
Perspectives and Critical Debates
edited by Arthur P. Mol and David Sonnenfeld

DILEMMAS OF TRANSITION
The Environment, Democracy and Economic Reform in East Central Europe
edited by Susan Baker and Petr Jehlička

ENVIRONMENTAL MOVEMENTS
Local, National and Global
edited by Christopher Rootes

POLITICAL THEORY AND THE ENVIRONMENT
A Reassessment

Edited by
MATHEW HUMPHREY
University of Nottingham

FRANK CASS
LONDON • PORTLAND, OR

First published in 2001 in Great Britain by
FRANK CASS PUBLISHERS
Crown House, 47 Chase Side,
London, N14 5BP, England

and in the United States of America by
FRANK CASS PUBLISHERS
c/o ISBS
5824 N.E. Hassalo Street
Portland, Oregon 97213-3644

Website: www.frankcass.com

British Library Cataloguing in Publication Data

Political theory and the environment : a reassessment
1.Green movement 2.Political ecology
I.Humphrey, Mathew II.Environmental politics
320.5

ISBN 0 7146 5181 8 (cloth)
ISBN 0 7146 8187 3 (paper)

Library of Congress Cataloging in Publication Data

Political theory and the environment : a reassessment / edited by Mathew Humphrey.
p. cm.
Published also as a special issue of Environmental politics, v. 10, no. 1, spring 2001
Includes bibliographical references and index.
ISBN 0-7146-5181-8 (cloth) – ISBN 0-7146-8187–3 (pbk.)
1.Green movement. 2. Political ecology. I. Humphrey, Mathew,
1962- . II. Environmental politics.
JA75.8 .P646 2001
320.5–dc21

2001028705

This group of studies first appeared in a Special Issue: 'Political Theory and the Environment: A Reassessment' of *Environmental Politics* (ISSN 0964-4016) 10/1 Spring 2001 published by Frank Cass.

Printed in Great Britain by
Antony Rowe Ltd., Chippenham, Wilts.

Contents

Reassessing Ecology and Political Theory

MATHEW HUMPHREY

The 'reassessment' referred to in the subtitle of this edited special edition of *Environmental Politics* refers, crucially, to a rethinking *from within*. The most important project currently under way in environmental political philosophy is the reconstruction of a positive environmental agenda which is cognisant of the various critiques of green political thought that have been articulated since the 'first wave' of green literature in the 1960s and 70s. The context of, and justification for, this edited collection is best provided by a brief intellectual history.

From the 1960s, green political thought (and environmentally inclined political thought more generally) has had its own developmental history. To say that there have been 'three waves' of literature is inevitably to simplify considerably, but this characterisation also captures an important truth. If we take Rachel Carson's *Silent Spring* as a fairly conventional starting point, we see a 'first wave' of literature that sought to alert a readership to a new set of environmental problems. This literature was distinguished from earlier writing on environmental themes in that these problems were taken to be structurally, rather than contingently, attached to conventional models of economic and technological development. They were also taken to be global in scope, and to imply absolute limits to the possibilities of economic development around the world [*Carson, 1965; Daly, 1973; Ehrlich, 1968; Goldsmith, 1972, Meadows et al., 1974*]. An important political corollary to this view, which developed as various writers tried to think through the implications of environmental degradation, was a sense of pessimism about the possibility of maintaining the liberal-democratic form of government in the light of these apparent ecological problems. A world in which people were free to choose modes of behaviour according to an understanding of their self-interest would inevitably conflict with the kind of ecological outcomes that were valued in this literature. The solution lay at the very least in 'mutual coercion mutually agreed upon', and possibly upon a coercive global government dedicated to ecological ends, and with the power to overcome the 'tragedy of the commons'. [*Hardin, 1968; Heilbroner, 1974; Ophuls, 1977*].

This 'eco-doomsday' scenario of the 1960s and early 1970s produced a predictable backlash, from a variety of sources. Mainstream economists maintained that the forecasts of resource depletion, maximum capacity sink-resource use, and the ecological stresses caused by human population growth in environmental literature were massively over-pessimistic (famously, Julian Simon won a bet with Paul Ehrlich over the future prices of a set of primary resources) [*Beckerman, 1974; Simon and Kahn, 1984*]. Socialists claimed that ecologists had overlooked the crucial question of resource distribution and social justice in their critiques of industrial society, and that the more correct target was still capitalism [*Ensensberger, 1974*; *Pepper, 1993; Weston, 1982*]. Meanwhile libertarians stressed the apparently authoritarian implications of the political measures advocated by environmentalists [*McHallam, 1991*].

It is clear that at least some of these critiques hit their target. However, rather than forcing an abandonment of the political-ecological project, they have instead led to a critical revision of green political thought on the part of both scholars and activists who share ecological concerns. The 'first wave' of literature alerted the public to a problem, and has placed environmentalism on the political map - permanently. The 'second', critical wave of literature provided the impetus to a needed rethinking of the position that ecologists and environmentalists wanted to adopt. Now a 'third' wave of literature has emerged, which again places environmental concerns at its core, but in a more reflective, nuanced, and critically aware manner than its first wave predecessor. (As I say, my account simplifies, I would not disagree with Dobson's contention that the critical literature has also become more sophisticated [*Dobson, 1995: 204*].) I would cite as exemplary in this regard the recent books by John Barry [*1999*], Andrew Dobson [*1998*] and Tim Hayward [*1998*]. The epistemological, ontological, economic and political assumptions of the first wave of literature all now stand questioned within the parameters of environmental political philosophy itself. This does not mean, however, that what I have called the second wave critique has itself been adopted uncritically – far from it, much of it stands rejected. What it has catalysed, instead, is an immanent critique from environmental theorists of their own concepts, ideas, and value commitments – and as a result these theorists are in the process of developing a more satisfying account of ecological political theory and philosophy.

This special issue of *Environmental Politics* seeks to carry this important project forward by providing a forum for a number of analyses offering a sympathetic, reconstructive critique of elements of existing environmental political philosophy. This is what gives intellectual coherence to a collection of essays that *in toto* survey a broad area of the ideational landscape.

The Contents of this Volume

The essays collected here fall, without an excessive amount of gerrymandering, into two broad categories of concern, which we might call 'blind-spots' on the one hand, and 'errors in argument' on the other. That is, the process of reconstructing political-ecological thought is held by the authors of this collection to require either

1) a 'correction of vision' on the part of green theorists such that particular areas, issues, or objectives come more clearly into view and are dealt with explicitly.

And/or

2) A 'correction of argument' in areas where green political theory is taken to have gone astray in its lines of reasoning, strategies, or failure to understand the implications of its own position.

On the question of 'blindspots', the first essay, from Andrew Light, seeks to shed light upon "the urban blindspot in environmental thought" in both environmental ethics and in political ecology. Light argues that, because most environmental ethicists (a paradigmatic example being a thinker such as Holmes Rolston III) tend to think of nature and culture as distinct spheres of ethical concern, and focus almost exclusively on the former, 'non-natural' environments are left lacking philosophical grounds for protection and are sometimes held up as examples of environmental disvalue. The picture in political ecology is more complex, as social ecology, in particular, has not ignored the urban environment. None the less in general an urban blindspot persists even here. Light offers us an argument to the effect that the anti-urban bias in environmental ethics and political ecology is counter-productive and needs to be overcome.

The second area in which environmental ethics is accused of suffering a blindspot is that of property theory. In particular, Breen's contribution to this volume holds that whilst ecocentric theorists have been "vigorous in rejection of dominant western ideas of property" they have been surprisingly neglectful of the task of developing an alternative theory of property in accord with their own ethical position. Breen's account attempts to inject some theroretical clarity into ecocentrism through an examination of its theoretical foundations. She then builds upon this an argument for an ecocentric theory of property based on a two-factor system of weighted interests.

The third contribution to the 'blindspot' section concerns ecofeminism, and what the author perceives as its failure to comprehend its own utopian aspirations and thus its own potential. Lucy Sargisson explores the implications of a coming-together of feminism and ecologism. They have shared thematic preoccupations, including challenges to traditionally conceived notions of the public and the private, the nature of the political, and a concern to imagine alternative ways of being. Both are, on Sargisson's reading, therefore utopian movements. Ecofeminism has, however, to date failed to capitalise upon its own utopian possibilities. The meeting of feminism and ecologism on the terrain of utopia permits the creation of a 'new/no conceptual space' in which creative thinking can flourish.

Niraja Jayal's study on the need to balance political and ecological values would have fitted well in either section, as she argues both that environmental ethicists have tended to disregard particular human and environmental problems that exist in the Third World, and that the relationship between ecological values and (broadly liberal) political values has not been adequately theorised to date. Through the use of environmental conflict in India as a case study, Jayal demonstrates that it is in the third world that we most forcefully encounter the lack of a neat 'fit' between a story of environmental degradation on the one hand, and human interests on the other. This divergence results in forms of social domination. Ultimately there is a need to work human specificities into an anthropocentric environmental ethic, such that differences in human locations and human histories, class, and gender can all be accounted for when ecological and liberal political values conflict.

Turning from blindspots to cases where green theory is held to be in error on the grounds of using mistaken arguments, this section begins with a paper on intergenerational justice. Terry Ball examines some of the problems involved in thinking about the problem of intergenerational justice. Ball argues that the two dominant views – that future generations have no demands based in justice because of lack of recipriocity, and alternatively that we need a radically new discourse if we are to understand our obligations to future generations – are both deficient. Deficient because they presuppose an untenable view of the process of 'conceptual change'. Liberal-individualistic conceptions of justice and rights are not fixed and frozen, but open to challenge and contestation from *within* the discourse of liberal individualism. Ball introduces the notion of 'punctuated reciprocity' to show that we can speak meaningfully and coherently about our obligations to act justly towards posterity through the recognition of two well established liberal principles, life and liberty.

The analysis by Avner de-Shalit examines failures of environmental activism, and asks how we can theorise these in order to understand their causes more adequately. Such failures are frequently attributed to the structural problems environmentalists face within a particular political system. De-Shalit asks, in contrast, to what extent environmental activists are themselves responsible for the failures of some environmental campaigns. He finds that there are ten crucial decision areas where the wrong choices increase the likelihood of campaign failure. Unfortunately for environmental activists, these mistaken strategies are pursued all too frequently.

Finally, Mathew Humphrey examines the notion of 'irreversibility' as it has been used in environmental discourse. He suggests that there has been a rather easy assumption on the part of some ecological theorists that the possibility of undergoing 'irreversible change' is a property unique to natural objects, or at least a close-to-unique property. The possession of this property is then used to bolster arguments for preservation, sustainability and the retention of option-value. Whilst accepting that there is a common-sense understanding of irreversibility by which these claims are true and important, it is worth investigating the theoretical effects that follow from taking seriously the proposition, from the philosophy of science, that irreversibility is a 'normal state of the universe' and as such applicable to a far wider class of objects than environmental goods. An appreciation of this understanding of 'strict irreversibility' may change some of the ways in which we think about relevant considerations in environmental decision making.

Theorising environmental politics is an ongoing process. There is no 'last word', at least partly because environmental theory has to keep pace with the physical changes to the natural world that human beings are capable of bringing about. Environmental political philosophy, as it develops, is also becoming increasingly sensitised to the requirement that it must acknowledge other political values than environmental ones, particularly questions of distributive justice, democracy, and freedom. This makes for more difficult and complex theory building, but, as a consequence, it also makes for more satisfying theory. This volume will, we hope, contribute something to these developments.

REFERENCES

Barry, John (1999), *Rethinking Green Politics*, London: Sage.

Beckerman, Wilfred (1974), *In Defence of Economic Growth*, London: Jonathon Cape.

Carson, Rachel (1965), *Silent Spring*, Harmondsworth: Penguin.

Daly, Herman (ed.) (1973), *Toward a Steady-State Economy*, San Francisco, CA: Freeman.

Dobson, Andrew (1995), *Green Political Thought*, Second Edition, London: Routledge.

Dobson, Andrew (1998), *Justice and the Environment*, Oxford: Oxford University Press.

Ehrlich, Paul (1968), *The Population Bomb*, New York: Ballantine.

Ensensburger, Hans-Magnus (1974), 'A Critique of Political Ecology', *New Left Review* 84, pp.3–32.

Goldsmith, Edward (1972), *A Blueprint for Survival*, London: Tom Stacey.

Hardin, Garrett (1968), 'Tragedy of the Commons', *Science*, Vol.162, pp.1243–48.

Hayward, Tim (1998), *Political Theory and Ecological Values*, Cambridge: Polity.

Heilbroner, Robert (1974), *An Inquiry into the Human Prospect*, New York: Harper & Row.

McHallam, Andrew (1991), *The New Authoritarians*, London: Institute for European Defence and Strategic Studies.

Meadows, D. Meadows, D. Randers, J. and W. Behrens III (1974), *The Limits to Growth*, London: Pan.

Ophuls, William (1977), 'The Politics of a Sustainable Society', in Pirages (ed.), *The Sustainable Society*, New York: Praeger.

Pepper, David (1993), *Eco-socialism*, London: Routledge.

Simon, Julian and Herman Kahn (1984), *The Resourceful Earth: A Response to Global 2000*, Oxford: Blackwell.

Weston, Joe (ed.) (1982), *Red and Green: the New Politics of the Environment*, London: Pluto.

The Urban Blind Spot in Environmental Ethics

ANDREW LIGHT

Sometime around 5:00 p.m. on a winter's day, I look up from my desk in my office at New York University, glance out of my south facing window and immediately think, 'the stars have come out, it's going to be a beautiful night'. This really is my first unreflective thought, even though what I am looking at are not points of light in the celestial firmament, but the twinkling windows of the top few floors of the twin towers of lower Manhattan, the World Trade Center. Now that the leaves have fallen from the oak tree outside, I can see the tops of the towers poking above the four-storey turn-of-the-century brick buildings across the street. It is an old urban metaphor to be sure, and maybe even a bit trite: the city lights bring the stars down from the heavens. But there is something to it. And the occasional flash from a tourist's camera, vainly trying to capture dusk over the city from the observation tower, helps the illusion. There is even a flashing red planet suspended above the structure, apparently, and conveniently, always at its perihelion. Everything one needs to capture a star gazer's imagination.

Still, as has become increasingly familiar in the last few decades, the lights of the city do not ignite the romantic imaginations of us all. The rise of environmental awareness in the US, continuing a steady climb from the publication of Rachel Carson's *Silent Spring* through the first Earth Day in April 1970, to the election of a self-styled environmental Vice-President in 1992, has brought along with it an anti-urbanism which sees the illumination of Manhattan as at best hazardous light pollution. At worst, the urban stars represent the technological hubris of humans foolish enough to think they are now independent from nature if not an outright embodiment of human domination over the natural world. Perhaps, it has even been argued, urban dwellers suffer from a moral corruption, disconnected as they are from what E.O. Wilson calls 'biophilia'. Certainly, it does not help matters much that the highest points in the particular urban galaxy I am looking at now are in the financial district.

But one wonders if it has to be this way? Is the city really the source of all environmental ills, covered only by a thin veneer of cultural accomplishment? Or is it in fact one of the most important front lines of environmental issues, a terrain of environmental values and which will be the true test of the ecological acumen and social pluralism of the environmental community? In order to seriously consider this last possibility, we must first acknowledge the blind spot, if not anti-urban bias in environmental thought. Only then, like the analysand on the psychologist's coach, will we realise that we have a problem worth confronting.

Many environmental social scientists and historians, including William Cronon, Mark Dowie, and David Schlosberg, have pointed to this urban gap in environmentalists' theories, practices and organisations. But philosophers have been relatively silent on the matter. Until recently, the literature on urban environmental ethics contained only a handful of articles, mostly on very specific topics such as the ethics of personal automobile use. We still await any word on the topic from the leading ethicists in the field today. By and large, cities are considered sources of environmental disvalue: a landscape either to be mined for examples to be avoided or ignored all together as a product of human intentions – an artifact rather than part of nature and so outside of the appropriate boundaries of the discipline.

The purpose of this contribution is to help to rectify this disciplinary lacuna. My goal is to first (in sections I and II), offer an explanation for why the urban environment has been discounted in environmental ethics (though along the way I will offer a bit by way of reasons for a similar lapse in the environmental movement in North America); second, provide a series of arguments for why an ecologically and socially responsible environmentalism must not overlook the importance of urban issues, and finally, offer an example of how the city can serve as a unique site for environmental education, if not ecological citizenship, over and above available resources in the countryside or the wild.

Environmentalists need not resort to a language that replaces the non-human world with an artificial one – for reasons romantic or not – in order to see the city as a source of environmental value. We only need to accept the task of self-criticism when faced with our prejudices concerning natural value and recognise the central and necessary importance of urban questions in ecological renewal. If environmental ethicists (and the larger environmental community) do not take up this task then we will fail in making any lasting contribution to the pursuit of long-term environmental sustainability.

I. The Non-anthropocentric Prejudice of Environmental Ethics

Over the last three decades the field of environmental ethics has come to organise itself around discrete sets of philosophical, political, and practical issues. But especially in North America, environmental philosophy has been dominated by a concern with more abstract questions of value theory, primarily focused on the issue of whether nature has 'intrinsic value', or some other form of non-instrumental value. If such value can be justified independent of human consideration then it is an instance of what environmental ethicists call 'non-anthropocentric' value, or sometimes biocentric or ecocentric value, as opposed to anthropocentric, or human-centred forms of valuation which have dominated the history of ethics in the West. If nature has such non-instrumental non-anthropocentric value (similar to the sort of value that traditional ethical theories attribute only to humans) then, so most of the major theorists in environmental philosophy would argue, a wide range of duties, obligations, and rights obtain in our treatment of it.

Curiously however, environmental ethicists are largely silent about urban environmental issues, let alone the normative status of urban environments. In a recent, and extremely rare article on the subject, Alastair Gunn reports that in three recent and top selling textbooks on the subject, out of nearly 200 readings between them, not one single selection deals explicitly with cities [*Gunn, 1998*].[1] Some authors even appear outright hostile to the potential of finding value in humanly produced cultural landscapes. My claim here is that this dismissal of the built world and urban environmental problems can be traced to the foundations of the field in the search for non-anthropocentric forms of non-instrumental value. What then is the attraction of non-anthropocentrism? Why would the field of environmental ethics so narrowly define itself so as to not be applicable to all environments? The answer is that for the vast majority of environmental ethicists, the embrace of non-anthropocentric foundations for an environmental ethics has entailed a necessary rejection of anthropocentric forms of value, and I would argue, consequently, of anthropogenically created landscapes. But understanding the importance of the rejection of anthropocentrism in environmental ethics takes some explanation.

Since the beginnings of the field in the early 1970s, environmental ethicists have rejected anthropocentric schemes of moral consideration as both part of the cause of the current environmental crisis and as an impediment to any solution to those problems.[2] While the rejection of anthropocentrism has been far from univocal in the short history of the field, it is still arguably true that the vast majority of environmental ethicists reject anthropocentrism as a plausible foundation for an environmental philosophy in general or a theory of the value of nature in particular.[3] The burden of proof in the literature is clearly on the proponents of anthropocentrism and not on the opponents. Non-anthropocentrism can be taken as an uncontroversial starting point in any of the major journals in the field more, I would claim, as an accepted prejudice than as a proven position.

What is the problem with anthropocentrism for an environmental ethics? If we take anthropocentrism to be a description of the 'attitudes, values, or practices which promote human interests at the expense of the interests or well-being of other species or the environment', then it is not difficult to see why the view is objectionable from a standpoint committed to environmental sustainability.[4] If the natural world is measured only by the yardstick of human needs then what moral justification will exist to preserve it? From the beginning of the field, several authors pointed out that this view necessarily had to be answered in order to proceed with the development of an environmental ethic. In his early article, 'Is There a Need for a New, an Environmental Ethic?' which was quite influential in laying the tasks of the emerging field, Richard Sylvan (then Routley) put it this way:

> It is increasingly said that civilization, Western civilization at least, stands in need of a new ethic (and derivatively of a new economics) setting out people's relations to the natural environment, in [Aldo] Leopold's words, 'an ethic dealing with man's relation to land and to the animals and plants which grow upon it'. It is not of course that old and prevailing ethics do not deal with man's relation to nature; they do, and on the prevailing view man is free to deal with nature as he pleases, i.e., his relations with nature, insofar at least as they do not affect others, are not subject to moral censure [*Sylvan, 1973: 205*].

Sylvan went on to term anthropocentrism 'the despotic view'. Importantly here for Sylvan, as for many others, the predominance of anthropocentrism was partly explainable by the history of Western philosophy which had upheld it as a defensible assumption if not a formal principle. In this sense, the philosophical rejection of the metaphysical and moral justifications of anthropocentrism which had emerged in the history of philosophy became one of the principle tasks of an environmental philosophy.

It is clear however that the original target of anthropocentrism was of a particular from of anthropocentrism, namely one that maintains that human interests will always prevail at the expense of non-human interests. But there seems to be no clear reason why this characterisation of anthropocentrism as despotism would exclusively capture all possible interpretations of the relationship between humans and nonhumans from a human point of view. In one of the early articles in the field trying to describe an alternative conception of anthropocentrism to the despotic view, Bryan Norton pointed out how anthropocentrism, as characterised by Sylvan, was necessarily connected to a pernicious form of instrumentalism, thus providing environmental ethics with a distinctive niche:

> ... the question of whether environmental ethics is distinctive [Sylvan's question] is taken as equivalent to the question of whether

> an environmental ethic must reject anthropocentrism. … Environmental ethics is seen as distinctive *vis-à-vis* standard ethics if and only if environmental ethics can be founded upon principles which assert or presuppose that nonhuman natural entities have value independent of human value. … Anthropocentrists are therefore taken to believe that every instance of value originates in a contribution to human values and that all elements of nature can, at most, have value instrumental to the satisfaction of human interests [*Norton, 1984: 182–3*].

From here Norton went on to describe an alternative foundation for environmental ethics, called 'weak anthropocentrism', which he claimed captured the sense that humans could, for a variety of reasons, find value in nature for human-centred reasons which would not lead to a crude description of nature as a mere instrumental resource for human ends. But interestingly enough, the view that anthropocentrism is wedded to a crude instrumentalism persists in some forms to this day even while the reliance on intrinsic value as the locus of non-anthropocentric descriptions of the value of nature is waning. In a fairly recent debate between Norton and J. Baird Callicott, a subjectivist about intrinsic value (one who argues that values, intrinsic or not, must originate in a valuing agent, human or nonhuman), it is clear that the connection between anthropocentrism and instrumentalism drives the continued rejection of appeals to human interests as appropriate foundations for an environmental ethic [*Norton, 1995; Callicott, 1996*].

What explains the continued rejection of anthropocentrism in environmental ethics? I believe that the answer still lies behind the worries about the reduction to instrumental valuation implied in Sylvan's work and drawn out by Norton. But important for me for this discussion is not so much that anthropocentric value is considered to be equivalent to the instrumental valuation of nature but that anthropocentrism is perceived as incapable of providing the grounds for a guaranteed rejection of certain cultural forms of valuing nature. At bottom, the worry of non-anthropocentrists is more over allowing environmental issues to be decided in terms of human preferences, preferences which are ground in cultural norms and social practices. The early critique of anthropocentrism because of its instrumentalism was in fact embedded within a critique of the perceived cultural relativity of most contemporary environmental policies. At the end of his original 1973 article Sylvan provides an example of just this sort of worry.

> … it would just be a happy accident, it seems, if collective demand for a state of the economy with blue whales as a mixed good, were to succeed in outweighing private whaling demands; for if no one in the base class happened to know that blue whales exist or cared a jot that

> they do then 'rational' economic decision-making [a form of anthropocentric instrumental valuation] would do nothing to prevent their extinction [*Sylvan, 1973: 210*].

Paul Taylor brings this claim for an acultural foundation for natural value home further, and more forcefully, by arguing that anthropocentric value is always 'entirely relative to culture: if any particular society did not hold ideals that could be symbolized in nature and wildlife (for example, if it happened to value plastic trees more than real ones), then there would be *no reason* for that society to preserve nature or protect wildlife' [*Taylor, 1984: 151, n5*].[5]

What is the connection though between the rejection by environmental ethicists of anthropocentrism and their silence about urban issues? The answer involves the fact that since many if not most environmental ethicists see the principle goal of their inquiry to involve the identification of an acultural non-anthropocentric value in or for nature, most theorists focus in their work on what they perceive to be pristine forms of natural value, such as wilderness areas, as exemplar forms of this value. If nature is to be considered as valuable in itself then, however the ground of that value is metaphysically or ontologically conceived, it will be best identified in those areas relatively independent of human intervention as opposed to those humanly shaped areas which exemplify exactly those culturally bound preferences that many environmental ethicists wish to reject.

II. Wilderness and the Geographical Dualism of Environmental Ethics

Take, for example, the work of Holmes Rolston III, widely considered to be the dean of North American environmental ethics. Any reader of Rolston knows of the focus in his work over the years on wilderness issues and most sympathetic readers regard this focus as entirely appropriate. In one of his more famous essays on the topic, 'Values Gone Wild', Rolston exemplifies the intuition that a nonanthropocentric ethic starts in the realisation of the value of wilderness and then moves on to re-evaluate other spheres of cultural value:

> Only about 2 percent of the contiguous United States remains wilderness; 98 percent is farmed, grazed, timbered, hunted over, dwelt upon, paved, or otherwise possessed. … But … when the wildness is almost conquered, we begin to awake to error in the mastery theory. Not all value is labored for, assigned, or realized at our coming. The anomalous 2 percent that we will to keep wild, and then realize to be valuable without our will, reveals that the theory of value that has governed our handling of the 98 percent is flawed, only an approximation over a certain range [*Rolston, 1989: 134–5*].

For Rolston, non-anthropocentrism in environmental ethics entails either an explicit or implicit conceptual division between nature and culture as divided spheres of moral and political concern. Nature is the source of value, and culture must now be reconceived as first, lacking the kind of value we find in pristine nature, and second, deserving of reassessment itself in relation to whatever value we find in culture. In a later essay considering the possibility of the human improvement of wild nature, Rolston's nature-culture division is evident: 'The architectures of nature and of culture are different, and when culture seeks to improve nature, the management intent spoils the wilderness. ... The cultural processes by their very 'nature' interrupt the evolutionary process: there is no symbiosis, there is antithesis' [*Rolston, 1998: 371*]. Such a nature-culture dualism is quite common in the work of other figures in the field as well [cf. *Katz, 1997*]. Those embracing this dualism tend to either discount the value of urban areas or ignore them, and hence urban environmental problems, altogether. Again, at the best a blind spot and at worst an anti-urban bias.

Philosophers are not alone in this focus on wilderness. Mark Dowie, in his excellent survey of the recent history of the environmental movement, points out that the image of the environmentalist as backpacker and tree-hugger has persisted throughout the history of environmentalism in America. While many see this focus as more a tendency of the so called first wave of environmentalists at the turn of the century, for example, John Muir and his followers, even the second wave of environmentalism, which got off the ground in the 1960s and 1970s, embraces this wilderness focus: 'Environmentalism means wildlife protection and wilderness conservation, while the environmental movement is identified with the Sierra Club and similar organizations' [*Dowie, 1996: 6*]. David Schlosberg confirms Dowie's findings and argues that the recent rise of the environmental justice movement has been in direct relation not only to the perceived lack of minority representation on the boards of the major environmental groups, but also to the focus of these groups. The 'more telling complaint centered on the movement's focus on natural resources, wilderness, endangered species and the like, rather than toxics, public health, and the unjust distribution of environmental risks', exactly those issues that are of interest to low-income communities and committees of colour, largely in urban areas [*Schlosberg, 1999: 9*].

At this point however, many will object that my suggestion of a connection between non-anthropocentrism and an anti-urban bias or blind spot is true only of philosophers like Rolston who seek to ground a theory of natural intrinsic value in an objective basis which easily imports a form of nature–culture dualism. It is certainly true that for Rolston, values in nature are objective and not subjective. The intrinsic value of nature exists as a preexisting fact about the world, independent of any valuing agent. It is also true that subjectivists who endorse a theory of intrinsic value, such as Callicott, have argued against the idea of 'wilderness' as a meaningful term precisely because it perpetuates a contentious nature-culture divide [*Callicott, 1998*]. None the less, Callicott maintains that the central theoretical question of environmental ethics is the issue of whether nature has intrinsic value. Echoing Norton's interpretation of Sylvan's understanding of the foundations of the field, Callicott claims, 'if nature lacks intrinsic value, then non-anthropocentric environmental ethics is ruled out' [*Callicott, 1999: 241*]. While Callicott's critique of the focus on wilderness is to my mind laudatory, it is not surprising given his commitment to non-anthropocentrism to find little in his work about non-natural landscapes or urban environmental problems (an exception is Callicott [*1992*], which argues that cities are as much a part of nature as ocean reefs, but still falls far short of articulating an explicitly urban dimension to environmental ethics). Further, other subjective nonanthropocentrists who endorse a theory of intrinsic value, such as Robert Elliot, admit to a distinction between the value of nature and the value of humanly produced landscapes which leads them to controversial positions critiquing not only the value of humanly produced landscapes but attempts by humans to restore damaged natural landscapes as well [*Elliot, 1997*]. Clearly, nonanthropocentrism in environmental ethics in general either leads at worst to direct reasons to disvalue culturally produced landscapes or at best the tendency to ignore them as appropriate questions for environmental ethics.

Here however we must proceed cautiously. Even the staunchest advocate of the importance, even *sui generis* quality of wilderness values such as Rolston, does not claim that there is no value in human culture or in cities as one of the more remarkable expressions of that value. In one of his more recent books, after stipulating that the earth contains three environments, urban, rural, and wild, Rolston follows with the Aristotelian claim that humans are a political animal and that their 'essence is to build a *polis*, a town.' 'The city is in some sense our niche; we belong there, and no one can achieve full humanity without it' [*Rolston, 1994: 12–13*]. From our history of living in cities, according to Rolston, comes literacy and advancement, many things which make us human. So far, so good.

But the existence of wilderness, as suggested above, brings us something else: the recognition that all values are not simply the human values cultivated in cities. While in itself such a claim does not represent much of a problem for the appreciation of urban environmental issues, Rolston goes much further in reversing the priority of forms of valuation over that which we would find in a more conventional Aristotelian account:

> No one can form a comprehensive worldview without a concept of nature, and no one can form a view of nature without evaluating it in the wild, deliberating over spontaneous nature and whether and how it can have value. In that sense, one of the highest of cultural values, an examined worldview, is impossible to achieve without wild nature to be evaluated as foil to and indeed source of culture [*Rolston, 1994: 15*].

Many will no doubt find this claim curious. The explanatory hurdles involved in demonstrating first that nature has such a value, and second that the value of nature exerts such a grounding of other human values, are substantial to say the least. But Rolston goes on to make a case for his argument, ground in a claim to the importance of the natural origin of human culture as emerging from wilderness. And regardless of the conceptual problems with the view, even an anthropocentric environmental ethicist like Norton admits to the enormous influence of Rolston's version of intrinsic value on the literature, and in the wider environmental community.[8]

What I find more worrisome though is the implication, however justified, in a view like this one for urban questions, specifically the issue of the ontological or moral status of urban environments and experiences in those environments. Shortly after introducing this notion of the grounding of cultural values in the appreciation of the value of wilderness, Rolston clearly states that a full human life cannot be achieved in the city alone. Without being specific about what he is referring to, Rolston offers an account of the prevalence of environmental concern among urban dwellers (as opposed to rural people) to the 'depravation' that they feel in the city. Whatever this depravation is, it causes them to look outside of the city and become concerned with the wild. Accordingly, the urban dweller who does not look outside the city for sources of value, or what Rolston terms a 'mere' urban person, is 'one-dimensional; three-dimensional persons will know how appropriately to respect urban, rural and wild environments' [*Rolston, 1994: 15*].

Now certainly, many in the environmental community will find this claim uncontroversial. After all, the suggestion appears to simply be that a full life is lived not in one kind of environment but in many, and Rolston is giving cities their due as the source of a uniquely human form of value which still has some positive content. Who then would want to object to the claim that, all things considered, a life is better where one can appreciate the three different environments that Rolston identifies? But Rolston is not claiming that all three environments are equal. It is not just that a human is comparatively worse off if they do not 'respect', the wild, but that a human life is incomplete, that a human life is not wholly human, without the self-conscious knowledge of this respect.

I find this to be a very curious position. But to realise the gravity of this point it is important to note that, for Rolston, we humans do not live in the wild [*Rolston, 1994: 14*]. The wild is not our home, for presumably if it was then it would not be the wild. So, it is not as if we have a choice to become better persons by living in the wild and then round out that experience by coming to appreciate our experience of the urban as a source of equal value. This makes it clear that Rolston's is not simply an appeal to the plural value of various environments. We can only live in the urban or the rural and still maintain the division of the three kinds of environments that Rolston identifies. If the urban, rural, and wild were equal then respecting only one of them as a resident would be equally as bad as only respecting any other one of them as a resident. But humans cannot live in the wild so wherever we live, in the rural or urban environment, it is the wild that completes us because the wild is the home of nature, or in a sense, the home of our home as an evolved product of nature.

Further, note that Rolston is a bit more careful in this later work not to use the term 'experience' in his description of the kind of interaction we should have with the wild. The term used is 'respect'. We must respect the wild. But what does this respect entail? In Rolston's earlier work (and there is no explicit repudiation of this point that I can find) a full human life is only possible through the actual experience of the wild: 'Society is crucial for one aspect of persons, wilderness for another. Never to plunge into wilderness, never to expose oneself to it, is never to know either forest or self' [*Rolston, 1989: 230*]. So it is not just that one must respect or understand the importance of the wild, the rural, and the urban in relation to each other in order to be a fully three-dimensional human, one must actually experience the wild. The claim is then not simply that a richer life is lived, all things considered, by respecting the three environments of the Earth, but that missing experience in one deprives one of a full life. An analogous claim might be that a full life cannot be lived without experiencing a high point of urban culture, such as hearing a live performance of Chopin's *Etudes*. If Rolston were willing to say comparable things about urban experiences, perhaps those of us bothered by this suggestion could be partly pacified. We must respect the wild. But for every suggestion that the place of humans is in the polis, there are other suggestions that the city is a source of disvalue, specifically in terms of understanding one's self. 'Lostness plagues the urban, mobile world', says Rolston [*1989: 224*]. And elsewhere:

> Big-city life in a high rise apartment – to say nothing of the slums – or a day's work in a windowless, air-conditioned factory represents synthetic life filled with plastic everything from teeth to trees. Such

> life is foreign to our native, earthen element. We have lost touch with natural reality; life is, alas, artificial [*Rolston, 1998: 36*].

All life, apparently in the city, is not natural, not a part of nature. It is something wholly different. Parks, trees, vestiges of streams, let alone buildings and cultural landscapes, are not a part of nature. They are anthropogenically derived and anthropocentrically valued. Humans too, in some sense are unnatural in the city, or at least one-dimensional, unrooted, unless they experience the wild, the source of all value.

Anthropocentrism then is not simply a moral predicament, a hurdle to an environmental ethic which seeks to find a legitimate basis for the human-independent value of nature, but the bulwark of an inferior anthropogenically produced landscape. But why a rejection of anthropocentrism in ethics must lead to a denigration of the city as at best a second-class environment, it not clear at all. Arguably though, the blind spot toward the city or lack of attention to urban problems in environmental ethics has its roots in the movement from non-anthropocentrism to the point we find ourselves at in Rolston's work. Even if one believes that the foundations of the field in non-anthropocentrism are well grounded, here, clearly we have an undefended prejudice – a move from a critique of crass human-centred forms of valuation to a rejection of humanly produced landscapes, landscapes which cannot possibly bear any semblance of acultural descriptions of value. Even those subjectivist non-anthropocentrists who reject an acultural, objective ground for natural value, appear to let the agenda of the critical issues up for discussion be decided by wilderness advocates, hence producing the urban blind spot in their work as well.[9] This is not to say that preservation of those statutorily designated wild areas is unimportant, nor are issues involving species preservation and biodiversity loss unimportant. It is only to say that there is much more at stake under the big tent of environmental philosophy than seems to be getting attention and the reasons for this predicament do not seem to be very good ones.

In addition to the readily apparent conceptual nature-culture value dualism that Rolston assumes in his environmental ethic, and which has been the subject of strong criticisms by anthropocentrists like Norton and subjective non-anthropocentrists like Callicott, I find another dualism here which is potentially more damning: a *geographical dualism* between wilderness and cities which represents a bifurcation of two realms of existence, one containing 'nature', however Rolston conceives of nature, and one not containing nature by definition. While simply pointing out that a theoretical position contains a dualism does not in itself justify its rejection, here the upshot of this dualism is distressing: natural values do not exist in cities because cities do not contain nature. As a consequence, what many people would call 'environmental problems', or problems which concern the natural world, also do not exist in cities.[10]

While we will see below that other environmental ethicists share this same bias against the urban world as a world containing nature, it is important at this point to note how much support there is for Rolston's position in other fields as well. It is not as if non-anthropocentric environmental philosophers are the only ones prepared to make the claim that the experience of wild nature, or nature under a specific description, is the grounding draw of the essence of value and the essence of a good human life. Though I do not have the space here to do the theory justice, E.O. Wilson's biophilia hypothesis is rife with similar suggestions.

For Wilson, 'biophilia' is the name of the connections that human beings seek with the rest of life. But this love of life is not a chosen love, instead it is a naturally evolved inclination of humans toward nature. For Wilson, like Rolston, the human evolution of emotional, aesthetic and even spiritual cravings to be close to nature is a result of our origins in nature. As a naturally evolved species who spent most of our history in nature, we are shaped by the forces and complexity of nature. The only question is whether we will let our natural origins shape our forms of life.

> Humanity is part of nature, a species that evolved among other species. The more closely we identify ourselves with the rest of life, the more quickly we will be able to discover the sources of human sensibility and acquire the knowledge on which an enduring ethic, a sense of preferred direction, can be built [*Wilson, 1992: 348*].

The evolutionary 'imprint' on us in the form of our genetic nucleotide sequences, representing our long struggle in and with nature, 'cannot have been erased in a few generations of urban existence'. Evidence for this claim is found for Wilson in the tendency of humans to acquire phobias to objects and circumstances which threatened them in their natural environments – snakes, spiders, open spaces – rather than more modern dangers such as guns and automobiles. Additionally, people tend to prefer living near water where parkland can be viewed, and spend more time in leisure in parks, zoos and aquariums than athletic events [*Wilson, 1992: 349–50*]. And we should not be surprised to learn, at bottom, that biophilia is connected to the idea of wilderness. People are attracted to wilderness because it 'settles peace on the soul', and is 'beyond human contrivance' [*Wilson, 1992: 350*].

Not surprisingly, several philosophers have connected Wilson's biophilia hypothesis to the search in environmental ethics for a non-anthropocentric intrinsic value to nature.[11] What I find more striking though, and more worrisome, are Wilson's conclusions about the proper direction of environmental ethics following on the heels of such analysis. Though he claims not to be arguing for an innate human nature in his recitation of the common human predilections toward green spaces, Wilson is adamant that the existence of this residual attachment to wild nature in human consciousness is sufficient ground to claim that the philosophical task at hand is to focus on 'the central questions of human origins in the wild environment' [*Wilson, 1992: 351*].[12] It would appear that many environmental ethicists completely agree.

III. Why an Urban Environmental Ethics?

At this point I expect that some readers will be ready to completely discount Rolston and other anti-urbanists out of hand. Others, particularly colleagues in the field, will not. How then to respond?

The traditional answer to Rolston's anti-urbanism (or his geographical dualism) would be to take on the philosophical merits of his case. If nature, specifically wild nature, is the source and locus of some kind of fundamental value then what is the ground of that value, how is it manifest? Other philosophers such as Norton or Callicott have taken up this task with mixed results. One reason is that metaphysical and epistemological debates are rarely resolved to anyone's satisfaction, they tend to either limp along in the literature or die out with little by way of resolution or concession by one or another party. While philosophically stimulating, they don't go very far in helping to set an agenda for environmental philosophy which will enable it to contribute to the resolution of environmental problems rather than only to metaethical and metaphysical debates on the value and status of nature.

Importantly however, whatever one thinks of the philosophical merits of Rolston's case, or the many other environmental ethicists who hold views which are sympathetic to his geographical dualism, an anti-urban bias in the field, and in the larger environmental movement, persists and is likely to persist no matter what philosophical resources are committed to answering it. As was briefly pointed out above, environmental historians and social scientists have documented the anti-urbanism prevalent in many environmental organisations. Hating the city, or at least ignoring it, is a fact of life in environmental circles which is only now being challenged, though largely from outside of the main environmental movement. I would argue that no matter what its philosophical problems, the rhetorical force of Rolston's claims about the value of wilderness will most likely persist in the face of strong philosophical objections, at least as this force is measured in terms of its impact on the larger movement. Environmentalists tend to be snapshot phenomenologists, generalising their positive experiences in the wild as proof of the importance of the value of the wild and the unimportance of the things we would compare to it. It is no surprise to me that Rolston's form of environmental ethics and the environmental ontology of others, such as the deep ecology of Arne Naess, relies heavily on the experiential dimensions of wild nature as the source of human attitudinal change. After all, figures like Rolston and Naess emerged not just out of philosophy departments, but the movement as a whole. Strantgely though, only rarely have environmental professionals confronted the obvious dilemmas that arise from such claims about the importance of people experiencing wilderness: if experiences in wild nature are required for a greater environmental consciousness, or even for complete human self-actualisation as Rolston suggests, then the attainment of such experiences by a majority of the population would threaten the stability and viability of exactly those wild areas which environmentalists cherish.[13] None the less, Rolston's claims are intuitively appealing to a broad swath of the environmental movement, and I suspect of the general public as well. The unfortunate other side of the coin however is that we have learned to denigrate the city at the expense of Rolston's wild areas, and environmental philosophy appears well placed to encourage this attitude. How many of us, after all, environmentalists and non-environmentalists alike, will want to wade through turgid arguments in epistemology and metaphysics to decide whether our intuitions about the relative importance of experiences in wilderness and cities are correct?[14]

The philosophical arguments over the importance and value of wilderness, the validity of non-anthropocentrism, and the supposed problems with anthropocentrism can and should persist in the literature. But another tack may be taken as well in response to the geographical dualism at work in much environmental ethics and the urban blind spot that it engenders. I propose that we focus on two things to overcome this blind spot, rather than an engagement in the metaphysical and epistemological issues: (1) the importance in ecological terms of environmental issues in the urban context, and (2) the regressive social dimensions of an anti-urban bias in environmental thought. Let us call (1) the ecological question and (2) the social question. On the ecological question, again recall that even the most adamant defender of the priority of wild values such as Rolston admits to the cultural values produced in the city. Further, though somewhat less appealing to them, Rolston and other wilderness advocates accept that preservation of the wild must be pursued hand in hand with the movement for sustainable human communities [*Rolston, 1998*]. If a complete environmental ethics must acknowledge the normative and axiological connections between the urban, rural, and wild environments, as Rolston maintains, then surely it must acknowledge their resource connections as well. Seen from such a perspective, living in a city must entail a form of ecological citizenship – which I will loosely define here as a ground of moral and political environmental responsibility for one's duties to the human and natural communities one inhabits and interacts with – as well as a form of political citizenship. More on this last point will follow in section IV.

Focusing on the social question however is more difficult. I doubt that many non-anthropocentrists sympathetic to Rolston's views will give up his geographical dualism. But perhaps they may come to recognise that the anti-urban connotations of their views endanger any hope of forming a broad political consensus on environmental problems as well as implicating their views in morally suspicious connotations. Environmentalism has a long history of association with nativism, if not racism, which it has never been able to afford, and has chaffed against. Those who refuse to admit this moral lapse cannot be pragmatically reconciled with those who do. But before getting into this issue, what are the ecological grounds for a call for more attention to urban environmental problems?

Ignoring urban environmental issues is a crucial mistake for at least three ecological reasons, all of them almost painfully clear. First – even from the perspective of exactly that wilderness oriented philosophy which is at the centre of much contemporary environmental ethics – because of population pressures there is a direct trade-off between the ability to preserve non-urban areas and the extent to which urban spaces can be made livable. As suggested above, and acknowledged by psychologist Peter Kahn, we cannot all expect to have experiences in what is taken to be pristine wilderness and still preserve the existence of such a thing. Cities therefore must become at least one potential home for the sorts of experiences Rolston wants, or if not Rolston, the sorts of experiences that ethicists less enamored of geographical dualism see as important. Stephen Kellert is convinced that such experiences are possible in the city, claiming that the suggestion that there is insufficient opportunity for 'meaningful contact with the natural environment' in the city (as required by biophilia) reflects 'a false dichotomy between cities and nature' [*Kellert, 1996: 192*]. Though again I do not wish to cross swords with Rolston here about his ontological conception of the primacy of wild value, it is telling that no less an authority in environmental ethics circles than Aldo Leopold certainly had different intuitions: 'The weeds in a city lot convey the same lesson as the redwoods. ... Perception ... cannot be purchased with either learned degrees or dollars; it grows at home as well as abroad, and he who has a little may use it to as good advantage as he who has much' [*Leopold, 1996: 266*]. And even with such sentiments we are not even scratching the surface of the educational opportunities regarding nature which exist in urban areas. The biodiversity exhibit at the American Museum of Natural History in New York City is a good case in point. But in order for the city to serve this purpose we must attend to the environmental issues found within it. This is something environmental ethicists have not been doing.

Second, cities, even without a concentrated attempt at conservation efforts, engender economics of scale which consume less energy than rural areas or regions which sustain human populations alongside wilderness areas. In a recent article about the loss of conservation gains made during the late 1970s and early 1980s in the US, *The New York Times* reported a study which showed that more urbanised states tend to consume less energy per capita than less urbanised states. The lowest consumption rate went to New York state (215 BTUs on average) because so many residents live in New York City apartments (sharing walls and hence sharing heat) and do not own cars (nor regularly using them if they own them). The highest consumption rate went to Alaska, with 1,139 BTUs on average, five times as much energy consumed as a New Yorker. While surely climatic differences in part explain this gap, other states with the highest individual consumption included states with more compatible weather, such as Wyoming, North Dakota and Montana. The lowest consumption rates included Rhode Island and Massachusetts [*Myerson, 1998*]. While this is only one variable, it is important to note how important a variable it is. Transportation costs for food and other goods are remarkably similar in most parts of the country. Most Americans now consume hot house tomatoes from California; the amount of energy expended to bring food to Montana or Manhattan is, per capita, essentially the same. Each consumer dollar spent in the US also releases petroleum, but consumption is no greater on average in large urban areas than in suburbs, small towns, most rural areas. The same is true of most production. The energy savings from effective public transportation and dense living are arguably the most important structural differences between cities like New York and other residential areas in the US, all else remaining equal. Assuming that population levels and consumption rates remain constant (which, of course, we can hope that they will not), moving away from density is one of the single biggest hurdles for achieving environmental sustainability. It is the suburbanisation of cities, and the flights of populations to the countryside, that must be dissuaded.

It would seem then that encouraging urban dwelling does more good for the environment – even if the inhabitants who stay there are not fully self-actualised on Rolston's account – than living in states which are the home to preserved wilderness. Certainly, the prevalence of extractive industries in less populated states helps to account for their increased energy consumption, but this does not discount the importance of concentrated urban centers for energy savings. Further, if we were to generalise Rolston's argument that experience in the wild helps one to become more fully human, grounded, etc., then we could argue that the more such experiences the better. Perhaps even living close to a wilderness area, as Rolston does, is even the best, most preferred lifestyle for true ecological self-actualisation. But if living lightly on the earth is indicative of environmental responsibility, ecological citizenship if you will, then surely Manhattanites are doing more for the planet than our colleagues in Colorado. And importantly, New Yorkers need not self-consciously embrace a sense of environmental responsibility in order to live an inherently more sustainable lifestyle. This is a critical point. If some sort of environmental consciousness raising (through experience with the wild or otherwise) is required for environmental responsibility, then one should be fearful that such a change in consciousness will happen soon enough, or on a great enough scale, to forestall the worst consequences of the cumulative impact of humans on the planet. We should therefore nurture those forms of life that are structurally more sustainable. This does not give urbanites in densely populated cities a free pass. Development of an explicit environmental consciousness would be better for them too. But, as things stand now, it is encouraging that all New Yorkers are in a weak sense 'environmentalists' without having to do anything other than live as they live now. The task of an expanded urban environmental ethics must therefore include one of distinguishing more ecologically responsible urban development patterns from those that are not responsible. Endorsing the ecological values of dense urban living will provide a critique of the sprawl found in cities such as Atlanta and Houston.

Finally, third, anyone interested in the sustainability of larger biotic systems has to be concerned with the sustainability of the urban environment as one of the largest concentrated impacts on those systems, simply because of the higher populations of urban areas (even assuming resource savings such as those just suggested). Social scientists like Kellert have taken on this issue head on, as have progressive environmental planners and architects. Others have not. I will return to this point below. The ecological and social questions become blurred when we take up the issue of population, so at the end of this section I will provide an example of an environmentalist critique of cities which seems to be overlooking the importance of both issues in its focus on population problems.

Let us turn now to the social question. As I suggested before, environmentalists best prepare themselves for some harsh social criticisms if they wish to hold on to something like Rolston's geographical dualism. Direct accounts of how the urban blind spot implicates environmentalism in a regressive history provide a strong motivation for expanding the notion of what counts as a legitimate object of environmental concern. Particularly compelling and appropriate for the discussion so far is Avner de-Shalit's critique of what he calls 'ruralism' in environmental thought [*de-Shalit, 1996*]. Largely directed at environmental historians like Anna Bramwell, who read the history of environmentalism as contiguous with the history of late nineteenth and early twentieth century right-wing ideologies, de-Shalit provides a ground for criticising this trend in broader environmental thought as well. But de-Shalit argues that what is being described by Bramwell and implied in other progressive critiques of environmentalism, by figures such as Murray Bookchin, is ruralism rather than environmentalism. A key to understanding ruralism includes a recognition of its anti-urban bias: 'By "ruralism" I mean the glorification of country life, and a dissatisfaction with urbanism not only from the purely ecological point of view (e.g., as a source of pollution), but also because it is said to represent an inferior moral condition, or even a state of degeneration' [*de-Shalit, 1996: 50*]. Clearly we might want to consider the ruralist thesis as applying to theorists like Rolston. Unfortunately it also applies to fascist and nativist groups that Bramwell identifies as environmentalists, groups with whom Rolston would wish to distance himself.

In contrast, what de-Shalit considers to be true environmentalism, 'rather than preaching the superiority of rural life', is also 'concerned with improving our urban life, without a rejection of industrialism' [*de-Shalit, 1996: 51*]. But while I wholeheartedly agree with de-Shalit that environmentalism should be concerned with urban life and not romantically glorify any alternatives, rural or wild, it is clear even from de-Shalit's discussion that most environmental ethics and most environmentalism is actually not concerned with urban issues even if it ought to be. Though not necessarily ruralist, many environmentalists evoke racist and fascist accusations for not explicitly denying the negative critique of urbanism contained in ruralism and for suggesting that those who only reside in cities are missing an opportunity at full humanity. Rolston is not alone here. Other figures in the field unwittingly step into the same position from very different starting points.

Take, for example, David Abram's fairly recent appeal for a phenomenological basis for a new environmental awareness, and presumably a new environmental ethic [*Abram, 1996*]. On Abram's account a new animism is needed to recognise our connection with what he calls the 'more than human' natural world, which I interpret as Abram's form of non-anthropocentrism. But in his explanation for how this animism can be derived from a reinvigoration of our bodily senses, as interpreted through the work of Merleau-Ponty, the city becomes less interesting the more one rejuvenates a carnal empathy with the land. Just the initial step of becoming more aware of the blending and expansion of one's senses (which Abram identifies as the 'synaesthetic' view) reveals something akin to Rolston's suggestion of the one-dimensionality of urban experience. If we reacquaint ourselves with our 'breathing bodies', according to Abram, the world transforms itself: 'countless human artifacts with which we are commonly involved – the asphalt roads, chain-link fences, ... – all begin to exhibit a common style, and so to lose some of their distinctiveness' [*Abram, 1996: 62*] Mass produced artifacts of civilization 'draw our senses into a dance that endlessly reiterates itself *without variation*' [*Abram, 1996: 64*].

Abram's account here is a perfect example of an environmental theory which is set up, intentionally or not, to offer reasons to reject human built spaces as beyond the pale of environmental enlightenment, without resorting to an overt form of ruralism. In a presentation of this critique of Abram's work, Abram responded that he does not 'diss' the city, and that his phenomenological view provides the ground for reform of urban architecture as much as it establishes a connection with nature through the human senses.[16] But even though he does slightly qualify some of his critiques of urban space in his book, there are no comparable criticisms in Abram's work of non-urban space. As such, there is in principle more wrong with the city than with any other environment because it is more distant from original, wild nature. Those bound to the city by race, class or circumstance are those trapped in a less ennobling experience. This is exactly the urban bias that environmentalism needs to avoid and the morally pernicious implications of it are clear. If Abram thinks that his view does apply to urban environments as well, then in anticipation of the possible association of his view with a similar anti-urbanism as that found in ruralism, he should provide some positive examples of urban experience. But the blame cannot be laid solely at Abram's feet. If environmental ethics and environmentalism more broadly were thought of as not being restricted to non-urban issues, then perhaps Abram would have provided those examples as a matter of course.

As I said before at the end of my discussion of the ecological question, issues involving population pressures often cross whatever line we may wish to draw between these ecological and social questions which may motivate bringing urban concerns to the fore in environmental ethics. While many studies duplicate the ecological findings suggested above, that there are precious few substitutes for intensive urban development coupled with expansive public transportation systems to generate lower human impacts on natural systems, questions about population pressures in cities often deflate such findings. While environmental worries about population in the US peaked with Paul Ehrlich's warnings about a population bomb (and later explosion) in the early 1970s, other issues such as immigration and new scaler studies of the impact of cities on ecosystems have stepped in to fill the gap. And just as Barry Commoner worried about the regressive social implications of Ehrlich's population bomb scenarios, we can be equally concerned today with the newer forms of this criticism as it has attached itself to cities.[17]

For example, take the recent work on what has come to be known as 'ecological footprint' studies. Ecological footprints are extrapolated maps of the environmental impacts of urban areas generated with the help of Geographical Information Systems (GIS) tracking inputs in cities in the form of resources brought in and outputs in the form of waste produced. The point of such maps is to demonstrate that the environmental stress caused by cities is far greater than the actual physical borders of the city [*Rees and Wackernagel, 1995*]. As such, footprint analysis provides a very good indicator of unsustainable consumption patterns and a very helpful spatial metaphor for urbanites to understand the larger ecological consequences of their consumption patterns. It also helps to demonstrate the unjust distribution of resources between first and third world countries.

But the rhetoric of the planners and geographers who first devised this technique often ends up sounding like the geographical dualism found in Rolston, including its unfortunate social implications. In a recent popular defense of the technique, William Rees suggests that the increased urbanisation predicted into this century (some 5.1 billion people living in cities by 2025) is evidence of humanity's 'technological hubris'. 'Separating billions of people from the land that sustains them is a giddy leap of faith with serious implications for ecological security' [*Rees, 1999*]. Urbanisation, we are told, removes people spatially and psychologically from the land that sustains them. This analysis best shows its true colours however in a series of impending 'dimensions of urban human ecology' which Rees runs through. According to Rees, we need to worry about cities because croplands and forests are being used more intensively to sustain urban populations, more hectares of productive land are being relied upon to sustain the populations of rich countries (presumably their cities), and, in a world of 'rapid change', cities are unsustainable since the lands in its footprint are not secure from ecological change or social hostility [*Rees, 1999: 2*].

But there is no reason to believe that cities themselves are making it easier for populations to grow. Rees's worries about urban populations, except for the strategic concern at the end, are all claims which apply generically to any population growth in the developed world, not just growth in cities. The convention of using the ecological footprint to critique cities amounts to little more than the old wine of population worries in the new bottles of GIS data [*Rees, 1999: 3*]. This suggestion ignores the evidence provided by Rees' own techniques which show that third world cities, with lower consumption rates, have smaller footprints. When considering the alternative argument that cities produce economies of scale that are needed for energy savings, Rees replies with his strategic worry: analysis which finds energy savings in urbanisation 'implicitly assumes that the city enjoys a stable and predictable relationship with its hinterland' [*Rees, 1999: 3*]. In the end, Rees uses this analysis to argue that sustainable cities should not only be sites of consumption, but also production as well, producing their own energy and food.

Certainly there is nothing wrong with this last suggestion. Cities certainly would be improved if they could incorporate their own sites of production. But the strategic worries that Rees raises are troubling. Is it the case that urbanisation is unwise for *ecological* reasons because surrounding lands may become politically unstable? Perhaps. Thomas Homer-Dixon has argued that environmental problems are more likely to create political violence in rural rather than urban areas [*Homer-Dixon, 1999: 155ff*]. At the same time, Homer-Dixon reports that, empirically, urban violence (at least political violence) does not necessarily increase with rural–urban migration. The extent to which urban advocates should worry about this consideration is at best unclear. What is clear is that Rees' reasons for seeing cities as examples of technological hubris are more social than ecological.

The anti-urban bias of environmentalists and the urban blind spot of environmental ethics is ripe for ruralist and racist abuse. At the end of the day, environmentalists must confront the fact that shortly into the next century more than half of the world's population will live in cities. As these people will be held there by the forces of capitalist production, those of us interested in the environment as a terrain upon which social justice is often decided have a responsibility to give reasons why the urban environment can be reclaimed as a rich social, and even physical sphere and not derided, to paraphrase Frank Lloyd Wright, as morally cancerous.

One of the biggest shames of environmentalism is that those who benefit most from ghettoization, from poverty, from unequal distribution of wealth and entitlements, from pollution, and from social unrest, are served by an environmental movement which apparently dismisses the inner city and its residents as much as these agents of oppression do. Too many contemporary environmental ethicists are only adding more fuel to this fire. An expanded environmental ethics that embraces the literal ground of these problems would help to redefine environmentalism and make a greater contribution to the sustainability of ecological systems and reform of social systems.

IV. Urban Ecological Citizenship, an Example: Restoring Nature

In closing, I will offer a brief example of an environmental issue which may have more potential in cities than in rural areas, and presumably is less important in wild areas. It also responds to the ecological needs of local environments and avoids the social problems just discussed. The example I have in mind is restoration ecology, the practice of restoring damaged ecosystems. It is the sort of issue that an expanded urban environmental ethic would focus on. But first, one caveat to set up the example concerning the importance of public participation in environmental practices.

Earlier I suggested that one of the goals of an environmental ethic sensitive to urban issues would be the development of a sense of ecological citizenship. If, again loosely speaking, such a sense of citizenship involves environmental responsibility for one's actions, one's fellow citizens, and one's environment, then how is that citizenship to be engendered? Taking responsibility for one's political community is familiar enough to us but how do we take responsibility for our environment as part of that community? The first and most important goal of the development of an urban ecological citizenship involves the stimulation of public participation in the maintenance of natural processes. While it would take further argument to prove than I have space for here, I believe that a direct participatory relationship between local human communities and the nature they inhabit or are adjacent to, including urban natural areas, is a necessary condition for encouraging people to protect natural systems and landscapes around them rather than trade off these environments for short-term monetary gains from development.

If I am in a normative and participatory relationship with the land around me I am less likely to allow it to be harmed further. But this does not mean that a relationship with nature is participatory only if it leads participants to make scarifies for nature. It only means that such participation is a necessary condition for protecting nature as a foundation of ecological citizenship. Why? One reason is that environmental protection, as is the case with other laws governing common resources, often admits to free rider problems. If all environmental legislation was mandated from above and local populations had no reason to take an interest in environmental protection, then little would motivate citizens from abstaining from free rides, or even out and out violation of environmental regulations. This problem has been proven over and over again in the history of environmental legislation. Most recently we have seen this in several well publicised examples in the developing world where drawing lines around an area and declaring it a national park or wilderness has done little to ensure environmental protection of the site. Deane Curtin gives a thorough account of some of these cases, including the failing attempt by the Nepali government to create the Chitwan National Park over the needs of local communities to collect firewood [*Curtin, 1999*] (see also Jayal, this volume, for examples from India). For reasons such as these I am tempted to gauge the relative importance of different environmental practices in terms of their ability to engender a more participatory relationship between humans and the nature around them. I believe that restoration ecology represents such a practice, and its greatest headway so far in terms of serving as a conduit for public participation in nature, has been in urban areas.

Restoration ecology is the practice and science of restoring damaged ecosystems, most typically ecosystems which have been damaged by anthropogenic causes. Such projects can range from small-scale urban park reclamations to huge wetland mitigation projects. On two common indicators of the importance of environmental activities – number of voluntary person hours logged on such projects and amounts of dollars spent – restoration ecology is revealed to be one of the most pressing and important environmental priorities on the North American environmental agenda, and in most other developed countries as well. In the US for example, the cluster of restorations known collectively as the 'Chicago Wilderness' project in the forest preserves surrounding the city, typically attracted over 2,000 volunteers per weekend to help restore the native Oak Savannah ecosystems which have slowly become lost in the area [*Stevens, 1995*].

In general, restoration makes sense because on the whole it results in many advantages over mere preservation of ecosystems that have been substantially damaged by humans. But it must be remembered that this is a technological practice, very different in kind from acts of wilderness preservation, for example, which are more purely environmental initiatives. Some non-anthropocentrists, such as Eric Katz (and Robert Elliot, as mentioned above), who have commented on restoration to date, have even gone so far as to argue that the objects produced by restoration are not natural at all, but instead artifacts because they are produced by humans [*Katz, 1997*]. While I disagree with this view, the logic it stems from is ground in the non-anthropocentric value dualism between nature and culture described above, and no doubt partly by the geographical dualism attributed earlier to Rolston (though I am happy to report that Rolston is much more open to the importance of restoration in an overall environmental management scheme than others).

But despite such objections, restoration is an institutional practice that is of top concern to governments, businesses, NGOs, and research universities. The practice is so common that it is almost unremarkable to note that every region of every developed country contains some restored landscape. But I think if we were to focus on the fact that restoration is taking place and chalk that up to proof of the importance of the sort of environmental issues which will motivate the development of an ecological citizenship, we would miss something quite important. What we would be missing is that the fact that landscapes are being restored is not nearly as important as the choices that we have to make about what to value in those restoration projects which produce those landscapes. Seen as an environmental practice it is easy enough to focus on the end products of restorations only and then use this focus to endorse the best technologies which can help to produce the best restored landscapes. I would argue however that as a human practice that involves our connection to nature, we need to think about what values are produced in that practice and how those values can best be made use of in the broader, long-term project of creating a sustainable society.

Now, to date, my intervention on questions concerning restoration has focused on the value of public participation in restoration projects as a positive pragmatic outcome of such activity [*Light and Higgs, 1996*]. When restorations are performed by volunteers then they are, in the sense I have described above, an important generator of the forms of responsibility associated with ecological citizenship. Even if it is true that humans cannot reproduce the value of nature as philosophers like Katz maintain, it is quite plausible that a moral ground justifying restoration projects can be found in the value of human participation in nature. The value of this participation is not however justified in a vacuum. In the case of restoration, participatory practices get us better restorations because they create the sorts of relationships with nature that I argued were a necessary condition for long-term environmental sustainability. Those restorations that are not produced by volunteers do not capture this participatory value and do not necessarily add the long-term project of creating communities committed to the protection of their local environments.

Sociological evidence available to date focusing on the Chicago restorations suggests that participants in restoration projects are more likely (as one might expect) to adopt a benign attitude of stewardship and responsibility toward nature as a result of such interactions with nature. The reason appears to be that participants in restoration projects learn more about the hazardous consequences of anthropogenic impacts on nature because they learn in practice how hard it is to restore nature after it has been damaged. This same research suggests that participants take the lessons of restoration with them on the road. When restorationists visit preserved areas, such as national parks or wilderness areas, they are more likely to act as more responsible environmental citizens while in those places.[18] The more interesting philosophical issue then becomes how to guarantee or further this value of participation in restoration projects. In terms of the values represented in the practice of restoration, there is a strong moral and political claim inherent to the practice for having more local participation in restoration projects as a sort of schoolhouse for environmental responsibility and a means of stimulating more democratic environmental practices. At its core participatory restorations amount to public participation in nature; it is a restoration not only of nature but also of the human cultural relationship with nature [*Light, 2000a*].

This sort of analysis gets us both short-term and long-term goals. On the short term we want to encourage laws which would mandate local participation in restoration projects which are publicly funded (something like a right of first refusal for local communities and neighborhoods) on the assumption that local participation in *all* restorations is part of the overall criteria for what counts as a good restoration. This criteria is just as important as scientific or technological proficiency in restoration and could even outweigh the value of proficiency in some instances. The reason again is that I would claim that in the long term we will only have environmental sustainability when we all have vested interests in our local environments.

But on the long term we will want to focus our attention as ethicists and environmentalists on those areas most likely to generate such foundations for ecological citizenship, namely those geographical areas which are most amenable to public participation in restoration. Larger rural restoration projects, such as the multi-million dollar projects undertaken by the US Army Core of Engineers to de-channellise rivers are too unwieldy for significant voluntary efforts. But urban restorations, such as the Chicago projects and the prairie restorations at the University of Wisconsin arboretum in Madison are perfect for serving this purpose. One could even claim that the massive public participation generated in Chicago was directly linked to the location of the city in relation to the restorations. Certainly, restoration should not be restricted to such smaller sites, but these sites may in fact be the best suited to fulfilling the full normative value of restoration – creating an opportunity for citizens to form relationships with their local environments. Though I do not have the studies to support the supposition, I would suggest that community gardens, and other common forms of urban environmentalism, are important for the same reasons (see Light [*2000b*].

But my example of restoration ecology as a demonstration of the importance of urban environmental issues and practices does not go far enough. If environmental ethics is to fully embrace the urban, then it must describe the brown space of the city to be as important a locus of normative consideration as the green space. An environmentalism expanded to include the city as an object of its concern needs to be founded in a specific set of moral and political positions rejecting the anti-urban bias and the urban blind spot that is endemic to traditional environmental views. As a consequence, we will only have a fully environmental ethic, which covers all environments, when we turn our attention to the preservation of richly textured urban spaces as often as we do to old growth forests.[19]

NOTES

1. The few other papers on urban issues in environmental philosophy include Jamieson [*1984*]; Lawson [*1995*]; and Light [*1995*]. Other environmental theorists who have written on urban issues include Avner de-Shalit, Clare Palmer, Roger King and Warwick Fox (especially Fox's collection [*2001*]).
2. While reasonable people can disagree about the exact start of environmental philosophy as a recognisable philosophical endeavour, I take as a watershed year 1973 when three critical papers in environmental philosophy were first published: Sylvan [*1973*]; Naess [*1973*]; and Singer [*1973*], though the latter, admittedly, has become more influential in the literature on animal welfare as opposed to environmental ethics proper. For those unfamiliar with this division, broadly speaking animal welfare/rights advocates consider the proper extension of moral consideration beyond humans to be to individual animals (hence these theorists are often called 'individualists') while environmental ethicists argue that the proper extension of moral consideration should be to entire ecosystems rather than individuals, consequently discounting the importance of attribution of value to individuals within a species (hence these theorists are often called 'holists'). Debates between individualists and holists crop up for example in disputes over whether an overpopulated heard of deer in an area can be culled in order to prevent destruction of the ecosystem they inhabit. Figures such as J. Baird Callicott have pressed this division home. Practical challenges to the upshot of the distinction have come most notably from Gary Varner, while theoretical challenges have been raised by Dale Jamieson. Without siding with any party as to the legitimacy of this distinction, the critique in this analysis will be directed at holist environmental ethics.
3. For alternative approaches to the dominant views on anthropocentrism in environmental ethics see Watson [*1984*]; Norton [*1984*]; Skolimowski [*1984*]; Hayward [*1997*].
4. The definition is Tim Hayward's [*1998: 173*].
5. Emphasis added. While quite interesting, it is striking that views like Taylor's and Sylvan's are false on broadly speaking both realist and anti-realist metaphysical grounds about moral claims. On realist grounds (which suggest that moral claims refer to existing qualities in or about the world), one would expect that if there are conceptions of the value of nature that can stand outside of culture and determine obligations and duties regardless of cultural predilections, then there is no *a priori* reason why there could not be a foundation for human obligations to nature which did not depend on the attribution of non-anthropocentric value. For example, it is conceivable that there is some all things considered better state of the human character which entails duties to nature while not articulating a value in nature independent of human valuing. (Such a view is at least as plausible as the claim that nature has a value in and of itself which can stand against a given culture's culturally bound appraisal of the value of nature, and I think it also has the same epistemic hurdles, or at least hurdles as high as the non-anthropocentric view.) And on anti-realist grounds (which suggest that moral claims do not refer to existing qualities in or about the world), if there is no foundation for human conceptions of the value of other humans then there cannot be a *sui generis* sense of the value of nature that somehow transcends culture. Perhaps the way out of this dilemma is to say that for Sylvan, Taylor and others, a non-anthropocentric conception of nature is by definition outside of culture since it is a view independent of human prescriptions of value, cultural or otherwise. More charitably then, what non-anthropocentrists want is a description of natural value that is acultural, rather than resistant to cultural relativism, since, after all, culturally driven approximations of the value of nature could be expressed in non-relativistic terms.
6. For another influential view which is infused with an admitted nature-culture division see Katz [*1997*].
7. For a nice summary of the common supposition that American environmentalism contains three waves from tum of the century reformers to today's interest groups (often accused of being co-opted by the business community), see Schlosberg [*1999*].
8. See Bryan Norton's review of *Conserving Natural Value* [*1996*]. Norton here offers some strong criticisms of the epistemological and ontological justifications of Rolston's theory of natural value. For an excellent discussion of Rolston's views and a sharp defense of them against Norton's criticisms see Preston [*1998*].

9. As one might expect, weak anthropocentrists like Hargrove and Norton are better on such questions, but not always and not without some prodding. Norton's early work on weak anthropocentrism sought to justify it as an adequate foundation for valuing just the sorts of wild places that Rolston is fixed on. See Norton [*1984: 184*]. Norton now focuses more on the importance of 'place' as opposed to 'nature' or 'environment', see Norton and Hannon [*1998*]. Still, there is little by way of explicit account in his work on urban problems. Even if there was though I would not want to necessarily tie my claim to the importance of urban issues in a robust environmental ethics to a rejection of non-anthropocentrism. Though I try to remain agnostic about the existence of non-anthropocentric intrinsic value in my own work, I believe that whether it does or does not exist is irrelevant to the question of whether we should attend to urban issues, for the reasons I will raise in the next section below. For a justification of my agnostic position on intrinsic value see Light [*1996*].
10. I should note here that while I have no statistical evidence to back it up, I find this geographical dualism geographically mappable. Environmental ethicists in the UK and much of the rest of Europe are far less concerned with wilderness and wildness since, I believe, there is not much there that one can point to by way of wild nature, even under a more liberal description of such environments. Australians, Norwegians and North Americans seem inordinately preoccupied with the issue; especially those theorists who live in proximity to such places. There is, in a certain sense, a kind of *western* bias in environmental ethics in North America, which may be attributable to the location of theorists like Rolston in the great western states.
11. See, for example, Agar [*forthcoming*].
12. It should be noted however that Wilson's colleague in work on biophilia, Stephen Kellert, at the Yale School of Forestry, is much more balanced in his portrayal of environmental priorities. Kellert is forthright about the existence of natural experiences in cites (something that Rolston would object to and Wilson may or may not): 'Even the most impoverished city offers extraordinary opportunities for experiencing natural wonder. ... Society's challenge is to make the positive experience of nature accessible to all rather than to dismiss its presumed relevance to an entire group', see Kellert [*1996:28*]. Kellert also does an admirable job of advocating the design of cities with nature in mind. Peter H. Kahn, Jr. claims that empirical studies on biophilia confirm the importance of these urban themes in Kellert's work. See Kahn [*1999*].
13. Kahn is an exception, directly taking on this worry, see Kahn [*1999: 223*].
14. No doubt some philosophical colleagues will find my claims here specious and unphilosophical. The persistence of a position as true in the face of arguments that it is false do not count as good reasons to accept the position. But to me, as I have argued elsewhere, the point of environmental philosophy is first to contribute to the resolution of environmental problems, which necessitates attention to a different set of issues, be they philosophical or not. For an example of this pragmatic approach to environmental philosophy (though not to all questions in applied ethics) see Light [*2001*]. A more complete defense of this pragmatist methodology will appear in my manuscript, *Pragmatism and the Reconstnsction of Environmental Ethics*. I do not believe though that the general call for an attention to urban problems in the field will necessitate a full blown acceptance of the position I call methodological environmental pragmatism.
15. This book is perhaps the best selling and most widely discussed book of environmental philosophy yet by the public published. In addition to coming out as a trade title in hard cover with Pantheon, the paperback was published by Vintage. Abram won two forty thousand dollar non-fiction literary prizes for this work. It is the book that I get asked about the most from non-philosophers and from my students.
16. My presentation was 'The Question of Style in Public Philosophy', at the Association for Literature and the Environment conference, Missoula, Montana, July 1997.
17. For an excellent recent overview of the Ehrlich-Commoner debate, see Feenberg [*1999: Ch.3*].
18. See the essays in Gobster and Hull [*2000*].
19. Presentations of this paper have been made at New York University, Clarion University, the University of North Texas, Lancaster University (UK), Albright College, Michigan State University, the University of Texas School of Architecture, and the University of South Carolina. Many thanks to all of these audiences for helpful comments, and especially to Baird Callicott, Irene Klaver, David Strauss and Brad Wilson.

REFERENCES

Abram, David (1996), *The Spell of the Sensuous: Perception and Language in a More-Than-Human-World*, New York: Pantheon.

Agar Nicholas (forthcoming), *Life's Intrinsic Value*, New York: Columbia University Press.

Callicott, J. Baird (1992), 'La Nature est morte, vive la nature!', *Hastings Center Report*, Sept.–Oct., pp.16–33.

Callicott, J Baird (1996), 'On Norton and the Failure of Monistic Inherentism', *Environmental Ethics*, Vol.18, No.2, pp.219–21.

Callicot, J. Baird (1998), 'The Wilderness Idea Revisited', in Callicott and Nelson [*1998: 2337–66*], *Debate*.

Callicott, J. Baird (1999), *Beyond the Land Ethic: More Essays in Environmental Philosophy*, Albany, NY: SUNY Press.

Callicott, J. Baird and Michael Nelson (eds.) (1998), *The Great New Wilderness Debate*, Athens, GA: University of Georgia Press.

Curtin, Deane (1999), *Chinnagounder's Challenge: The Question of Ecological Citizenship*, Bloomington and Indianapolis, IN: Indiana University Press.

De-Shalit, Avner (1996), 'Ruralism or Environmentalism?' *Environmental Values*, Vol.5, No.1, pp.47–58.

Dowie, Mark (1996), *Losing Ground: American Environmentalism at the Close of the Twentieth Century*, Cambridge, MA: MIT Press.

Elliot, Robert (1997), *Faking Nature*, London: Routledge.

Feenberg, Andrew (1999), *Questioning Technology*, London: Routledge.

Fox, Warwick (ed.) (2001), *Ethics and the Built Environment*, London: Routledge.

Gobster, Paul and Bruce Hull (2000), *Restoring Nature: Perspectives from the Social Sciences and Humanities*, Washington, DC: Island Press.

Gunn, Alastair (1998), 'Rethinking Communities: Environmental Ethics in an Urbanized World', Environmental Ethics. Vol.20, No.4, pp.341–60.

Hayward, Tim (1997), 'Anthropocentrism: A Misunderstood Problem', *Environmental Values*, Vol.6, No.1, pp.49–63.

Hayward, Tim (1998), 'Anthropocentrism', *Encyclopedia of Applied Ethics*, Vol.1.

Homer-Dixon, Thomas F. (1999), *Environment, Scarcity, and Violence*, Princeton, NJ: Princeton University Press.

Jamieson, Dale (1984), 'The City Around Us', in Tom Reagan (ed.), *Earthbound*, Philadelphia, PA: Temple University Press, pp.38–73.

Kahn, Peter H. Jr. (1999), *The Human Relationship with Nature*, Cambridge, MA: MIT Press.

Katz, Eric (1997), *Nature as Subject*, Lanham, MD: Rowman & Littlefield.

Kellert, Stephen (1996), *The Value of Life: Biological Diversity and Human Society*, Washington, DC: Island Press.

Lawson, Bill E. (1995), 'Living for the City: Urban United States and Environmental Justice', in Laura Westra and Peter Wenz (eds.), *Faces of Environmental Racism*, Lanham, MD: Rowman & Littlefield, pp.41–55.

Leopold, Aldo (1996), *Sand County Almanac*, New York: Oxford University Press.

Light, Andrew (1995), 'Urban Wilderness', in David Rothenberg (ed.), *Wild Ideas*, Minneapolis, MN: University of Minnesota Press, pp.195–211.

Light, Andrew (1996), 'Callicott and Naess on Pluralism', *Inquiry*, Vol.39, pp.273–94.

Light, Andrew (2000a), 'Ecological Restoration and the Culture of Nature: A Pragmatic Perspective', in Paul Gobster and Bruce Hull (eds.), *Restoring Nature: Perspectives from the Social Sciences and Humanities*, Washington, DC: Island Press, pp.49–70.

Light, Andrew (2000b), 'Elegy for a Garden: Thoughts on an Urban environmental Ethic', *Philosophical Writings*, Vol.19, pp.41–7.

Light Andrew (2001), 'Taking Environmental Ethics Public', in D. Schmidtz and E. Willott (eds.), *Environmental Ethics: Introductory Readings*, Oxford: Oxford University Press, forthcoming.

Light, Andrew and Higgs, Eric (1996), 'The Politics of Ecological Restoration', *Environmental Ethics*, Vol.18, No.3, pp.227–47.

Myerson, Allen R. (1998) 'Energy Addicted in America', *The New York Times*, 1 Nov. 1998, Week in Review, p.5.

Naess, Arne (1973), 'The Shallow and the Deep: Long-Range Ecology Movements', *Inquiry*, Vol.16, pp.95–100.

Norton, Bryan (1984), 'Environmental Ethics and Weak Anthropocentrism', *Environmental Ethics*, Vol.6, pp.131–48.

Norton, Bryan (1995) 'Why I am Not a Nonanthropocentrist: Callicott and the Failure of Monistic Inherentism', *Environmental Ethics*, Vol.17, pp.341–58.

Norton, Bryan (1996) 'Book Review: "Conserving Natural Value", *Environmental Ethics*, Vol.18, No.2, pp.209–14.

Norton, Bryan and Bruce Hannon (1998), 'Democracy and Sense of Place Values in Environmental Policy', in Andrew Light and Jonathan M. Smith (eds.), *Philosophy and Geography Ill: Philosophies of Place*, Lanham, MD: Rowman & Littlefield, pp.119–214.

Preston, Christopher J. (1998), 'Epistemology and Intrinsic Values: Norton and Callicott's Critiques of Rolston', *Environmental Ethics*, Vol.20, No.4, pp.409–28.

Rees, William E. (1999), 'Life in the Lap of Luxury as Ecosystems Collapse', *The Chronicle of Higher Education*, July 30, p.1.

Rees, William E. and Mathis Wackemagel (1995), *Our Ecological Footprint*, New York: New Society.

Rolston, Holmes III (1988), *Environmental Ethics: Duties to and Values in the Natural World*, Philadelphia, PA: Temple University Press.

Rolston, Holmes III (1989), *Philosophy Gone Wild*, Buffalo, NY: Prometheus Books.

Rolston, Holmes III (1994), *Conserving Natural Value*, New York: Columbia University Press, pp.12–13.

Rolston, Holmes III (1998), 'The Wilderness Idea Reaffirmed', in Callicott and Nelson [*1998*].

Schlosberg, David (1999), *Environmental Justice and the New Pluralism*, Oxford: Oxford University Press.

Singer, Peter (1973), 'Animal Liberation', *New York Review of Books, 5* April.

Skolimowski, Henrik (1984), 'The Dogma of Anti-Anthropocentrism and Ecophilosophy', *Environmental Ethics*, Vol.6, pp.283–8.

Stevens, William K. (1995), *Miracle Under the Oaks*, New York: Pocket Books.

Sylvan, Richard (then Routley) (1973) 'Is There a Need for a New, an Environmental Ethic?' *Proceedings of the World Congress of Philosophy*, pp.205–10.

Taylor, Paul (1984), 'Are Humans Superior to Animals and Plants?,' *Environmental Ethics*, Vol.6, pp.149–60.

Watson, Richard A. (1983), 'A Critique of Anti-Anthropocentric Biocentrsim', *Environmental Ethics*, Vol.5, No.3, pp.245–56.

Wilson, Edward O. (1992), *The Diversity of Life*, New York: W.W. Norton.

Ecocentrism, Weighted Interests and Property Theory

SHERYL D. BREEN

As a political and ecological philosophy, ecocentrism argues that nature in systemic terms exists for its own sake rather than for the benefit of humans' economic, scientific or recreational designs. The ultimate goal, ecocentrists argue, is the holistic wellness of regional and global ecosystems; a primary barrier is anthropocentrism, which is perceived as infecting everyone from urban planners to farmers to mainstream environmentalists. Like more moderate approaches to environmental conservation, ecocentrism began rising into Western public consciousness in the late 1960s and early 1970s, primarily in Western Europe, North America and Australia. Unlike other environmental thinkers, however, ecocentrists have demanded an ideological revolution based on dynamic ecosystemic relations rather than incremental policy reforms based on human actions and needs.

Ecocentric thinkers have been busy in their role as opposition, but reciprocal critiques also have been numerous and much needed. Non-ecocentric commentators, including both disdainful nay-sayers and sympathetic scholars, have reproached some or all ecocentrists for irrationality or misanthropy. Ecocentrists have responded vigorously and, in some cases, have refined their arguments in valuable ways. An additional critique is needed, however, for ecocentric theorists have been disturbingly lax regarding crucial questions of property and ownership. From Plato to Locke and Marx, conceptions of property have been central to our visions of political liberty, equality and order. Questions of property are particularly relevant to environmental debate, especially as that debate turns from a focus on pollution toward issues of land use, development and ownership rights. However, although ecocentrists have been vigorous in rejection of dominant Western political and property theory, amid their repudiation of much else, they have been considerably less devoted to the task of considering their own ideology's demands in the area of ownership. Specifically, they have paid surprisingly little attention to the development of an alternative ecocentric theory of property. Issues of property have arisen, of course, but the ecocentric approach largely has been politically anecdotal – for example, this forest should not be logged – or theoretically ethereal – for example, the trees belong to themselves. Still lacking in ecocentric thought is a cohesive theory of property that could lay the groundwork for a coherent platform of ecological land use.

For the sake of theoretical clarity and future public policy, the ideological demands of ecocentrism on issues of property require closer examination. As part of this scrutiny, the task for ecocentrism is to articulate the means by which the core principles of ecocentrism can lead to a theory of property that is meaningful in theory and workable in practice. In this article, in the hope of bringing us nearer that goal of clarity, I propose a system of weighted interests and then examine pivotal ways in which such a system can support an ecocentric theory of property. I argue that the concept of interests, articulated through a two-factor system that allows the weighted designation of interests among individuals, species and ecosystems, satisfies the ecocentric demand for a holistic universe of shared moral standing while allowing decision-making on issues of property through a set of workable, pluralist criteria.[1]

Interests

Interests address those factors conducive to an entity's well-being, so that *A* has an interest in *X* if *X* contributes to *A*'s functioning or flourishing.[2] Interests therefore operate within the context of needs and welfare that give an entity moral standing in itself rather than merely for its instrumental value to others. As summarised by Gary Varner:

> [T]o say that an entity has interests is to say that it warrants direct moral consideration because its needs, desires, etc. (whatever we take to define its interests) ought, other things being equal, to be fulfilled or satisfied, and that for their own sake. To say that a thing has interests is to say that it has a good of its own, a good which moral agents have direct, *prima facie* duties to protect (a duty of non-maleficence) and further (a duty of beneficence) [*1990: 268 n. 2*].

If the concept of interests is to be useful to ecocentric theory, however, two factors must be determined in sequence: who (or what) can be said to *have* interests and how should these interests of these bearers be *weighed* when they conflict?

Determining the Bearers of Interests

An entity's interests constitute those ways in which it can be benefited or harmed, but whether consciousness (real or potential), desires or other factors are required for the allocation of interests and moral standing has been much disputed. At risk of overly simplifying the complexities of the debate, it is useful to consider four positions regarding the necessary and sufficient conditions for recognition of entities as bearers of interests. These positions can be considered as a set of four concentric circles, with each ring encompassing more within the universe of moral standing and interests as we move outward toward the holistic foundations of ecocentric theory.

Ring 1: For advocates of the first position, humanness constitutes an admission ticket for inclusion in the realm of interests, so that conscious, senile, brain-damaged and comatose people as well as infants can be accorded moral consideration as interest-bearers.[3] This first position is broadly shared in Western political and moral culture, although variations have been offered regarding the unique characteristics that define humanness. R.G. Frey, for example, insists upon the criterion of desire – which he restricts to humans – as the necessary condition for determining bearers of interests.[4] This first ring restricts the moral universe to humans and so is the most exclusive of the four listed here, but the placement of humans within a unique category does not mean advocates of this position can condone or even ignore cruel treatment of non-humans. As Lawrence Johnson has pointed out, the assumption that humans are the exclusive holders of interests does not mean that animals can be mistreated without moral tinge but rather that our humane treatment of them must be ethically based on our own interests [*1991: 2*].

Ring 2: A second circle extends the universe of interests and moral standing beyond the species of *homo sapiens*. Peter Singer, following Jeremy Bentham's utilitarian lead, argues that the sufficient and necessary criterion for interests is not humanness but sentience. Those animals that can feel pain can be said to have interests, while those entities that do not suffer (a category that includes at least invertebrates and plants, he argues) do not have interests in themselves [*1990*]. Other philosophers drawn to the area of animal liberation or rights, including Joel Feinberg, have argued along similar lines [*1974*], and debate remains active as to whether sentience or another criterion should define the outer boundary of this second circle. For example, while David DeGrazia recently has argued that only sentient beings can be said to have interests [*1996*], Warren Neill has presented an 'emotocentric' theory of interests that limits recognition to entities with the capacity for affective response [*1998*].

Ring 3: Ecology-oriented commentators have found such theories of limited moral inclusion just as unsatisfactory as human exclusiveness, however, leading to a third position that stipulates life as a sufficient and necessary condition for bearers of interests. One persistent criticism of sentience arguments has been that any boundary used to accord interests to some forms of life while denying them to others faces the problem of marginal cases. In response to that issue and others, biocentrists have endeavored to remove margins altogether, arguing that moral standing cannot be determined simply by species membership or an elitism of human-like characteristics. Instead, they argue, all living beings – not just antelope and orangutans but also amoebas and oaks – have a good of their own and, therefore, can be said to be bearers of interests. The capacity to suffer is a *sufficient* criterion for moral standing, as Kenneth Goodpaster writes, but not a *necessary* one [*1978: 316*]. Either the concept of interests must be extended to include all life, he argues, or we must arbitrarily select an element of psychological capacity (such as Frey's criterion of desires), an option that is neither warranted nor plausible [*1978: 320*]. Arguments for this third ring regarding interests were offered in the 1970s by biocentric philosophers such as John Rodman [*1977*] and Richard Routley and Val Routley [*1995*], followed by a series of influential works during the 1980s by Robin Attfield [*1981*], Paul Taylor [*1983, 1986*] and Holmes Rolston III [*1988*]. The field of moral thought regarding biocentric interests remains both vigorous and articulate, and Attfield [*1995*] and Varner [*1998*] have produced particularly clear, thoughtful and well-developed arguments in recent years.[5]

Ring 4: So far, the circles that define who (or what) can be considered interest-bearers have reached far enough to include humans, other sentient animals, invertebrates and plants. Now the ring of interests and moral inclusion must widen even further to a fourth position, marking the divide between individualistic and holistic theories. Whereas a biocentric approach can accommodate all individual forms of life as bearers of interests, a holistic theory such as ecocentrism demands recognition of species and ecosystems as entities with morally significant interests of their own. Just as individual seaweed and salmon have interests, ecocentric theory demands, so do the species and ecosystems of which those individuals are a part.[6] Biocentrism has been a valuable and radical form of theoretical progress, according to the ecocentric view, but like the first and second positions, it fails to see the filigree of connections that bind human to human, animal to plant and organism to soil and water. We not only live *in* our environment but are constituted *by* our ecological interdependencies, which means that 'the world is an intrinsically dynamic, interconnected web of relations in which there are no absolutely discrete entities and no absolute dividing lines between the living and the nonliving, the animate and the inanimate, or the human and the nonhuman' [*Eckersley, 1992: 49*].[7]

Ecocentrism has met deeply rooted biases against this fourth and most-inclusive position. Western scientific and linguistic traditions, which view species and ecosystems as aggregates of individuals rather than as dynamic entities in themselves, foster widespread refusal to recognise independent ecosystemic interests. To be valuable in both theoretical and practical terms, the ecocentric campaign for acceptance of this fourth ring must be propositional rather than simply oppositional. Faced by these traditions, the intellectual task for a holistic theory such as ecocentrism is not to discard them – for as Johnson points out, 'there is a great deal which is *right* about our ways of thinking about the world' [*1995: 843*] – nor to turn from scientific and observational thinking toward mysticism or sentimentalism, but rather to correct and augment. We have learned much about ecological relationships and dynamics by breaking the world down into discrete, measurable pieces, moving from one level of analysis to the next in small, logical steps, and this is a learning process that does not inherently violate the intrinsic principles of ecocentrism, contrary to the anti-rationalist, anti-scientific denials of some members of the ecocentric camp. Yet caution and correction certainly is needed, for implicit in this predominant vision of scientific method is the troubling assumption that we can understand ourselves, our ecosystems and our universe as assemblages of tiny bits, much as we might analyse a child's playroom construction through knowledge of the multicoloured, multishaped Legos of which it is made. How, then, can advocates of ecocentrism correct and augment these collective-of-individuals traditions and bring argumentative force to this fourth position? At least three endeavours are needed, I believe.

First, ecocentrists must provide specific arguments to support the assertion that wholes are more than the sum of their constituent parts. Second, if species and ecosystems are entities in themselves, ecocentrists must argue convincingly that they have discrete moral standing and interests as well. Finally, ecocentrists must answer the question, 'why does this matter?' In other words, if species and ecosystems have interests of their own, distinct from the interests of individual entities, how does recognition of these holistic interests provide a valuable analytical tool in either theoretical or practical terms?

Johnson has led the way on the initial endeavour. First, he undermines the assumption that species are collections of individual organisms that share relevantly similar features or 'family resemblances'. On the contrary, among members of many species that display a wide enough range of variations and life forms, 'there may be no feature whatever that they all have in common'. Furthermore, the assumption of family resemblances seems to be applied after the fact: 'Instead of the species being what it is because it has certain characteristics, a scheme of characteristics is settled upon describing what the species happens to be. What, then, if anything at all, is a species?' [*1992: 146*]. Second, the claim that species are a class finds trouble in the constantly changing membership of the group through birth and death. If a class is to be defined by its membership rather than as an entity in its own right, it cannot change membership in this way and still constitute the same class. While species evolve, branch out and often become extinct, '[c]lasses don't do things like that. Actually, classes don't *do* anything' [*1992: 147*]. Either a fundamentally new definition of class must be concocted – and the definition of species already is not clear even within the field of the philosophy of science[8] – or the conception of species as a class of individuals cannot fit.

The second endeavour, which contends that holistic entities have moral standing and interests of their own, must counter a series of arguments from biocentrists who believe the outermost boundary of interest-bearers must remain at the individualist third ring. Attfield, for example, argues that ecosystems or the biosphere cannot be regarded as living organisms without evidence that they possess the equivalent of 'the genetically determined capacities which confer upon living organisms their recurrent patterns of development and growth, and thus allow them to have a good of their own' [*1995: 26–7*]. Varner employs a similar argument: Even if an ecosystem could be considered to be an organism, which 'no sober ecologist' would accept, he writes, it still could not be accorded the essential admission criterion of biological interests 'inasmuch as its component subsystems could not have acquired any biological functions via natural selection' [*1990: 268*]. Richard Dawkins, in turn, argues that species cannot have traits (and therefore interests) in their own right because traits are selected at the individual rather than the species level . Harley Cahen agrees, arguing that because we cannot consider ecosystems to be genuinely goal-directed, they cannot be extended moral standing as interest-bearers unless we find that group selection occurs at the holistic level [*1988*].

Again, Johnson provides a series of counter-arguments.[9] First, although most recent attention to the category of species has been devoted to their evolutionary role and genetic lineages, this focus on genes fails to provide us with sharp boundaries that limit identity as interest bearers to individual organisms. As Johnson argues, although a living being's identity is strongly *shaped* by both its genes and its environment, it is not *determined* by either or constituted as a sum of its genetic properties. Organisms are not simply genetic 'things' but rather processes of life maintenance within dynamic and often hostile ecosystems [*1992: 150*]. Second, living individuals and the biosphere (unlike tractors and computers)[10] share two crucial characteristics: first, 'organic unity', in the sense that their characters are an 'integrated expression of [their] subsidiary systems', and, second, self-identity, in the sense that these entities' forms of existence and what serves to maintain them are determined by their own nature. Just as no typology of interests can legitimately separate humans from nonhumans or sentient animals from non-sentient animals, restriction of interests and moral standing to the individualist level alone must fail as well [*1992: 150*]. Third, even if biocentric critics were correct that evolution could not proceed on the species level, species still can be said to have interests of their own. Natural selection takes place on the level of individual organisms through gene manifestation based on the degree to which that manifestation is beneficial to the individual's reproduction and, hence, proliferation; accordingly, a species trait would be manifested on the individual level. It does not follow, however, that a species trait is simply a summation of the traits of individuals, and Johnson turns to the evolutionary characteristic of genetic diversity as a case in point:

> It would be absurd to say that individual organisms have genetic diversity in the sense that species do, though individual organisms might instantiate that diversity. Genetic diversity is important to the long-term welfare of many bisexual species, which accordingly have an interest in maintaining it. In their breeding arrangements and in their internal chemistry, bisexual species go to quite some lengths to maintain their genetic diversity. In the past it has been in the interests of individual organisms to have the traits by means of which genetic diversity is maintained, although on the level of individuals the interests were different interests in different traits. While genetic diversity is manifested through and selected for through individual organisms, the diversity that is beneficial to the species as a whole is by no means a matter of the aggregated interests of individual organisms [*1992: 152*].

Finally, Johnson argues, although evolutionary selection can be said to take place at the level of the gene in fundamental terms, natural selection involves far more than simply genes in competition with other genes. Both genetic and non-genetic environment must be considered, as genes are manifested not in isolation but in relationship with their ecosystem. Generally speaking, genes are selected and evolve in reference to their ability to 'get along' with the manifestations of other genes in the same organism or other beings, which means that, as a rule, genotypes are selected when their manifestation in the organism encourages replication. However, because genotypes evolve within organisms within specific environments, any specific manifestation that aids replication of a particular genotype may be neutral (for example, sexually attractive characteristics) or detrimental (for example, the stinging response of bees) to the life of the individual organism of which it is a part [*1992: 153*]. The interests of ecosystems and species thus can be contrary to the interests of members as individual lives.

Predator-prey models, such as the interrelationship surrounding the wolf population in northern Minnesota, are particularly apt for illustrating the existence of interests at both the individual and holistic levels. On an individual level, each white-tailed deer in this forest ecosystem has an interest in remaining alive rather than becoming prey to a wolf. On both the species and ecosystemic levels, however, reduction in the population of predators and expansion of deer habitat over the past century due to human encroachment has caused significant problems, allowing cycles of deer overpopulation to reach historic levels and, hence, rising ecological pressures.[11] In this situation, while individual deer have an interest in continued life, the species and ecosystem have interests in individual deer being prey. In this case, as in others,[12] the species and ecosystem hold significant interests of their own that cannot be considered merely as the sum of their members' interests. In contrast to Attfield, Varner, Dawkins and Cahen, therefore, we must not discount the indications of well-being, biological interests, traits and group selection – and therefore interests and moral standing – at the holistic level as stipulated in ecocentrism's fourth and outermost ring.

The third endeavour yet remains: Why do these holistic interests matter? The answer, I believe, is that recognition of interests at the species and ecosystemic levels gives us a means by which theoretical and policy judgements can be made. When integrated within a system that allows different entities' interests to be weighed when they come into conflict, the concept of holistic interests provides us with an analytical tool through which ecosystems can play a primary role in questions of environmental decision-making. Such a tool is especially relevant when those questions concern property ownership and use, for the clashing interests of humans, non-human individuals and species and ecosystems are at the heart of contemporary ecological land-use debates.

Determining the Weight of Interests

If all individual and holistic living entities are said to have interests, any political or ethical admonition to take those interests into consideration remains empty without some method of judging their relative weight.[13] Without a weighting technique, we find ourselves engaged in a form of interest egalitarianism in which one person's interest in living is equivalent to that of another's interest in a college education and both are equivalent to an oyster's interest in unpolluted waters. Some ecocentrists seem to argue precisely that point,[14] but just as common sense and traditional moral codes tell most of us that college and continued life are not equally important, so we also have a familiar sense that some of the interests of an oyster do not weigh as heavily as some of those within the human community. If we are to apply an ecocentric concept of interests to property theory and, ultimately, coherent practical politics, we must go beyond the issue of moral *standing* to the question of moral *significance*. If all life has interests, can we assign workable priorities when these interests collide? I believe we can and must do so.

Donald VanDeVeer's theory of interspecific justice [*1979*] provides a valuable point from which to begin. In his proposal for 'Two Factor Egalitarianism', VanDeVeer constructs a classification of interests based on, first, the role of an interest in a living entity's life and, second, the entity's psychological complexity. He distinguishes three types of interests: (1) basic interests of life, which are required to function in a 'minimally adequate' way; (2) serious interests, without which it is difficult or costly to an entity's well-being to survive; and (3) peripheral interests, without which an entity does not thrive. In general, according to VanDeVeer, basic interests should outweigh serious interests and they, in turn, should rank above peripheral interests. In the absence of a second weighting factor, however, this classification would demand that a cockroach's basic interest in food be given greater priority than a human's serious interest in a hygienic kitchen. To avoid this conclusion, VanDeVeer presents what he calls the 'Weighting Principle', which holds that 'the interests of beings with more complex psychological capacities deserve greater weight than those with lesser capacities – up to a point' [*1979: 70*]. In his defence of this weighting principle, VanDeVeer offers three clarifications. First, when like interests of a human and nonhuman come into conflict, we must recognise that humans are subject to some kinds of suffering that other animals are not, so that long-term disutilities should be taken into consideration as well [*1979: 70–1*]. Second, it is a morally significant fact that the prospects for satisfaction are generally larger for humans than for nonhumans due to 'opportunity costs' that result from greater psychological complexity [*1979: 71–2*]. Third, a weighting principle may take threshold points into account, precluding differential treatment in some cases and justifying certain forms of interspecific and intraspecific discrimination in others [*1975: 75*].

Admittedly, this method of assigning interest priorities using two factors – types of interest and psychological complexity – does not offer more than a tentative comparability among vastly divergent interests. Furthermore, as a biocentrist, VanDeVeer addresses only those conflicts that emerge between members of different species and does not consider the implications of interests at the species or ecosystemic level. An expanded and reformulated method of judgement that incorporates ecocentric principles is in order. Building from VanDeVeer's model and a revision suggested by Attfield, I propose the following two-factor system for weighing interests among individuals, species and ecosystems in accordance with ecocentric principles.

When conflicts of interest arise between members of different species, it is morally permissible, *ceteris paribus*:

(1) to sacrifice the interest of individual *A* to promote a like or more important interest of individual *B* if *A* lacks significant psychological capacities possessed by *B*,

(2) to sacrifice a basic interest of individual *A* to promote a serious interest of individual *B* if *A* substantially lacks significant psychological capacities possessed by *B*,

(3) to sacrifice the peripheral interest to promote the more basic interest if the individual beings are similar with respect to psychological capacity (regardless of who possesses the interests).[15]

However,

(4) because beings who are members of species incapable of consciousness also have moral standing, the lower weight of their individual interests adds up to a higher priority when the basic interests of a large number of beings (or the possible existence of many future beings) are at stake.[16]

When conflicts of interest arise between individual beings and an ecosystem or species,[17] it is morally permissible, *ceteris paribus*:

(5) to sacrifice the interest of an individual or species to promote a like or more important interest of an ecosystem,

(6) to sacrifice the interest of a species (S^1) to promote a like or less important interest of an individual if and only if the individual is a member of a species (S^2) that has significant psychological capacity and the species (S^1) is the cause of invasive disease.

This set of weighted interests accords primary weight to ecosystems' well-being while recognising the priority conferred by the relative importance of interests and the degree of individuals' and species' psychological capacity. Likewise, although the interests of species generally carry heavier weight than those of individuals on the premise that we 'ought not to superkill a species without a superjustification' [*Rolston, 1990: 304*], species do not carry universal trump power. Overall, the weighting system provides a means by which to address the issue of judgements from a pluralist, holistic perspective. As I will now examine, this system of weighted interests also provides a way in which to define and apply an ecocentric theory of property.

An Ecocentric Theory of Property

The issues of property rights and land-use restrictions are both visible and volatile in contemporary political and environmental debate, and environmental regulations and land-use restrictions regularly meet strident cries that autonomous private ownership should not be threatened (although complete autonomy from public intervention has never existed in fact). As the environmental debate in Western industrialised nations continues to shift its emphasis from questions of pollution control toward issues of land use, an ecocentric theory of property can help frame the debate around land-management proposals' implications in terms of individual and holistic weighted interests.

To determine how it would do so, we must first examine how an ecocentric definition of 'property' differs from dominant Western understandings. According to the liberal tradition that looks to Sir William Blackstone and John Locke, '*A* owns *P*" means three things: first, *A* has a right to use *P*; second, others may use *P* if, and only if, *A* consents; and third, *A* may permanently transfer the rights under the previous two rules to other persons by consent [*Snare, 1972: 202–4*]. In this view, property is viewed as an inert commodity of consumable and/or trade value, and control over that commodity is a prevailing concern. Applying the principles of ecocentric theory to the concept of property yields a definition with a distinctly different emphasis: *A* owns *P* within the overall goal of ecosystemic well-being. *A*'s rights of use, exclusion and transfer, as stipulated in the Blackstonian/Lockeian tradition, are not negated (as property-rights advocates often allege in land-use debates) but are filtered by a system of weighted interests. Ecocentric property ownership thus means control of land to the extent that such control allows nature to flourish according to its various levels of interests, not according to its value as a commodity. This understanding of property does not inherently demand universal 'wildness' or lack of human presence (again, contrary to property-rights advocates' allegations) but does require limitations of human use according to holistic priorities. The ecocentric definition of property also means that whereas natural-rights advocates often see the right to property as more important than the property itself, ecocentrists view the ecosystems of which that property is a part as more important than either the property or ownership rights.

Furthermore, an ecocentric theory of property based on weighted interests is neither intrinsically reactionary nor necessarily anarchist in terms of property institutions. While ecocentrism requires a high degree of wariness toward civil property institutions on the grounds of anthropocentrism and abusive uses of power and hierarchy, it does not demand wholesale rejection of political and legal structures. An ecocentric theory of property can accommodate human-designed property institutions, whether through government action (for those ecocentrists who favor democratic centralism) or community consensus (for those who lean toward decentralism and anarchism), as long as those structures incorporate the weighing of interests according to pluralist, holistic priorities. In other words, while property-rights theorists contend that constitutional and civil guarantees are designed to protect property owners rather than the property they own,[18] ecocentrism explicitly charges property institutions with the role of ensuring that owners protect ecosystemic interests. Thus, private ownership (in individual, group and corporate forms) does not disappear in an ecocentric theory of property, nor does such a theory stipulate that common or public ownership is always more attentive to holistic interests. Instead, an ecocentric approach allows a variety of institutions of ownership to function in accordance with judgements incurred by a system of weighted interests. Within institutions of property ownership that recognise weighted interests, individuals, groups and governments have the ability (if not always the wisdom) to restrict actions that violate weighting criteria and enable those that promote a pluralist, holistic scheme.

Even if private, public and common ownership can survive within an ecocentric understanding of property, however, a system of weighted interests clearly challenges other legal and common-use meanings of land ownership. Contemporary conceptions of property cannot change overnight and any ecocentric project to reconfigure popular or political opinion will be a long-term endeavour. Even at this preliminary stage, however, we can summarise several crucial implications regarding an ecocentric application of weighted interests to questions of property:

(1) *Central priority of ecosystemic well-being.* Humans' interests cannot be ignored on either the individual or species levels, or else charges of misanthropy against ecocentric theory will be confirmed. Neither, however, can they be given universal priority. By incorporating two factors – degrees of interest and psychological complexity – into the process for land-use decision-making, we can greatly alleviate the tension between respect for life at the systemic level and respect for property ownership.

(2) *Property ownership as a cultural and social construct.* Locke saw ownership as a natural right that government is designed to protect, and while that vision has been resoundingly influential, it is by no means impregnable. As Eric T. Freyfogle points out, the institution of private property is a means rather than an end in itself and therefore 'makes sense only to the extent that its consequences are good ones' [*1994: 483*]. Weighted interests provide a method to judge those consequences.

(3) *Land ownership as membership in an ecosystem.* Conceptions of land as an inert commodity must give way to an understanding of membership that includes not only the animal and plant inhabitants of the broader ecosystem but also the soil and water signified by Aldo Leopold's 'land ethic' and the interlocking network of human owners. Because of the dynamic interrelationships within any ecosystem, such an understanding will emphasise the ways in which actions of human power cause reactions, for good or ill, that will affect the rest of the system and future generations. An understanding of land ownership as constituting membership in an ecosystem promotes recognition and satisfaction of the duties of non-maleficence and beneficence to individual and systemic bearers of interests, as described by Varner.

(4) *Attention to peculiarities of place.* Predominant institutions of ownership tend to view land as exchangeable parcels without giving sufficient attention to subtle but important variations. A system of weighted interests encourages local judgement rather than universal guidelines, thus allowing us to fashion land-use management approaches more specifically to the interests and complexities of different locations. For example, the system demands that we weigh the interests of an individual wetland in the migratory flyway patterns, the habitat provided by a rural region's remaining hedgerows, the density of a particular housing subdivision plan and the tradeoffs implicit in specific pollution or development credit transfers. Decisions regarding land-use restrictions, requirements and ownership structure can follow according to the peculiarities of each distinct place.

(5) *Attention to expanding ecological knowledge.* Changes in biological and evolutionary knowledge over the past few decades emphatically underline the extent to which ecological science is a dynamic field. As our understandings of the intricate interrelationships within ecosystems expand, so can our judgements incorporate new insight regarding the individual and holistic interests connected to land-management decisions.

The proposal for weighted interests presented here is a preliminary sketch, to be sure, and work remains to be done on the theoretical and policy levels. An ecocentric approach to property questions merits just such continuing development, I believe, for the urgency of land-management questions within the current ecological debate highlights the need to scrutinise property-ownership assumptions in general and the implications of an ecocentric property theory in particular. Ecocentric opposition to accepted portrayals of nature and humanity has served a crucial role, especially in the early days of radical theorising. The time for greater rigour has arrived, however, and a clearer proposition of an ecocentric theory of property should be part of that constructive task.

NOTES

1. I offer this proposal not in the role of ecocentric thinker (although I am sympathetic in many ways, as arguments presented here will show) but rather as an advocate of theoretical consistency and practical politics. If we are to take the ecocentric approach seriously, as its advocates certainly argue we must, we also must unearth its implications for the crucial yet largely unexplored realm of property theory.
2. My gratitude is extended to Terence Ball for offering this definition.
3. Some moral philosophies, of course, are unwilling to accommodate even this first position. A Kantian ethic, for example, is willing to grant moral standing only to autonomous individuals capable of rational reflection, which means that not all humans can be said to have interests of their own. Debate also continues regarding how far the definition of 'humanness' should be extended. For a brief but engaging overview of the arguments regarding future, possible and former people, see Attfield [*1995: 13–18*] and Terence Ball, 'New Ethics for Old? Or, How (Not) to Think About Future Generations', this collection, pp.89–110.
4. Frey argues that interests arise from desires, which require bçliefs, which are constituted by language. According to Frey, nonhuman animals are not language-users and so cannot be said to have beliefs and desires of the kind required for interests [*1980*].
5. Those who argue for limited interests and moral standing, such as DeGrazia and others in the first and second positions, pose the 'machine problem,' which contends that granting interests to plants and bacteria forces us to grant them to tractors and other artefacts as well. Such an extension clearly cannot be accepted, DeGrazia argues, and thus we must reject biocentric interests as well *(1996:229]*. The problem is laid out in considerable detail in Kaufman [*1994*]. Variations of this challenge have been rejected on several grounds; see especially Attfleld *(1981]*, Bernstein [*1992*] and Vamer [*1998: Ch. 3*].
6. The holistic foundation of ecocentrism has been manifested both in this pluralist form, which accords importance to both the ecosystem and its myriad living inhabitants, and, unfortunately, in a misanthropic monolithic form, which explicitly or implicitly denies standing to individual lives, whether human or nonhuman. The monolithic view – most commonly expressed by the misanthropic wing of the deep ecology movement – holds that the biosphere alone has significant interests and moral standing and that the value of individual lives depends upon their contributions to the well-being of the Earth as a whole. This monolithic approach is not required by holistic foundational principles and demands frequent and focused rejection by ecocentric theorists and activists.
7. This focus on interrelationships prompts an increasing number of ecocentric theorists to reject the label of 'environmentalism', arguing that the mainstream movement's focus on piecemeal reform misses more fundamental changes that must be made. Environmentalism and ecologism must not be confused as synonyms, Andrew Dobson and others have warned. While environmentalism works to solve ecological problems through managerial techniques that can overlay our present lives as consumers and producers, ecologism demands radical alterations in our conceptions of nature, our relationships with nonhuman life and our standing in local, regional and global ecosystems. The term 'environment' is used to describe the aggregate of physical, social and cultural conditions that surround individuals and their communities, ecocentrists say; 'ecology', in contrast, focuses on interrelationships and the interdependence of living organisms and their habitats. Persistent conflation of environmentalism and ecologism, Dobson states, has been 'a serious intellectual mistake' [*1995:1*].
8. For an overview of the current debate, see *Species: New Interdisciplinary Essays* [*Wilson, 1999*].
9. Johnson's most extensive examination of ecosystemic interests and moral standing can be found in *A Morally Deep World: An Essay on Moral Significance and Environmental Ethics*

[*1991*]. For additional examples of arguments regarding the interests and moral standing of species and ecosystems, see Callicott [*1995*], Rolston [*1988*] and Mathews [*1995*].

10. Johnson thus joins thç argument against the 'machine problem' as described in n. *5*.
11. Somewhat paradoxically, the expanding boundaries of suburban and rural housing development have helped increase rather than decrease the deer population. Deer find these developed areas congenial due to a lack of wild and human hunters and relatively easy access to food.
12. Johnson cites the well-known case of the Kaibab Plateau of northern Arizona. When mountain lions were removed, the deer population exploded, leading to conflicting interests between individual deer and their species as a whole [*1991: 163–6*].
13. This point is an adaptation of Elliott Sober's similar observation about discussions of needs [*1995: 239*].
14. I place the blame in these cases on their weak ecocentric theorising rather than on the foundations of ecocentric theory.
15. Points 1 through 3 are VanDeVeer's formulation [*1979: 63–4*]. My only modification in this part is the addition of 'or more important' in the first point This change is for clarification and does not alter the first point's implications.
16. Point 4 arises from Attfield's critique of VanDeVeer's formulation, in which Attfield proposes two revisions: (1) beings with greater psychological capacities receive priority only when the exercise of those capacities is at risk of endangerment; (2) the interests of conscious creatures normally take priority over interests of creatures incapable of consciousness; however, because unconscious beings also have moral standing, the lower weight of their individual interests adds up to a higher priority when thç basic interests of a large number of beings (or the possible existence of many future beings) are at stake [*1991: 172–7*]. Attfield argues that without his first revision, VanDeVeer's formulation would allow the continuation of factory-farming. I have not incorporated this revision, believing that factory-farming can be combated through the system of weighted interests proposed in this article and that Attfield's addendum is overly restrictive in its elimination of interest conflicts that do not involve endangerment to psychological capacity – for example, a human's serious interest in swatting a biting mosquito, thus sacrificing the insect's basic interest in life. I have incorporated Attfield's second revision, with the clarification that 'unconscious beings' means beings who are members of species incapable of consciousness.
17. In this system of weighted interests, 'species' continues to be used in its systemic sense. The phrase 'basic interests' thus refers to the life-sustaining interests of the species as a whole and not those of a collection of its members. In addition, the term 'ecosystem' must be applied with common-sense discrimination as signifying, in originator Arthur Tansley's sense, an ecological entity of significant – and complexity with both biological and non-biological elements and characterised by a cycling of nutrients and continuous, dynamic energy flow.
18. This argument has been especially prominent in US legal and political debates regarding 'takings' theory. For arguments in support of government compensation to property owners affected by environmental restrictions, see Epstein [*1985*] and Thompson [*1990*]. For an overview of conflicting arguments from environmentalists and proponents of the land-rights movement in the Westem US, see Brick and Cawley [*1996*].

REFERENCES

Attfield, Robin (1981), 'The Good of Trees', *Journal of Value Inquiry*, Vol.15, pp.35–54.

Attfield, Robin (1991), *The Ethics of Environmental Concern*, Second Edition, Athens, GA: University of Georgia Press.

Attfield, Robin (1995), *Value, Obligation, and Meta-Ethics*, Amsterdam: Rodopi B.V.

Bernstein, Mark (1992), 'Towards a More Expansive Moral Community', *Journal of Applied Philosophy*, Vol.9, pp.45–52.

Brick, Philip D., and R. McGreggor Cawley (eds.) (1996), *A Wolf in the Garden: The Land Rights Movement and the New Environmental Debate*, Lanham, MD: Rowman & Littlefield.

Cahen, Harley (1988), 'Against the Moral Considerability of Ecosystems', *Environmental Ethics*,

Vol.10, pp.195–216.
Callicott, J. Baird (1995), 'Animal Liberation: A Triangular Affair', in Elliot [*1995*].
Dawkins, Richard (1986), *The Blind Watchmaker*, Harlow, England: Longmans.
DeGrazia, David (1996), *Taking Animals Seriously: Mental Life and Moral Status*, Cambridge: Cambridge University Press.
Dobson, Andrew (1995), *Green Political Thought*, Second Edition, London: Routledge.
Eckersley, Robyn (1992), *Environmentalism and Political Theory: Toward an Ecocentric Approach*, Albany, NY: State University of New York Press.
Elliot, Robert. (1995), *Environmental Ethics*, Oxford: Oxford University Press.
Epstein, Richard A. (1985), *Takings: Private Property and the Power of Eminent Domain*, Cambridge, MA: Harvard University Press.
Feinberg, Joel (1974), 'The Rights of Animals and Unborn Generations', in W.T. Blackstone, *Philosophy and Environmental Crisis*, Athens, GA: University of Georgia Press.
Frey, R.G. (1980), *Interests and Rights: The Case Against Animals*, Oxford: Clarendon.
Freyfogle, Eric T. (1994), 'Owning the Wolf: Green Politics: Property Rights, Ecology Rights', *Dissent*, pp.481–7.
Goodpaster, Kenneth (1978), 'On Being Morally Considerable', *Journal of Philosophy*, Vol.75, pp.308–25.
Johnson, L.E. (1995), 'Species: On Their Nature and Moral Standing', *Journal of Natural History*, Vol.29, pp.843–9.
Johnson, Lawrence E. (1991), *A Morally Deep World: An Essay on Moral Significance and Environmental Ethics*, Cambridge: Cambridge University Press.
Johnson, Lawrence E. (1992), 'Toward the Moral Considerability of Species and Ecosystems', *Environmental Ethics*, Vol.14, pp.145–57.
Kaufman, Frederik (1994), 'Machines, Sentience, and the Scope of Morality', *Environmental Ethics*, Vol.16, pp.57–70.
Mathews, Freya (1995), 'Value in Nature and Meaning in Life', in Elliot [*1995*].
Neill, Warren (1998), 'An Emotocentric Theory of Interests', *Environmental Ethics*, Vol.20, pp.163–82.
Rodman, John (1977), 'The Liberation of Nature', *Inquiry*, Vol.20, pp.83–145.
Rolston, Holmes, III (1988), *Environmental Ethics: Duties to and Values in the Natural World*, Philadelphia, PA: Temple University Press.
Rolston, Holmes, III (1990), 'Property Rights and Endangered Species', *University of Colorado Law Review*, Vol.61, pp.283–306.
Routley, Richard and Val Routley (1995), 'Against the Inevitability of Human Chauvinism', in Elliot [*1995*]. (First published in K. Goodpaster and K. Sayre (eds.), *Ethics and Problems of the 21st Century*, Notre Dame, IN: University of Notre Dame Press, 1979.)
Singer, Peter (1990), *Animal Liberation*, New Revised Edition, New York: Avon.
Snare, Frank (1972), 'The Concept of Property', *American Philosophical Quarterly*, Vol.9, pp.200–206.
Sober, Elliott (1995), 'Philosophical Problems for Environmentalism', in Elliot [*1995*]. (First published in B. Norton (ed.), *The Preservation of Species: The Value of Biological Diversity*, Princeton, NJ: Princeton University Press, 1986).
Taylor, Paul W. (1983), 'In Defense of Biocentrism', *Environmental Ethics*, Vol.5, pp.237–43.
Taylor, Paul W. (1986), *Respect for Nature: A Theory of Environmental Ethics*, Princeton, NJ: Princeton University Press.
Thompson, Barton H., Jr. (1990), 'Judicial Takings', *Virginia Law Review*, Vol.76, pp.1449–544.
VanDeVeer, Donald (1979), 'Interspecific Justice', *Inquiry*, Vol.22, pp.55–79.
Varner, Gary E. (1990), 'Biological Functions and Biological Interests', *The Southern Journal of Philosophy*, Vol.28, pp.251–70.
Varner, Gary E. (1998), *In Nature's Interests? Interests, Animal Rights, and Environmental Ethics*, New York: Oxford University Press.
Wilson, Robert A. (ed.) (1999), *Species: New Interdisciplinary Essays*, Cambridge, MA: MIT.

What's Wrong with Ecofeminism?

LUCY SARGISSON

Where to begin? Ecofeminism is essentialist, biologist and it lacks political efficacy. Ecofeminism is inconsistent, intellectually regressive and it lacks rigour. Ecofeminism is the fluffy face of feminism. Challengers of this view of ecofeminism insist that ecofeminism is scientific, profound, and essential to human and non-human survival. Criticisms of ecofeminism, they insist, are inaccurate, infected by patriarchy and/or simply naïve. They tell us that ecofeminism is political [*Salleh, 1997*]; ecofeminism is practical [*Sturgeon, 1997*]; ecofeminism is complex [*Birkeland, 1993*]; ecofeminism is ethical science [*Mies and Shiva, 1988*]; and that ecofeminism is the salvation of the world [*Spretnak, 1990; Plant, 1989*]. Women are said to be closer to nature than men are, and so only they can save the planet [*Starhawk, 1990*].

Debates regarding the efficacy and rigour of ecofeminism are well established and I have little to add to them. Critiques like those offered by Janet Biehl are thorough and thoughtful [*Biehl, 1991*]. Such critiques of ecofeminism are on the whole accurate and appropriate but, I suggest, what's really wrong with ecofeminism is that it denies its full potential. Ecofeminism is utopian in all senses of that term and it fails to acknowledge and exploit this. Understanding of this allows us to see both the value and the dangers of ecofeminist thought. Utopianism is both the beauty and the beast of ecofeminism.

Utopianism

(1) Utopians are the world's dreamers. Utopias are inspirational. Utopias offer imaginative alternatives to real political and social dilemmas. Utopias are the creative expressions of political desire.

Utopias work from the margins of fantasy whilst addressing political desires and frustrations of the present. Utopias permit the politically discontented to view the present from afar and to think critically about this from another perspective. Many historical utopias employ the convention of a 'visitor' as a vehicle for this. It provokes a certain sense of estrangement, which has a subversive political function. Krishan Kumar suggests that utopias are a particularly subversive form of political commentary, and notes that their authors have often experienced imprisonment and/or torture as political dissidents. He explains thus: 'Utopia challenges by supplying alternatives, certainly. It shows what could be. But its most persistent function, the real source of its subversiveness, is as a critical commentary on the arrangements of society' [*Kumar, 1991: 87–8*]. As estranged texts, utopias are able to view from an imaginary distance the society whence they originate. In this way they present a particular challenge to the *status quo*.

The creativity – and fictive nature – of much utopian writing also has a potentially transformative function. Utopias present theory as fiction and *vice versa*. They create a space in which philosophical ideas can be imagined, tested, and explored. These are all specific functions that I have elsewhere linked in an approach to utopianism that stresses its transgressive function [*Sargisson, 1996*]. Briefly, I suggest, utopian thought is transgressive in three ways: it steps over boundaries that order and separate. Examples might be boundaries between disciplines, or conceptual boundaries, or boundaries that establish the norms of social behaviour. It thus renders them meaningless or emphasises their porosity. This permits the creation of a space where previously there was none, in which new and different ways of relating to the world can be practised. These spaces are the new place that is no place: utopias.

In *Demand the Impossible* Tom Moylan offers a conceptualisation of what he calls the critical utopia [*Moylan, 1986*]. This is a useful device. It stresses the dual function of utopian thought that, historically, has offered simultaneous political critique *and* the creation of something new. Utopian thought, he finds, unsurprisingly, is rooted in discontent: 'It is, at heart, rooted in the unfulfilled needs and wants of specific classes, groups, and individuals in their unique historical contexts' [*Moylan, 1986: 1*]. Its function is oppostional: utopia opposes what he calls 'the affirmative culture' [*1986: 1*]: 'Utopia negates the contradictions of a social system by forging visions of what is not yet realised either in theory or in practice. In generating such figures of hope, utopia contributes to the open space of opposition' [*1986: 1–2*]. Unlike many commentators, who are concerned at the diversity and ambiguity of contemporary utopian writing, Moylan finds delight in this multiplicity. He sees it as historically specific and appropriate. For him, the multiple and diverse nature of recent utopias and utopian theory enables effective opposition to what he perceives as capitalist hegemony. These utopias, he says, are critical in two senses: '"Critical" in the Enlightenment sense of *critique* – that is expressions of oppostional thought, unveiling, debunking, of both the genre itself and the historical situation. As well as "critical" in the nuclear sense of the critical mass required to make the necessary explosive reaction [*Moylan, 1986: 10*].

In order to be effectively critical in these ways the utopia must, says Moylan, destroy, transform, and revive the utopian tradition, which, in its past and present state was and is inadequate to the task of provoking social transformation. A fixed, finite and universal utopia of perfection cannot adequately oppose a fixed, finite, and universal capitalist system. Only an understanding of utopia that destroys old perceptions of the genre, transforms them into something new and thus revives utopianism can adequately reflect the concerns, needs, and wants of contemporary malcontents. The critical utopia does not blueprint, but rather it privileges social change in process. It retains imperfection.

Moylan connects this critical utopianism to what he optimistically calls a 'new historic bloc' of political opposition [*1986: 11*]. This, he says, consists of a historically specific collection of groups, linked by the source of their discontent. He finds the values of feminism, ecology, and democratic socialism to infuse this bloc. These are manifested in an opposition to certain core values embodied in capitalist economy: 'Whatever the particular set up of social images each text sets forth, the shared quality in all of them is a rejection of hierarchy and domination and the celebration of emancipatory ways of being as well as the very possibility of utopian longing itself' [*1986: 12*]. An important function of utopias then is that of transformative opposition. In some ways, I suggest, ecofeminism may perform this function.

(2) Utopias are intellectually challenging. Utopians cross disciplinary borderlines, utopians combine fiction with their politics and desire with the exercise of reason.

Utopias are invariably fictions. They imagine alternative realities; they stretch the conventions of the present; they re-present the world to us for inspection from another perspective; they imagine worlds transformed. As such they are an ideal place from whence to engage in political critique, and in which to explore alternative approaches to the world. The fact that they are fictive does not, however, mean that they are invariably articulated in the *form* of fiction. Utopias are expressed in a multitude of forms. Ernst Bloch identifies utopianism (a utopian impulse) as immanent in popular culture. His sources range from architecture to medicine; music to religion; art to philosophy [*Bloch, 1986*]. For Vincent Geoghegan, the 'classic' utopia (the literary model established by Thomas More) is 'but one manifestation of utopianism' [*Geoghegan, 1987: 2*]. Ruth Levitas, in her thorough examination of the canon, finds the focus on literary form to issue an unnecessarily narrow definition [*Levitas, 1990: 4*]. Lyman Tower Sargent, the major bibliographer of this field, has recently studied the utopias of the religious right in America as well as those of indigenous societies. This makes the study of utopianism a potentially endless process.

This interdisciplinarity gives to utopian studies a special place in contemporary and historical traditions of scholarship. Research from even the narrowest approach to utopia (as a piece of fiction) involves cross-disciplinary work. In order to pay attention to the content of a given utopia we have to engage in multi- or cross-disciplinary study of, say, theology, politics, and literature. Ecofeminism is quite extraordinary in its diversity of form and forces upon the scholar similar challenges. Its utopias find expression in poems, stories, academic (and pseudo-academic) essays, to name but a few.

(3) Utopianism has a dark side: utopians can be dangerous, utopias can be totalitarian. The imposition of a utopian blueprint can produce political exclusion, stagnancy and negation. Utopias in this sense are the death of politics.

I have elsewhere suggested that this is indeed so and that utopias of perfection which have a blueprinting function are politically and intellectually dangerous. However, not all utopias blueprint an ideal future, not all utopians desires to realise a vision of perfection, and not all utopianism is culpable of the 'crime' of closure and the imposition of a will to power. Despite the fact that most contemporary feminist utopianism evades such closures, ecofeminism does, I suggest, manifest some of these darker tendencies.

Ecofeminist Utopianism

(i) Style

Ecofeminism is inspirational in a number of ways but absolutely not for its blueprints. Ecofeminism adopts a visionary tone. Ecofeminists dare to dream.

Exploration of one ecofeminist utopian vision might perhaps help us to understand this. The work of Starhawk identifies a lack in politics: this is spirituality. Also, she proposes a shift in our consciousness of time. In an essay 'Power, Authority, and Mystery: Ecofeminism and Earth-based Spirituality', Starhawk suggests that the Pagan model of time is appropriate to a sustainable politics of social change:

> From a Pagan perspective, there is no end of time. Time is a cycle, and cycles come around and they go around and come back again. ... That, I think, is the kind of model we need for politics. We need to see the process of changing our society as a lifetime challenge and commitment. Transforming consciousness so that we can preserve and sustain the Earth is a long-term project [*Starhawk, 1990: 78*].

This shift would facilitate awareness that the project is of unending duration. It would profoundly and appropriately alter our attitude to ecological politics. An understanding of the interconnectedness of the issues facing environmentalists is, she says, an essential step towards lasting transformation. Starhawk explains by reference to a diagram, in which are illustrated:

> … the tree of life and the magic circle. The magic circle is a circle of the elements: air, fire, water, and earth. The tree has roots and a core, a center, a heart that's the same as the circle, and it has branches. If we think about it, all of these issues then we see as being so interconnected can fit into that magic circle [*Starhawk, 1990: 80*].

Community, says Starhawk, is a necessary perquisite for this. Community permits the individual to give energy when she can and promotes sustained input. This, she says, is because even if one person needs to rest there are others who will feel active. The community as whole, then, creates sustained movement. 'There are going to be times when we're active and it's exciting and we're obsessed by action, and there are going to be times when we pull back and nurture ourselves and heal and take care of ourselves' [*ibid.*]

Her emphasis is on being kind to ourselves but also of creating social and political situations and contexts in which individual commitment and effort is most effectively utilised. Community nourishes the individual and vice versa. In addition to this pragmatic utilitarianism is a certain mysticism: 'Finally, I think that the spell we need to cast, the model we need to create, has to be open to mystery, to the understanding that we don't know everything about what's going on and we don't know exactly what to do about it' [*ibid: 79*].

The poem below articulates Starhawk's vision of where all of this might take us:

> And so the time comes when all the people of the earth
> can bring their gifts to the fire
> can look into each other's faces
> unafraid
>
> …
>
> Hear the earth sing
> of her loveliness
> her hillock lands, her valleys
> her furrows well-watered
> her untamed wild places

She arises in you
As you in her
Your voice becomes her voice
Sing!
… .

This dream of communion with the earth is typical of ecofeminism, as is the use of varied forms and style through which to communicate their utopian desires.

The strength of this utopian expression is *not*, I suggest, in its potential to found a program of political action. In this ecofeminism is lacking. Rather, it adds creativity to feminist critique. Much feminist thought is angry, critical, and relentless. There is, I suggest, a need an extra dimension that is provided by the dreamers who combine pragmatism with expressions of barely imaginable desires. 'All we can do is try to speak it, try to say it, try to save it' [*LeGuin, 1989: 47*].

Utopianism is playful. Good examples of this can be found especially in the work of early expressions of 'ecofeminist' desire – those written before 'ecofeminism' became codified by political theorists into a system of categorisation. Mary Daly's Gyn/Ecology, for instance plays wilfully and consciously with language to an extent that reading becomes a new process: 'Wild Crone-centering is rigorous play/work, which is utterly Other than the rigor mortis of gamesmanship exhibited in phallocratic plays and works' [*Daly, 1978: 417*]. The aim here is to invent a way through restrictive language games and scholarship. Neologisms, revaluation, and density of text force our focus onto language itself so that style becomes a form of political praxis.

Ecofeminist texts disrupt academic expectations in terms of form and style. Novelists write tracts of theory, fictions contain political messages and poems litter the pages of conversational prose essays:

Daughters, the women are speaking
They arrive
over the wise distances
on perfect feet

> The women are speaking: so says Linda Hogan of the Chickasaw people … The women are speaking … And what they say is: 'We are scared' … Listen, they do not say: 'Nature is scared.' Because they distrust that word, Nature. Nature as not including humanity [*LeGuin, 1989: 46*].

Ursula LeGuin combines many forms of expression in her prose essays, which attempt to evoke an account of the world and women's place in it.

Others present theory in the form of an imaginary narrative: 'First there was the Great Egg and, inside it, the promise of all life. That promise of life began to stir, to swell, to grow, and the shell holding the promise began to stretch. The shell cracked and, from inside the egg, the water of life began to flow: a single river of hope and commitment' [*Cameron, 1989: 54*]. Anne Cameron's ecofeminist creation myth serves a particular function of utopian invention and creation of alternatives to apparently hermetically sealed systems of thought.

One possible outcome of such an approach is bad poetry, bad fiction, and bad political theory and indeed some of the collections of ecofeminist essays contain material of somewhat dubious quality. Jill of All Trades haunts ecofeminism. Eclecticism slides easily into intellectual incontinence.

Ecofeminism has its own peculiar vocabulary. Ecofeminism speaks in terms of natural bodily functions such as birth: its flows, cycles, and rhythms. This is overlaboured at times (forgive the pun) but it does illustrate a further attempt at evoking style as praxis or politics. The bodily functions evoked by such terms are those excluded by the sterile discourse of liberalism. Ecofeminists, in introducing such terminology into theory analyses, consciously attempt to articulate the politics of exclusion noted by other forms of feminism. This is a utopian attempt at producing a new language for politics.

Out of the point, the swelling
Out of the swelling, the egg
Out of the egg, the fire
Out of the fire, the stars
Out of the rain of stars
the congealing, molten world

...

She is alive in you as you in her
Warm your human hands at the watchfire
See the stains on the cloak
Feel the wounds too deep for healing
[*Starhawk, 1989: 115*].

This may not be effective, and certainly does not work for everyone - some find this inspirational, others find it nauseating – but it does nonetheless create a space within political thought for the exploration of alternative means of expression.

(ii) Content

I stated above that utopianism is visionary. It sees beyond the horizon. It demands the impossible. It articulates (sometimes incredible) desire. Examples of this can be found in utopian responses to the apparently intractable problem of dualistic thought. This is said to construct a paradigm the effect of which is oppositional, hierarchical and foundational for a politics of domination. It is said to ground a worldview that is driven by a dynamic of violence.

Val Plumwood's response to this is both interesting and creative. In *Feminism and the Mastery of Nature* [*1993*] she engages in a deconstruction of green political thought (and deep ecology in particular) that shows its reliance on existing paradigms of thought. Her own 'solution' to this problem (of how to think differently when the way that we think constructs the way that we think ...) rejects easy inversion (for example, valorisation of the feminine, and/or nature) and takes the more difficult road of rejecting dualism *per se*. This involves retaining the concept of distinction – reason and emotion can therefore be retained as distinct, but rejecting the notion of difference as deviance:

> the distinction [between reason and emotion] should not be treated in terms of radical exclusion: emotions need not be treated as unreasonable, nor reason as so divorced form emotion, as they are in dualistic construction … The expulsion of the master identity from the western construction of reason requires not the abandonment of reason itself, but an effort to install another, less hierarchical, more democratic and plural identity in its place [*Plumwood, 1993: 189*].

Generally speaking, when it comes to the analysis of concepts, ecofeminism is a mixed bag. Some, like Plumwood, offer sophisticated and imaginative responses. Other internal features of ecofeminism that can inspire and inform include the subversion of conceptions of 'the political' as issues as diverse as menstruation [*Plant, 1989*], and theology [*Daly, 1978*] are brought on to the political (public) agenda. Much ecofeminist intellectual energy is invested in identifying source of oppression, which are said to be shared between 'woman' and 'nature' and here analysis tends to be weak. Some of these draw a crude causal connection:

> Our pain for the death of the forests is simply, and most fundamentally, compassion for the shameless destruction of life … It is no accident that the minister of forests is a man, that the logging company is owned and run by men, that the logging truck is driven by a man. For after all, this is a man's world. Our language says it all, a virgin forest is as yet untouched by the hand of 'man' [*Plant, 1989: 1*].

> We know that when we resist the rape of the earth, we are fighting the same mentality that allows the rape of women [*Plant, 1989: 49*].

Like their radical feminist predecessors and allies, some ecofeminists identify men as the source of oppression.

Others take a more analytical approach and attempt to interrogate the conceptual system that is patriarchy. Here, relations of Self and Other are of primary importance:

> In their analyses of oppression, socialists, animal liberationists, ecologists, and feminists each distinguish between privileged and oppressed groups, where the privileged are upper- or middle-class, human, technologically and industrially 'developed', male, and the oppressed are poor or working-class, nonhuman animal, 'undeveloped' nature, and female, respectively. Ecofeminism describes the framework that authorises these forms of oppression as patriarchy, an ideology whose fundamental self/other distinction is based on a sense of self that is separate, atomistic [*Gaard (ed.), 1993: 1–2*].

> The categories "woman" and "animal" serve the same symbolic function in patriarchal society. Their construction as dominated, submissive "other" in theoretical discourse (whether explicitly stated or implied) has sustained human male dominance. The role of women is to serve/be served up; women and animals are the used [*Gruen, 1993: 61*].

Exploitation, domination, oppression: these are core themes of contemporary feminism.

Ecofeminist practice claims to 'dig at the roots' of oppression [*Gruen, 1993: 84*]. Oppression, they say, is not a simple matter. Lori Gruen identifies four connecting narratives that comprise frameworks of legitimate oppression. The objects of oppression are, she says, women and animals. The narratives are: (1) evolution stories in which male humans are characterised as developing hunting skills and being or becoming in some way significantly the stronger sex; (2) evolution stories that locate a moment of significance in the shift from nomadic to sedentary living which brought a further sexual separation of roles; (3) religious narratives that construct nature as a source of fear and man as its conqueror; (4) an empirically based belief system in which mechanistic and (a certain kind of) scientific world views further separate man from nature. Each narrative – and most so called emancipatory discourses (liberal feminism, Marxist feminism, socialist feminism, radical feminism, animal liberation theory all 'accept normative dualisms that give rise to a logic of domination' [*Gruen,*

1993: 79]. They are thus trapped in (and complicit with?) a world view that constructs the Other in opposition and responds to it with violence. This is a consistent theme in ecofeminist analyses of oppression:

> We who are born into this civilisation have inherited a habit of mind. We are divided amongst ourselves (*Griffin, in Plant* [*1989: 7*]).
>
> Civilised Man says: I am Self, I am Master, all the rest is Other – outside, below, underneath, subservient. I own, I use, I explore, I exploit, I control. What I do is what matters. What I want is what matter is for [*LeGuin, 1989: 45*].

Of course, other analytical and political traditions also identify dualistic thought to be a source of oppressive social and cultural relations. Ecofeminism cannot rightly claim sole possession of this perception. Nor is it the sole source of utopian alternatives. In Deep ecology, for instance, Arne Naess's concept of an ever opening all embracing Self attempts at resolution of the split and combative capitalist liberal (Judeo-Christian) Self [*Naess, 1989*]. A caustic corrosion of dualistic thought is at the heart of the work of Nietzsche. Good and Evil are banalities but they are potent in their contribution to a dominant slave morality which shamelessly moderates human behaviour [*Neitzsche, 1923*]. Derridian post-structuralism takes binary opposition as a starting point of deconstruction. So-called French Feminism does likewise and postmodern philosophy and anti-philosophy also takes this as a given.

Not regarding these bodies of work and thought, special claims are made for ecofeminism. Ecofeminist compassion is claimed as the source of salvation. Ecofeminism is said to be especially open to Otherness and difference: 'ecofeminist theory will recognise sympathy and compassion as a fundamental feature of any inclusive, liberatory theory' [*Gruen, 1993: 80*]. Compassion, it is claimed, enables us to 'undo' oppositional thinking. This strikes the same dissonant chords as does the work of early radical feminists. The shift that is demanded here is surely utopian: it seeks to totally change the way that we think and offers a model of and ideal (feminine) alternative. It is, however, not desirable. The danger of blueprints was briefly articulated above. Blueprinting utopias easily replace one system of domination with another, they stop process, and they manifest desire in a totalising and totalitarian manner. If women are possessed of a special and different attitude towards the world (loose references are made by those making these claims to the work of Carol Gilligan) then perhaps they had better be given the reins to run the world [*Gilligan, 1982*]. Would that it were so easy. Inversions of this kind do not address domination, oppressions and hierarchy *per se*, but they might impose an alternative version in which women are on top.

Ecofeminism is not perfect but is necessary:

(1) to feminism

Ecofeminism presents to other forms of feminism some serious criticisms. Maria Mies, for instance, is critical of the feminist utopia of a self-determining autonomous woman. First, she says, this takes as a prerequisite (male dominated) reproductive technology. To avoid enmeshment in the patriarchal construct of the nuclear family, the autonomous woman must 'free' herself from her tendency to reproduce: 'we now deal with the question of "emancipation" from the uncontrolled reproductive potential of the female body, of "emancipation" from our female nature.' Secondly, she notes, this particular utopia is not universal: '"Third World" women criticize the demand for self-determination for still another reason. The utopia of the independent, isolated and autonomous female individual is not attractive to them. ... They do not wish to live free and alone in the anonymity of big cities, to die, finally, as we shall, in a home for the old' [*Mies, 1988: 220*].

Ariel Salleh is ambivalent towards other forms of feminist thought, accusing them of 'racing ahead ... for their turn on the info superhighway' instead, she characterises her particular contribution (embodied materialism) as 'womanist' [*Salleh, 1997: ix*]. Feminism is often accused by ecofeminism of a lack of attention to 'nature', of technophilia, of an inappropriate alliance with male oppressive technology.

It may be that other forms of feminism have adequate responses to such criticisms. In fact, they do: the liberal feminist utopia caricatured by Mies, for instance is neither (i) universal nor (ii) actually offered anywhere as an authentic utopia. It is none the less healthy to continue internal critique and reflexivity within feminist thought. Ecofeminism lacks the strength and rigour of sustained critique to perform Moylan's critical function on feminism (the critical utopia works from the inside to transform and recreate, in this it is a form of immanent critique). However, it is possible to say, in true liberal fashion, that ecofeminism enables other forms of feminism to be reflective and cautious about their claims.

(2) to ecologism

Ecofeminism provides a critique of ecologism and the points that it makes are important: 'The deep ecology movement is shockingly sexist' [*Doubiago, 1989: 40*]. The green utopia *Ecotopia* is surely one of the more sexist of the genre. Women on tap fill Ernst Callenbach's novel [*Callenbach, 1975*]. However, much of this critique is deeply essentialist: 'Deep ecologists "are willing to listen to their inner voices," Warwick Fox declares. As everyone knows (and as many have deplored), Woman traditionally listens to her inner voice' [*Doubiago, 1989: 40*]. Claims are unproblematically made for a universal Woman, thereby replacing deep ecological sexism with ecofeminist deep essentialism.

A more sophisticated analysis comes from Val Plumwood whose *Feminism and the Mastery of Nature* poses a serious challenge to green political theory. Deep ecological environmental ethics, she claims, fail to engage with feminist critiques of rationalism. Green theory is gender blind and this affects its efficacy in creating alternatives to the paradigms that construct nature as Other [*Plumwood, 1993: 164–89*]. Privileging reason denies an ethic of dependency and constructs its other as 'unreliable, unreflective, irrational and sometimes uncontrollable force reason must dominate [*ibid.: 189*]. It could be that deep ecology might benefit from such input.

Some suggest that deep ecology and ecofeminism make ideal bedpartners. Judith Plant, for instance suggests that the green utopia of bioregionalism shares common ground with ecofeminist politics of community. Again, this is grounded in a deep essentialism that draws upon the alleged special and privileged qualities of a universal Woman.

Conclusion

Much of the content of ecofeminist thought is deeply essentialist: insisting on profound, intractable and significant differences in the nature of men and women. Further, it is regressive – pulling us back towards the models of femininity constructed by the canons of western political thought and theology. Some ecofeminism is, frankly, awful and few ecofeminist publications are of the high quality of the book length contributions of Janet Biehl and Val Plumwood, but even the fluffier faces of ecofeminism have a role to play. They can inspire and subvert and offer to those so inclined a (safe, enclosed) space in which further utopian imagining can occur. The poems, the stories and the imaginings have a place and a function that should be denied.

Ecofeminism has utopian potential. For many their first encounters with Mary Daly's *Gyn/Ecology* or Susan Griffin's *Woman and Nature: The Roaring Inside Her* or Rachel Carosn's *Silent Spring* or Marge Piercy's *Woman on the Edge of Time* are defining moments of inspiration and hope. These texts, which do not attempt integration into political theoretical discourse, which do not desire acceptability are, ironically, still the most potent offerings of ecofeminism.

> Since we have come through the sombre Passage of reconizing the alien/alienating environment in which women hating rituals vary from *suttee* to gynaecological iatrogenesis, we can begin to tread/thread our way in time and space. This knowing/acting/Self-centering Process is itself the creating of a new, woman-identified movement. It is the beginning of *Gyn/Ecology* [*Daly, 1978: 315*].

REFERENCES

Biehl, Janet (1991), *Finding Our Way: Rethinking Ecofeminist Politics*, New York: Black Rose Books.

Birkeland, Janis (1993), 'Ecofeminism: Linking Theory to Practice', in Gaard (ed.) [*1993*].

Bloch, Ernst (1986), *The Principle of Hope*, Oxford: Blackwell 1986 edn.

Callenbach, Ernst (1975), *Ecotopia*, Berkeley, CA: Banyan Tree Books.

Cameron, Anne (1989), 'First Mother and the Rainbow Children', in Plant (ed.) [*1989*].

Carson, Rachel (1965), *Silent Spring*, Harmondsworth: Penguin.

Daly, Mary (1978), *Gyn/Ecology: the Metaethics of Radical Feminism*, Boston, MA: Beacon Press.

Diamond, Irene and Orenstein, Gloria Feman (1990), *Reweaving the World: The Emergence of Ecofeminism*, San Francisco, CA: Sierra Club Books.

Doubiago, Sharon (1989), 'Mama Coyote talks to the Boys', in Plant (ed.) [*1989*].

Gaard, Greta (ed.) (1993), *Women, Animals, Nature*, Philadelphia, PA: Temple University Press.

Gaard, Greta (1993), 'Living Interconnection with Animals and Nature', in Gaard (ed.) [*1993*].

Geoghegan, Vincent (1987), *Utopianism and Marxism*, London: Methuen.

Gilligan, Carol (1982), *In a Different Voice*, Cambridge, MA: Harvard University Press.

Griffin, Susan (1978), *Woman and Nature: the Roaring Inside Her*, New York: Harper & Row.

Griffin, Susan (1989), 'Split Culture', in Plant (ed.) [*1989*].

Gruen, Lori (1993), 'Dismantling Oppression: An Analysis of the Connection between Women and Animals', in Gaard (ed.) [*1993*].

Kumar, Krishan (1991), *Utopianism*, Buckingham: Open University Press.

Levitas, Ruth (1990), *The Concept of Utopia*, Hemel Hempstead: Phillip Allen.

LeGuin, Ursula (1989), 'Women/Wilderness', in Plant (ed.) [*1989*].

Mies, Maria and Vandanan Shiva (1988), *Ecofeminism*, Melbourne: Spinifex.

Moylan, Tom (1986), *Demand the Impossible: Science Fiction and the Utopian Imagination*, London: Methuen.

Naess, Anne (1989), *Ecology, Community and Lifestyle*, Cambridge: Cambridge University Press.

Neitzsche, Fredrich (1923), *Beyond Good and Evil: A Prelude to a Philosophy of the Future*, Third Edition, London: Allen & Unwin.

Piercy, Marge (1979), *Woman on the Edge of Time*, London: The Women's Press.

Plant, Judith (1990), 'Searching for Common Ground: Ecofeminism and Bioregionalism', in Diamond and Orenstein [*1990*].

Plant, Judith (ed.) (1989), *Healing the Wounds: The Promise of Ecofeminism*, Philadelphia, PA: New Society Publishers.

Plumwood, Val (1993), *Feminism and the Mastery of Nature*, London: Routledge.

Salleh, Ariel (1997), *Ecofeminism as Politics*, London: Zed Books.

Sargisson, Lucy (1996), *Contemporary Feminism Utopianism*, London: Routledge.

Sargisson, Lucy (2000), *Utopian Bodies and the Politics of Transgression*, London: Routledge.

Spretnak, Charlene (1990), 'Ecofeminism: Our Roots and Our Flowering', in Diamond and Orenstein [*1990*].

Starhawk (1989), 'A Story of Beginnings', in Plant (ed.) [*1989*].

Starhawk (1990), 'Power, Authority, and Mystery: Ecofeminism ad Earth-Based Spirituality', in Diamond and Orenstein [*1990*].

Sturgeon, Noel (1997), *Ecofeminist Natures: Race, Gender, Feminist Theory and Political Action*, London: Routledge.

Balancing Political and Ecological Values

NIRAJA GOPAL JAYAL

Ecological and Political Values

This account seeks to revisit the relationship between ecological and political values, with a view to questioning the assumption of an apparently seamless continuity between these two arguably distinct types of values. While tensions between ecological and economic values (such as economic growth and property rights) have been recognised and extensively debated, there has been a tendency among environmental ethicists to view environmental goods and political goods as largely compatible, and to assume that the one translates fairly smoothly into the other. Even as it recognises the complexity of the interaction between ecological and political (especially liberal) values, this account suggests that at least some of the practical tensions that arise around environmental issues, which appear to require trade-offs between political and ecological values, pose important questions for environmental political theory. Through an empirical account of the by now familiar conflicts between parks and people, the analysis seeks to raise and answer questions such as the following: are political and ecological values always and necessarily compatible? How do we account for the areas of overlap as well as those of tension between them? Are the contradictions between them explicable in terms of their distinct philosophical premises?

Ecological values are frequently defended from the vantage-point of liberal political values. As such, substantive political values like rights and justice are often, unproblematically and even axiologically, extended to encompass an environmental ethic, making it possible for us to invoke discourses of justice or rights in relation to the natural environment. The most obvious example of ecological values being defended on the basis of liberal political values is the extension, to animals, of the assumption that rights are the best moral instruments for recognising the autonomy of human individuals. Moral consistency, it is argued, requires that we extend to animals the same respect for sentience that we accord to human beings, and that the recognition of animal rights is therefore the best way of ensuring that animals are not exploited. Of course, the limitations of the Benthamite argument of sentience become apparent when environmental ethicists are compelled to seek alternative justifications for respecting non-sentient natural phenomena such as plants or wilderness areas.

Conversely, political values (albeit not exclusively liberal ones) are also sometimes justified on the basis of ecological values, as when communitarian principles are endorsed by reference to ecological holism, or when biological diversity is invoked to justify political pluralism, as the authentic or 'natural' way of being. Indeed, despite some discomfort arising out of the easy translation of ecological holism into conservative politics, the dominant tradition in environmental ethics has tended to espouse radical political values. This broadly homologous relationship – even convergence - between ecological and political values thus often issues in the endorsement of political values such as those of democracy, justice and rights.

Sometimes, the defence of both ecological values and political values may spring from a common source, as with the appeal to the Aristotelian ethic of 'flourishing' or happiness being a good for humans, non-humans and future generations alike [*O'Neill, 1993*]. It is not surprising that there should be important similarities in the elaboration and enunciation of political and ecological values, because – rather like medical or business ethics - environmental ethics is cast in the mould of mainstream ethical theory, sharing not merely its form but also many of its assumptions [*Smith, 1995: 53*].

Are, however, ecological and political values as seamlessly continuous, and as capable of harmonious cohabitation, as they are often presumed to be? Just as there are tensions among liberal political values (most famously, that between liberty and equality) which may be philosophically consistent with each other, there is also empirical evidence to suggest examples of tensions and conflicts between ecological values and political values, which are not easy to arbitrate or negotiate in practice. This study seeks to identify some sources of such tensions, to examine whether and, if so, how and to what extent, it is possible to negotiate and resolve these in philosophical terms. The next section of the account raises the following questions: are ecological and political values intrinsically different types of values? Are their sources and bases distinct? Does the fact that they are attached to different sorts of entities create the tensions that we are addressing? The third section of the paper presents evidence from a case-study which exemplifies such a conflict, while the final section returns to the lessons that environmental political theory might draw from these.

Are Ecological and Political Values Intrinsically Different?

Despite many apparent similarities between them, it could plausibly be maintained that ecological and political values are intrinsically different types of values. Ecological values seek to justify *the worth of the existence of natural phenomena* and living beings of various species, while political values such as rights or freedom are based on a prior presumption of individual human worth and, at least since Kant, no longer concerned with justifying that worth. It is in the justification and recognition (or otherwise) of *equal* worth that political differences may arise, as when the presumption of equal worth issues in strong egalitarianism, and may conflict with the value of freedom. As such, political values have to do with the way in which human beings evolve the principles and institutions that govern their collective life in social and political organisation.

Despite this nominal difference, however, to the extent that political values speak to the question of the self-realisation of human beings in a polity, and ecological values to the question of the flourishing/self-realisation of living beings in nature, there is also a fundamental similarity between them. It is possible to identify at least two important respects in which political and ecological values inhabit a common philosophical space. The first consists in the *types of justification* that are commonly offered for both ecological and political values, and the second in the *moral pluralism* that implicitly underlies both. (a) Environmental values are frequently sought to be justified in terms of arguments of human interest. These take the form of justifying, to human beings, why it is in their *interest* to hold ecological values. This is not dissimilar from the way in which liberal political values like justice are defended. Most famously, John Rawls' [*1972*] account of how the two principles of justice as fairness are arrived at, was animated by the desire to eschew perfectionism, and to present an argument that was neutral between conceptions of the good life. This led Rawls to resort to the device of the social contract. In his original position, people situated behind the veil of ignorance would choose these principles on what turned out to be more or less prudential grounds, as when they invoked the maximin rule of choosing that alternative which would be least harmful if - when the veil of ignorance was removed - they found themselves among the most disadvantaged in society. In this account of justice, the principles of equality and fraternity were more or less unintended consequences of an essentially self-regarding decision, as Rawls's individuals chose the principles of justice as fairness not because they were animated by the ideals of equality and fraternity, but because they were the principles that people perceived as being least detrimental to their interests.

Tim Hayward's defence of ecological values in terms of human interests is an argument in similar vein. An appeal to the enlightened self-interest of individuals, rather than to the intrinsic value of nature, Hayward argues, is the soundest basis for ecological values. He posits the most fundamental interest of human beings as an interest in 'integrity', which stands for 'wholeness, unity, and health in one's physical, mental and spiritual being' [*Hayward, 1998: 88*]. Both rational self-interest as well as enlightened self-interest (in which the self appears as part of a greater whole, related to all other selves without claiming any particular privileges) can, on his view, be harnessed to environmental ends.

(b) The second respect in which ecological and political values share common philosophical ground is that moral pluralism is central to ecological values as well as to many kinds of political values, most notably in the liberal and communitarian traditions. The anti-perfectionism of liberal political theory is premised on the recognition that there are many contending conceptions of the good life, which should be negotiated by the processes of politics (ideally, processes of deliberative and dialogical democracy) rather than by the state, which ought to be neutral between them. Value-pluralism is based on a refutation of the idea of a human essence that can yield agreement on an indisputable human good, whether personal or political. Cultural relativists approach this somewhat differently, emphasising the fact that conceptions of human needs and human agency, and therefore moral beliefs and values, will differ across societies and cultural traditions. This belief in the social embeddedness of values has a certain affinity with the communitarian position in political theory, issuing in the belief that diversity and difference are intrinsically worth valuing.

In environmental ethics, too, we find a parallel recognition and even celebration of pluralism, arising out of the diversity of the biotic world. The immense diversity of nature – with the attendant, though empirically contestable, presumption that it is characterised by harmony, co-operation, balance and an absence of conflict and hierarchy – is frequently offered as an exemplar for social and political life.[1] Thus, for instance, the notion of the ecological commons (in air, water or pastures) is interpreted as being suggestive of a community-centred social and political entity, whose rootedness in community negates control by national governments or transnational corporations [*Morrison, 1995: 16–17*]. Though the holism of Deep Ecology tends towards a conservative direction, the virtues of democracy, egalitarianism, decentralisation, and even socialism, are frequently extrapolated from the way in which nature is 'naturally' constituted.

Nevertheless, there are arguably differences in the moral premises underlying our attachment to ecological and political values, leading to necessary differences in the identification of the sources of such values. Political values are generally premised on the assumption of individual autonomy, and the individual's capacity for rational thought and agency.

Ecological values, on the other hand, cannot so easily rest upon arguments of autonomy or agency.[2] Hence, the search for the source of value in nature – whether it lies in nature itself or in the consciousness of the human evaluator – typically invokes a variety of arguments, ranging from intrinsic value to instrumental value, as also flourishing, diversity and community.

Another important difference stems from the fact that ecological and political values are attached to entities that are qualitatively different. Thus, ecological values are values held *by* humans, which inhere – intrinsically or otherwise – in natural phenomena, and are ascribed to them. As such, ecological values are descriptive of nature, or of human perceptions and valuations of it. Political values, on the other hand, are values evolved and held by human beings for their own species, which are the products of reflection about how public authority should be constituted and social and political relationships regulated. This implies that ecological values are evolved – howsoever altruistically – by human beings for other species, and this holds true even when humans ascribe intrinsic value to natural phenomena. As such, one of the basic distinctions between ecological and political values lies in the beings or entities to which they are attached. This may be an important source of the tension between ecological and political values. Is it possible to resolve these tensions in policy, through political procedures of decision-making, and if so, does it compel us to modify some of our theoretical assumptions?

Evidence from a Case study

Conservation[3] is self-evidently an unimpeachable ecological value. In many Third World contexts, however, the commitment of environmentalists to conservation is severely tested by the countervailing force of their simultaneous commitment to political values such as justice and rights. In India, this tension is most starkly manifested in the conflicts between, on the one hand, the conservationist policy agenda of setting up protected areas such as national parks and wildlife sanctuaries and, on the other, the subsistence and livelihood rights of local communities which have historically lived in these areas and enjoyed access to the natural resources afforded by them. When, as is often the case, these local communities comprise ethnically distinct and largely marginalised social groups such as *adivasis* (tribal people), the environmentalist dilemma is acute, and the conservationist ethic is placed under greater strain. In this section, we shall survey some of the problems that have arisen in protected areas such as national parks and wildlife sanctuaries in different parts of India, and extrapolate from these examples issues that are relevant for our argument.

The predisposition of those who hold political power to exercise control over natural resources is, of course, as old as recorded history. The attempt by rulers and ruling classes to *conserve* natural resources (especially forests) is also a phenomenon of some antiquity. In India, for example, the Maratha rulers of western India had followed policies that could be called robustly conservationist in the early eighteenth century. By the middle of the nineteenth century, the East India Company – which had once, in a symbolic display of political superiority, razed to the ground a teak plantation in Ratnagiri nurtured by a Maratha admiral – was being encouraged to adopt policies of forest conservancy, by scientific advisers who linked deforestation to drought and the possibility of social and economic breakdown [*Grove, 1990: 22*]. The colonial state sponsored the merciless cutting down of forests, first for shipbuilding and later to furnish its railway network. However, the anxiety about timber supply led the British to offset their profligacy by some conservationist measures. To facilitate greater state control over the forests – which, in many parts, were common property resources managed and regulated by community sanction – the Indian Forest Act of 1878 was enacted. This legislation represented a victory for the 'annexationists', whose advocacy of stringent state control over forest resources was at least partly justified by recourse to a conservationist argument, according to which the chief threat to the forests came from the local communities whose access to these resources was now severely restricted, if not altogether curtailed [*Gadgil and Guha, 1993: 123–34*]. The main motivation, of imperial and commercial interests, reflected also a prejudice against tribals who peopled much forest land.[4]

The categories of classification of ownership and control over forests in contemporary India remain the same as under colonial rule: reserved forests, protected forests and village forests. It is therefore startling to discover that, despite retaining the colonial legacy in almost every dimension, when it came to adopting a model for wildlife conservation, India chose to follow the American practice rather than the considerably more enlightened British one. While National Parks in Britain recognise existing rights, maintain established farming systems and provide mechanisms whereby local residents can participate in processes of decision-making, the American practice has been one of creating sanitised reserves in which local people are treated as poachers or encroachers responsible for ecological decline, rather than as people with prior rights to these areas [*Colchester, 1994: 4*].

The conservationist impulse in India did not, however, emanate exclusively from within a colonial state whose material interests were bound up with the regeneration of forests. It came also from many rulers of princely states who, as keen game hunters, were alarmed by the rapid depletion of some species, and began to borrow and apply game laws devised by the British to their own hunting reserves. As early as 1910, thus, the Maharajah of Kashmir ordered the removal of the human population of the Dachigam deer reserve. In 1934, the government of British India enacted the Indian National Parks Act, which – without commenting on the local communities that lived in these areas – essentially specified the terms and conditions on which licensed visitors – read hunters – could enter game parks. India's first national park, the Corbett Park was established in northern India the following year. Also in 1935, at a conference organised by the United Provinces Wildlife Preservation Society along with the Bombay Natural History Society, enthusiastic conservationists – princes, urban naturalists and even Jawaharlal Nehru – argued strenuously for more effective wildlife preservation, through the setting up of more national parks, and more funds for controlling poaching.

In independent India, the marked acceleration in the process of setting up national parks – inspired by the new global environmental consciousness, as also by a recognition of the alarming rates of forest depletion and genetic loss – began in the 1970s, and gathered momentum in the next two decades. The number of sanctuaries and national parks went up from 65 in 1960, to 521 in 1995. The 76,000 square kilometres of area which were under protection in 1980, virtually doubled to 148,000 square kilometres by 1995, an annual expansion rate of 620,000 hectares. [*Khare, 1998: 90*] Because the creation of parks frequently involves the removal of human populations, this increase has unsurprisingly had a severe impact on the local communities inhabiting these areas. Today, as India approaches its target of placing five per cent of its land under such reserves, 19 per cent of the total forest in India, home to a fifth of the total *adivasi* population of the country, is already under sanctuaries/national parks.

The constitution and management of these parks is governed by the Wildlife (Protection) Act of 1972, which spells out the distinction between these two major categories of protected area. National parks and sanctuaries encompass reserved forests, protected forests, and revenue land, including areas used as common property resources. In National Parks, all rights to the land included within the park are acquired by the government, giving rise to involuntary displacement. Grazing of animals is forbidden, and no wildlife can be destroyed, exploited or removed. In sanctuaries, by contrast, people may enjoy limited rights of access to forest resources in the protected area. The displacement of local communities from such areas has, in recent years, drawn attention to the inadequacies and problems in the process of the 'settlement' of their rights.[5] Once an area is notified as a national park or sanctuary, the collector is required to determine the nature and extent of rights held by the people in or over the notified land. S/he has then to publish, in the local press, information regarding the boundaries of the land to be notified, and invite rights-holders to submit, within two months, written claims regarding their rights. By and large, claims are rarely brought forward for determination, because the people are ignorant of the law, and unaware of the publication of such notices. But the major obstacle is that rights, existing from pre-colonial times, are largely unrecorded, and formal law does not, for the most part, take cognisance of rights of usufruct and ownership enjoyed under customary law and usage. A public interest litigation relating to these issues is pending before the Supreme Court, which recently directed that settlement processes should be completed within one year of the notification of a protected area. This order had a curious effect on some state governments, which began to quickly denotify sections of national parks wherever the process of the settlement of rights appeared to be knotty or complex. The consequence of this is that local populations are deprived of their rights, even as the objectives of conservation remain unaccomplished. In the following paragraphs, we take examples from different parts of India to illustrate some of the conflicts generated by national parks and sanctuaries, and to extrapolate from these the issues relevant for environmental ethics and political ecology.

Involuntary Displacement

It has been estimated that as many as 600,000 people have been displaced as a direct consequence of the establishment of national parks and sanctuaries in India [*Colchester, 1994: 19*]. Displacement incurred in this way takes many forms, which include: involuntary displacement (with or without resettlement and rehabilitation); confinement to a buffer zone[6] (with or without access to forest produce); secondary displacement; disguised displacement; and even ostensible but in actuality meaningless options to stay on. Studies of displacement and resettlement have repeatedly shown that forced relocation causes not merely material impoverishment, but also social, psychological and physiological stress, as communities face the breakdown of a familiar moral order and consequently social disarticulation.[7] In the following paragraphs, we survey some instances of these.

The Gir National Park – the last surviving natural habitat of the famous Asian lion – is located in the state of Gujarat in western India. Less than a fifth of this protected area is a National Park, while the remaining (approximately 1,200 square kilometres) is presently a sanctuary, though the latter portion is under notification for conversion into a National Park, entailing eventually the total removal of human habitation. The main human inhabitants of this area over the past five hundred years have been a community of pastoralists called the Maldharis, officially given the status of tribal people. In 1972, approximately 800 Maldhari families were identified as eligible for resettlement, but just over half were actually resettled. Even this resettlement programme has been a failure, as the lands allotted to these people were uncultivable and without a water source, leading many families to make their way back. Resettlement of the families which continue to live in the 54 remaining 'nesses' (or pastoralist hamlets) and villages is fraught with difficulty, chiefly because of the unavailability of land in the region, and lack of access to water resources or grazing land for their cattle. Above all, these pastoralists are unfamiliar with the practices of settled agriculture and hence unable to adapt to a different lifestyle [*Choudhary, 2000*].

The removal of the Maldharis, along with their livestock, has also meant decreasing access to livestock for a steadily increasing population of lions (presently estimated as 304), and therefore an extension of the 'home range', the area within which they hunt. Meanwhile, the mining of limestone, blackstone and granite in about 20 villages of the buffer zone, bordering the sanctuary, is being undertaken by contractors for cement companies in the region. This is probably a greater source of disturbance to the Gir ecosystem than the human population that has inhabited this area for the better part of five hundred years.

In the Melghat Tiger Reserve in Maharashtra (declared a sanctuary in 1973, and then notified as a tiger reserve in 1987), while actual displacement has not yet taken place, the chiefly tribal population in 22 villages of the area lives in constant fear of forcible eviction. Public services in the area have gradually been suspended, which is always a sinister signal. The villagers are not allowed to enter the sanctuary or graze their cattle, and are liable to pay a stiff fine if their livestock stray into the reserved area. They are also prohibited from collecting wood, herbs and wild fruits from the forest, or bamboo to repair their huts or construct houses. There is a poignant irony in the fact that though a museum in the region proudly displays wooden handicrafts made by the Korku tribe of this area, the villagers are today no longer able to create such artefacts as a means of livelihood [*Centre for Environmental Law, WWF-India vs. Union of India and Others*: *Application for Intervention, Annexures VI–VIII*]. Despite their repeated petitioning of government authorities to be consulted and informed about the project, they have been largely ignored.

In the Koyna sanctuary in Maharashtra, most of the 50 villages that fall within the sanctuary area are those which suffered displacement as a result of the construction of the Koyna dam in 1960. These people now face a secondary displacement, caused by the notification of the area as a sanctuary. Though they are at present permitted to cut grass and other shrubs, and even allowed to extract non-timber forest produce such as honey and dead wood, their rights to these are unrecorded and hence likely to be taken away when the official procedures of recognition are applied.

Finally, there is the case of the Nagarhole National Park in Karnataka, said to be among the most productive areas world-wide in terms of animal biomass, and rich in tigers, elephants and other animals. The Ecodevelopment project in this park was launched by the World Bank, and reviewed by the latter in October 1998, on the request of the 6,000 *adivasi* people who have traditionally inhabited this area. The purpose of the Ecodevelopment project was twofold: to simultaneously support the management of protected areas which are significant from the point of view of global biodiversity and to protect the interests of local people living in and around these areas. As such, the planning process was expected to involve the local people in the management of the parks, as also to take into consideration their wishes regarding relocation. The Inspection Panel of the Bank found that only three per cent of the tribal population of the park had chosen to relocate, and the remaining, who had opted to stay, nevertheless feared forceful eviction from the project area. It also found, however, that while people had the option to relocate or to stay, the 'stay option' was 'very tenuous, to the point of perhaps not being a real option at all' [*International Bank for Reconstruction and Development, 1998: 19*]. This the panel attributed to the 'serious tension' between the provisions of the Wildlife Protection Act and the legal covenants of the Ecodevelopment project not to carry out any involuntary resettlement of people living within the protected area. It noted also the fact that these *adivasi* peoples do not have any property rights over the forests and lands on which they live, because these rights were extinguished by the colonial state and not restored after independence. Subsequently, after the passage of the Wildlife Protection Act, their rights of usufruct (collecting firewood, leaves, honey, and non-timber forest produce) were also taken away, as were their grazing rights. Thus, tribals living within the park do not own any cattle now, while those living in villages adjacent to the park boundary do, and continue to graze them in the park! It was taking all this into account that the Inspection Panel observed:

> This combination of the 1972 Wildlife Act, the 1997 Supreme Court decision, official expectations concerning the present and future choices of tribals, and the elimination of their rights to use the land and forests in which they dwell, taken together, conspire to undermine the reality of the stay option. They also seriously jeopardise the fundamental premise underlying the Ecodevelopment project. [*International Bank for Reconstruction and Development, 1998: 22*].

Rights of Local Communities, Especially Indigenous Peoples

As we have seen, the establishment of protected areas frequently entails the removal of human communities who have, in most such cases, lived in these environs for centuries. Many of these are *adivasi* communities, whose plight is not dissimilar from those of indigenous peoples in many other countries of the South. The assumption underlying the removal of these communities is that they are chiefly responsible for the degradation of natural resources, and therefore these resources need to be protected against depredations by them. This ignores, of course, the fact that had these communities – as in many such cases – not followed reasonably sustainable patterns of natural resource use, there would have been no area left to protect. As things stand, even when these communities are not subjected to involuntary displacement, they routinely suffer the denial of their customary rights to natural resources. Many of the conflicts generated by the establishment of protected areas are directly related to such denial and their attempts to maintain these rights, if necessary by resort to invasion, poaching, and even violence against parks authorities and forest guards. In at least one important case, this resentment has resulted in a political insurgency of compelling magnitude.

The most common form of conflict in and around the parks and sanctuaries is directly related to the prohibition on collecting wood from the jungle for building and repairing the huts of the forest-dwellers. Similarly, the ban on collecting food in the form of roots, tubers, and fruit; firewood as cooking fuel; fodder for livestock; and medicinal herbs, amounts to taking away the basic elements of their sustenance from the *adivasi*. It also strikes at the root of their livelihood, where the collection of minor forest produce[8] is a source of income and employment for them. In the Phoolvari ki Nal sanctuary in Rajasthan, the local people, who were dependent on the resources of the forest for their sustenance for nine months in the year, were instantly rendered destitute when the area was converted into a sanctuary. For this population of 30,000 persons, mainly *adivasis*, the ban on collecting minor forest produce meant that they could no longer collect and sell *tendu* leaves which was a major source of livelihood for them. Now, it is reported that local forest officials, in connivance with contractors, have been involved in the plucking and smuggling out of the *tendu* leaves. Here, as in almost every other such area, a common complaint of the unlettered *adivasis* is that corrupt forest officials harass and extort bribes from them for the alleged contravention of park rules, of which they are ignorant.

A similar insensitivity to the subsistence needs and customary rights of local peoples is visible in parks set up to protect biodiversity. The Nanda Devi Biosphere Reserve in the Himalayan region of Uttar Pradesh was declared a sanctuary as long ago as 1939, but was classified as a biosphere reserve only in 1988. Traditionally, this Valley has been divided into two parts: an upper portion which has always been kept free of human activity by, among other things, religious sanctions, which regard as sinful the unnecessary and wasteful use of the sacred valley; and a lower part where the local people customarily grazed their sheep and also collected minor forest produce for their subsistence needs. Even the collection of herbal flora for medicinal purposes was regulated by social norms which determined the seasons in which these could be plucked, the part of the plant that could be removed, and so forth. The careful use of the natural resources of this region come as close to an ethic of sustainability as is possible.[9] While some changes in the social and ecological profile of the area had become apparent since the Nanda Devi peak became a favourite of mountaineers and tourists in the 1930s, it is in recent years that the changes have become truly dramatic. With the declaration of Nanda Devi as a national park, biological diversity came to be privileged over human and cultural diversity, and local communities were denied their customary rights of access. Consequently, grazing activities had to be suspended, and with them the livestock economy of the local people. Suddenly, the people of this area found themselves without any source of income, and began migrating in search of alternative livelihoods [*Society for Participatory Research in Asia, 1993: 8–9*].

Possibly the most controversial conservation programme of all is Project Tiger, which has resulted in the alienation of local communities, and succeeded in creating hostility towards the animal rather than sympathy for the conservationist cause. The animosity towards animals in the Betla Tiger Reserve in Bihar, for example, is provoked by the fact that while the killing of an animal in the park invites a stiff penalty (often quite arbitrary, ranging from unrecorded fines to physical torture), in the event of a human being killed by an animal, little sympathy is forthcoming from the authorities who adopt a coldly mechanical attitude in the processing of claims for compensation. Restrictions on movement within the parks and on the right to carry traditional weapons have affected not only the livelihoods of these people but also rendered them, their livestock and crops vulnerable to attacks by wild animals. In southern and north-eastern India, crops damaged by elephants cause damage worth millions of rupees every year, while large numbers of cattle in all parts of the country fall prey to lions, tigers and leopards every year. The killing of human beings by elephants and tigers is obviously of even greater concern. Wild elephants have been estimated to kill an average of 200 people annually, while in the Sunderbans region alone, nearly a thousand human lives were taken by a steadily increasing tiger population in just two decades [*Gadgil and Guha, 1992: 234; Sukumar, 1994: 305–6*].

Apart from the loss of their customary rights which, in many cases, are closely bound up with *adivasi* cultures, there are also other rights of citizenship in a modern state which the people affected by the establishment of protected areas may legitimately claim. The right to be informed and notified in advance of displacement, and the right to represent their claims – which are technically provided for in the Wildlife Protection Act – are rarely, if ever, respected. The process of settlement of rights is yet to be completed in a majority of protected areas, despite the Supreme Court's 1995 directive to some state governments, to determine and settle the rights of the *adivasis* to land, and to ensure that they are not dispossessed till such time as these cases are disposed of.

The notices served for this purpose are displayed at the remote offices of the Forest Department, instead of being publicised through the more customary methods of public announcement and drum beating at the village marketplace. They are either in a language that is unknown to the local population, or drafted in incomprehensible legalese. The question of who is eligible to make a claim – that is, only the propertied or the propertyless as well; only those inside the boundaries of the sanctuary, or also those outsiders who depend upon it in various ways – is unclear. It is often the case that even forest officials have little understanding of what is involved, and panic strikes the people who believe that they are being served eviction orders. In the case presently pending before the Supreme Court [*Centre for Environmental Law, WWF-India and Others vs. Union of India, Civil Writ Petition No. 337 of 1995*], an intervention was filed by a number of voluntary organisations, asking the court to decide whether the affected people have a right to be heard; whether the governments have an obligation to explain in the local language the entire procedure for the settlement of rights; whether rights should include the unrecorded traditional and customary rights of the people, rather than only their recorded rights;[10] and whether a more transparent method should be adopted for this process of settlement. The intervention was dismissed by the Supreme Court in 1999, though the substantive case is still to be decided. The fate of the three million people who live in and around the 525 parks and sanctuaries hangs in the balance.

It has been argued that the section of the Wildlife Protection Act which relates to the determination of rights can be subject to both a narrow and a broad interpretation. On the narrow interpretation, the recognition of rights can be based only on land records. The broad interpretation, however, can plausibly entail the recognition of any right relating to the land or the water bodies within the sanctuary. This could include the rights that accrue from long practice and custom, for any community that lives within and around the sanctuary area. In practice, courts have generally tended to endorse the narrow rather than the broad interpretation, thereby depriving local communities of their customary rights to the collection of forest products for domestic use [*Upadhyay, 1999*].

Even as local – mostly *adivasi* – communities have either been deprived of, or face the prospect of losing, their customary rights, a variety of commercial interests have continued to thrive despite the creation of protected areas. The limestone and other illegal mining activities taking place on the periphery of the Gir sanctuary have already been mentioned. In the Great Himalayan National Park in north India, over a thousand hectares of land originally encompassed by the park have been denotified as protected area, ostensibly on account of the two villages located within it. In reality, however, it is well-known that this has been done to facilitate the setting up of the Parbati Hydel Project in the same area. This shows how notification and denotification alike are realms of bureaucratic discretion and arbitrariness, often disguising a variety of material interests of wealth or power. The ambiguities of the Wildlife Protection Act[11] make this easier. Ironically, the same provision of the Act is invoked, to support purposes that are sometimes conservationist, and at other times manifestly anti-conservationist. In the Rajaji National Park, for instance, Section 29 was first invoked to deprive the *baan* (rope) workers of their access to the *bhabar* grass with which the rope is made. Three years later, under public pressure, the same provision was invoked to allow a few headloads of the grass per person, on the grounds that if the *bhabar* is not removed, forest fires may occur!

A notable exception to this largely dismal tale is that of Sariska, also a tiger reserve in the Aravali hills, which was declared a national park in 1978. This led to forced migration on a massive scale, with the men moving to the cities as migrant labour, while the women and children stayed behind to work in the dolomite mines, over 200 of which fell fully within the protected area, and another 40 partly in it. The mines had already led to considerable denudation of forests in the area, as also barren pastures and polluted water. In 1990, a local non-governmental organisation called the Tarun Bharat Sangh moved the Supreme Court against mining in Sariska, and obtained a favourable order. However, with the protection of the Rajasthan state government, which wanted to continue the mining, mine-owners attacked the TBS volunteers, filed dozens of false cases against its volunteers, and even made three attempts on the life of its leader. Though the Supreme Court had directed the Union Government to declare the Aravali range a fragile ecosystem and ban mining, the mine-owners managed to get the notification watered down to exclude the particular regions of interest to them, and also engineered the scrapping of a clause banning mining in the 25 kilometres around the forest boundary. With the support of the Court, the TBS began its battle to win back the rights of the people of the sanctuary area to farm their lands. Gradually, through the formulation of community rules for the protection of the forest and for water-harvesting structures, the regeneration of the area has begun [*Pushkarna, 1998: 30*–32].

Political Insurgency

In some cases, the resentment against conservationist measures has even resulted in political insurgency. The Maria tribals evicted from their lands when the Kutru Tiger and Buffalo Reserve was established in Madhya Pradesh in 1984, are believed to have joined the ranks of the Naxalite (Marxist-Leninist) militants in the region. In Assam, the Bodo tribals belong to an area which was first brought under tea plantations by the British, and is now partly enclosed by the Manas Tiger Reserve. In recent years, there has been considerable Hindu and Bengali (that is, non-Bodo) migration into this area from Bangladesh. The Bodos now find themselves an ethnic minority in their own homeland, and have been demanding an independent state. Harnessing the resentment of local Bodos (who lost their lands to the reserve) to political advantage, insurgents have driven out the park guards. They are also reported to be killing wildlife in order to raise money to arm their movement, and three-quarters of the rhinoceroses from the Manas Reserve are believed to have been killed for their horns since 1989 [*Colchester, 1994: 23*].

Violence and Incendiarism

Other forms of violence are encountered almost routinely in and around the parks. In the Kanha national park, protest has taken the form of setting fire in large areas of the park as a retaliation for the denial of access to forest produce. In the Nagarhole sanctuary in Karnataka, 20 square kilometres of forest were set on fire as wildlife guards were accused of killing a poacher. Between 1979 and 1984, 117 incidents of violent conflict were reported from the parks and sanctuaries [*Gadgil and Guha, 1992: 234*]. Violence against park officials is also not uncommon.

Disruption of Ecological Balance

An ethical premise of biodiversity conservation is that this heritage is part of the global commons and hence for the good of all humankind, and indeed for the good of future generations as well. In ethical terms, it is difficult to conceive of a morally plausible trade-off between the rights of local communities as against the requirements of inter-generational equity. In reality, we find that despite sacrificing 'human interests', the conservationist objective may not even be achieved, as the creation of protected areas tends to disturb the traditional balance between humans and their environment, sometimes leading to more rather than less environmental degradation.[12] In the Betla Tiger Reserve, for example, local people were disallowed from bamboo trimming, an activity that previously brought them some income. Not only has this ban resulted in the loss of a source of income, it has also increased the threat of forest fires, because untrimmed bamboo is more prone to fire and helps it to spread rapidly and often uncontrollably.

Probably the most graphic illustration of how ecological balance can be disrupted despite conservation initiatives is the experience of the Keoladeo National Park in Rajasthan. This is a man-made wetland, home to 350 species of birds, which was formally, though somewhat incongruously, inaugurated by Lord Curzon with a duck shoot in 1902! Today, it is best known for the migratory birds, especially the Siberian crane, which visit it in the winter months. The ten villages surrounding the Park are home to about 16,000 people, mainly pastoral communities which depend on the sale of milk and milk products. When Keoladeo was declared a national park in 1982, grazing of livestock was banned, as was the collection of fuelwood and minor forest produce. The villagers opposed the ban, and in the police repression that followed their protest, seven villagers were killed [*Subramanian and Vlasoff, n.d.*]. Meanwhile, the visits of many migratory birds, such as the migratory waterfowl which have been among the chief attractions of the sanctuary, became scarce. It was only later that a study of the Bombay Natural History Society demonstrated that it was the absence of buffalo grazing that had contributed to the excessive growth of the *paspalum* grass, causing it to choke the marshes, which in turn discouraged the birds from visiting [*Kothari, 1997: 11*]. Subsequently, some cutting of the grasses by the villagers has been permitted in the park.

The argument of ecological balance is however interpreted rather arbitrarily by officialdom, and with varying motivations. The Chief Wildlife Warden of Uttar Pradesh, for example, has permitted the removal of grass and fallen timber from national parks and sanctuaries by local people, on the grounds that this is a sound measure for fire prevention. The Gujarat government has gone a step further, and allowed a paper mill to cut bamboo from the Shoolpaneswar Sanctuary, on the grounds that the clearings that result are good for wild herbivores! [*Upadhyay, 1999: 18*] The first of these two apparently similar actions, based on apparently identical motivations, benefits local communities, while the other clearly privileges commercial interests. Meanwhile, the fear that the focus on creating reserves, especially wildlife sanctuaries, provides a virtual license for the continued degradation of the areas outside of these parks, is not altogether unfounded.[13]

One response to the tensions between the claims of conservation and those of local communities was the strategy of 'ecodevelopment' supported by agencies like the World Bank. But the manifest inadequacies of ecodevelopment projects under implementation [*Baviskar, 1999*] have given way to the currently regnant wisdom of Joint Protected Area Management, an institutional innovation that seeks to extend the collaborative model of Joint Forest Management to the protected areas [*Kothari et al., 1996*]. This, too, is beset with difficulties, as the different agencies involved in the process have distinct and even conflicting priorities, and also because the inequalities of power relations within local communities are not addressed. Lacking political power and control over financial resources, local communities tend to remain 'very junior partners in decision-making' [*Colchester, 1994: 34*].[14]

Lessons for Environmental Political Theory

The impulse to conserve diversity, and preserve species of flora and fauna, has been an important element of the environmental agenda in all parts of the world. Conflicts of the kind detailed above are also not specific to India, and may be found in many parts of Asia, Africa and South America.[15] In several South American countries, the removal – and therefore resettlement – of residents from national parks is a statutory requirement, regardless of whether or not there is evidence to suggest that their continued presence constitutes a threat to the ecosystem of the region. In Uganda, the mass expulsion of 30,000 indigenous people to create a wildlife corridor between a forest reserve and a national park, led to 'serious human rights violations, mass impoverishment, burning, looting, the killing of livestock, and deaths of indigenous peoples' [*Colchester, 1994: 14*]. In Thailand, governmental coercion to evict villagers to make way for national parks and wildlife sanctuaries has, since the 1980s, witnessed the eruption of a number of clashes between people and authorities, as also a rise in protest movements against such projects [*Ghimire, 1991*].

In the countries of the South, therefore, the creation of protected areas is not an activity without serious human costs, which may entail the sacrifice of cherished political values. We may, for example, believe that the rights of *adivasi* (in other contexts, indigenous) people, being displaced by the creation of protected areas, to their land is an historically validated right; or that their rights to cultural community and to their unique way of life must be protected. We may also believe that, as citizens of a modern state, they have a legitimate claim to the fair application of the principles of justice on an equal footing with their fellow-citizens. Our commitment to democracy may lead us to argue, further, that these communities are entitled to voice and participation in decisions about the location of human habitation within parks and sanctuaries. Above all, we may be compelled to recognise that a political value as fundamental as freedom is denied in situations of involuntary displacement and that, even where the option to 'stay' ostensibly exists, it is not available as a meaningful choice.

Clearly, those who have an absolute commitment to ecological values and an equally absolute commitment to the human and social concerns of rights and justice, are confronted with a problem that appears to involve unhappy trade-offs. In situations of this kind, it is hard to endorse the trade-off of this wide gamut of political values, which we may view as fundamental and integral to the quality of human life in society, in exchange for the value of conservation *qua* conservation (rather than a value ascribed to nature on account of the interests of governments and transnational corporations). How, then, may this conflict be theoretically negotiated?

A possible, though not altogether satisfactory, way of approaching this dilemma is to allow the nature and depth of one's environmental commitment to guide the choice. As such, a deep ecologist might privilege ecological values, assert the overriding importance of conservation, and recommend only that governments adopt a more sensitive approach towards the people displaced by the park. On the other hand, an anthropocentric approach may yield the argument that human interests have a certain priority which must be respected in the way in which we choose to give effect to our conservationist objectives. Because we value nature not intrinsically, but instrumentally, we must perforce order our ecological concerns accordingly. In this case, we would allow political values to trump ecological values. This could be done in more than one way. We might place some rights on a list of non-negotiable core rights which cannot be sacrificed under any circumstances, howsoever compelling. Or else we might require that the independent arbitrating principle in such situations of conflict be that of self-determination through participatory democratic mechanisms. If the latter, we could ensure environmentally acceptable consequences only if participation were combined with environmental awareness, through the widespread dissemination of the idea of the worth of conservation. Committing ourselves to asserting the priority of human interests and therefore of political values in cases where these conflict with ecological values, is a logical consequence of arguing that human interests are the best means of justifying the latter. The anthropocentric ethic may, without much difficulty, accommodate such an affirmation of political values as trumps.

Our empirical evidence, however, poses two additional challenges to environmental political theory in general, and the anthropocentric ethic in particular. The first of these suggests the importance of working into it human specificities, such that differences of location (North and South, urban and rural); of history (coloniser/colonised or tribal/non-tribal); and of class and gender, can be accounted for and treated as relevant.[16] Only such a differentiated conception of the human in relation to nature, can lend force to the point that conflicts of the kind we have examined do not represent a necessarily adversarial relationship between human beings and their natural surroundings. The essentialism implicit in the view of humans as incorrigible authors of environmental destruction assumes that there is only a singular type of human-nature interaction, and underpins the argument that nature needs to be conserved and protected *from* humans. The evidence however suggests that such a view deserves to be qualified by the recognition that there are many types of human-nature interaction, not all of which are of necessity ecologically destructive, and that an anthropomorphic essentialism can only damage the environmental cause in the long run.

Human beings, as we all know, are capable of both degrading as well as conserving the environment. Some human beings – more often that not, commercial interests – may be responsible for exploiting nature far beyond the limits of ecological sustainability. Others, such as urban elite conservationists, may be enthusiastic supporters of wildlife and biodiversity preservation for a variety of reasons, including aesthetic ones. However, in some of the cases discussed above, the interests of both these categories of human beings – the predators and the conservers, so to speak – are equally unmindful of and even hostile towards those of a third category of humans, namely those belonging to the local communities which have historically inhabited the areas subsequently demarcated as protected. Of these local communities, in turn, some have practised sustainable patterns of natural resource use, which have long been inscribed into their culture, customs, and ways of life. Others may arguably be less conservationist in their practices, and yet it would be unusual to find a protected area that has been degraded but is still worth protecting. Indeed, if, in the now protected areas, local communities had indulged in over-exploitation of their resources, there may arguably have been nothing left to protect.[17] Today, however, as populations in and around the forest areas experience rapid increases, it is difficult to assume that it is possible or feasible to return to traditional and sustainable patterns of natural resource use.

If there is no singular model of the interaction of human beings with nature, the idea that there is only one model of conservation may also be interrogated. It has, for instance, been argued that the classical conservationist model is a western cultural construct, not necessarily shared by people in other cultures who have customarily seen the relationship between man and nature as one of coexistence rather than of duality and discordance [*Sarkar, 2000: 60*]. On the other hand, quite independently of the question of its cultural origins, this approach to, and model of, conservation can also be faulted for being exclusionary. A rethinking on alternative *ways* of effecting conservation, without questioning the worth of the goal, may therefore be desirable.

Secondly, the positive value attached to the project of conservation tends to obscure the important fact that conservationist initiatives are usually dependent on the agency of the state. Though environmental political theory recognises the emancipatory potential of deliberative democracy as well as of discourses of rights and justice, it is curiously reluctant to engage with the dimension of politics as power, except in the minimal sense of recognising that environmental degradation is a consequence of the exercise of humankind's power over nature. Environmental historians, by contrast, have readily identified the power of dominant social groups and classes, states and bureaucracies, as important variables in their enterprise of chronicling the impact of human life on nature. They have also provided rich accounts of the imperatives of forest conservation by colonial states which first scripted the degradation of the environment through the commercial exploitation of forest resources and then sought to restore these. The story of how mixed forests in colonial India were clear-felled and systematically replaced by single-species stands is well known, as is the long-term impact of this policy on the subsistence needs of local people.

Political ecologists have relatively less difficulty in identifying the role of states and dominant classes in environmental destruction. But even they do not, as a rule, point the same critical spotlight at the politics of conservation. This prevents them from observing the curious fact that conservationist attempts to insulate protected areas from human interference actually seek to effect this by deploying the authority of the state. The tasks of deciding which area is to be demarcated for protection, how the buffer and core zones will be delimited, which parts may be denotified from a protected area and with what justification, are not innocent of political, bureaucratic or commercial interests. The heavy dependence of conservationism on centralising modes of management and technocratic means of control makes it unsurprising that its social consequences should include violent conflict and political insurgency.

When, therefore, conservationism entails the removal of local communities or the denial of their customary rights, it recasts the discourses of democratic citizenship and political obligation. The more marginalised the citizens in question, the easier it is for the state to prevail, using ostensibly conservationist arguments to extend and consolidate its control. Environmental political theory has, on the whole, fought shy of engaging with such concerns about power, despite the fact that most of the liberal political values to which environmental political theory routinely appeals do reflect such concerns. Rights, liberty, justice and democracy, for instance, are not merely values intended to inform and inspire morally superior forms of political practice. They are also bulwarks against anarchy, on the one hand, and the arbitrary exercise of political power, on the other. Political values thus implicitly reflect a concern for the myriad possibilities of power. There appears to be little reason why environmental political theory should not attempt to do the same. Even as we search for principles by which the rival claims of ecological and political values may be balanced, we should seek also a more multi-dimensional integration of the ecological and the political.

NOTES

1. The diversity of ways of life and cultures is especially privileged by ecocentric theorists. However, as Michael Freeden has argued, 'even if biodiversity is an empirical fact of the natural world, it still remains a construction of a reality in which diversity is the perceived organising principle' [*Freeden,1996: 539*].
2. It has been argued that while green values can be grounded in a defence of autonomy, green theory would still be faced by the challenge of evolving principles by which to reconcile human and non-human autonomy. Further, even if the principle of autonomy can be extended to cover ecological entities, rights discourse has limited potential in this respect [*Eckersley, 1996: 179–80, 194*].
3. The customary distinction between *conservation* (protection of nature inspired by considerations of human interest) and *preservation* (initiatives for the protection of nature for its own sake) is not reflected in the Indian discourse on conservation. Officials, activists and scholars alike use the term conservation to describe both programmes which are motivated by prudential, human-interest reasons, as also those which are inspired by the desire to preserve something for its own sake. Indeed, despite the (anthropocentric) official nomenclature of 'conservation', there is an alarming stringency in applying measures *against* local communities. This has led environmentalists like Ramachandra Guha to argue forcefully that 'the emphasis on wilderness is positively harmful when applied to the Third World ... wildlands preservation has been identified with environmentalism by the state and the conservation elite; in consequence, environmental problems that impinge far more directly on the lives of the poor – for example, fuel, fodder, water shortages, soil erosion, and air and water pollution – have not been adequately addressed' [*Guha, 1996: 284–5*].
4. Richard Grove has pointed out that early environmental critiques not only facilitated control by the colonial state over the forests, but also paralleled and reinforced current prejudices against the tribals, identified as the social group chiefly responsible for environmental degradation [*Grove, 1990: 23*]. Similar animosities are frequently encountered even in contemporary conservationist discourses in India.
5. Before the advent of colonial rule, the nature of ownership in forests was based in customary law, though sometimes communities were also given occupancy rights on account of their ancestral dominion over the lands they 'worked'. With Anglo-Saxon jurisprudence, came the introduction of the concept of property, and the annexation of forests as the property of the Crown. Those who inhabited these areas were now legally rendered 'encroachers' and 'trespassers'. For the rest, the doctrine of eminent domain permitted the state to acquire the property of rights-holders for 'public purposes', with due compensation being determined and paid to them under the provisions of the Land Acquisition Act of 1894.
6. Protected areas are generally zoned in terms of a strictly protected core area and a buffer zone in which varying levels of human use may be permissible. A buffer zone is defined as 'any area where special measures are taken to ensure land use which enhances the conservation of a totally protected area.' Buffer Zones perform chiefly two functions: (a) extension buffering, which extends the potential habitat area of the core species; and (b) socio-economic buffering, which takes care of the resource dependence of the local people by providing for sustainable ways of meeting their natural resource requirements.
7. See Downing's [*1996*] argument about 'the social geometry of the displaced'.

8. 'Minor forest produce' is officialese for everything except timber and firewood. It accounts for between a quarter and a half of the food needs of 80 per cent of *adivasis*. It is often also the exclusive source of income for forest dwelling people who collect and sell leaves, bamboo, and grasses for cash. There is some merit in the argument that what government designates as 'minor' forest produce is actually, from the point of view of the *adivasis*, major forest produce.
9. It is important, however, to remember that not all communities everywhere have been conservationist. There are many which have been and are so, but it is as well not to exaggerate these phenomena to the status of a myth.
10. Tribals are not legally entitled to land because forest lands are not and traditionally have never been, covered by revenue records. In the absence of documents establishing 'ownership' (a notion alien to the tribal, for whom this land is a source of life, sustenance, and livelihood in a more fundamental sense), tribal communities are officially considered 'encroachers' on government land. This ignores both the fact of their historically validated claims to this land, their dependence on natural resources for every aspect of their life, as also the psychological impact on tribals of their alienation from the natural resources by which they have always lived.
11. Section 29 of the Wildlife Protection Act provides that the Chief Wildlife Warden may, in the case of both sanctuaries and national parks, construct roads, bridges, etc. or take other such steps for the security of wildlife, or in the interest of wildlife, or for the improvement of its habitat, on the basis of independent scientific investigation.
12. Ghimire and Pimbert assert that 'the parks approach to conservation has frequently resulted in the degradation of a much larger surface than the area actually protected and has made local communities less responsible in their usually sustainable practice of natural resources management' [*1997: 33*].
13. With the bulk of conservation budgets being swallowed up by what have been called 'charismatic megafauna', namely animals like tigers, lions, elephants and rhinoceros, parks set up for the protection of biodiversity are less lavishly funded [*Colchester, 1994: 9*].
14. The complete absence of dialogue, and even consultation, is described in Chandana Dey's study of the Jaldapara Wildlife Sanctuary in West Bengal [*Dey, 1997*].
15. This is hardly surprising given that 70 per cent of protected areas worldwide, and 86 per cent of those in Latin America, are inhabited.
16. Such issues have, however, been raised in the context of environmental *movements*, as in Robert Bullard's analysis of racism and the environmental justice movement [*Bullard, 1996*].
17. Of course, this argument may be met by another counter-factual: namely, that presumably there were other areas rich in flora and fauna, which have been degraded beyond recognition, and hence lost to the cause of conservation.

REFERENCES

Baviskar, Amita (1999), 'Participating in Ecodevelopment: The Case of the Great Himalayan National Park', in Roger Jeffrey and Nandini Sundar (eds.), *A New Moral Economy for India's Forests? Discourses of Community and Participation*, New Delhi: Sage Publications.

Bullard, Robert (1996), 'Environmental Racism and the Environmental Justice Movement!', in Merchant [*1997*].

Choudhary, Kameshwar (2000), 'Development Dilemma: Resettlement of Gir Maldharis', *Economic and Political Weekly*, Vol.XXXV, No.30, 22–28 July.

Colchester Marcus (1994), 'Salvaging Nature: Indigenous Peoples, Protected Areas and Biodiversity Conservation', Geneva: United Nations Research Institute for Social Development, mimeo.

Dey, Chandana (1997), 'Women, Forest Products and Protected Areas: A Case Study of Jaldapara Wildlife Sanctuary, West Bengal, India', in Ghimire and Pimbert (eds.) [*1997*].

Downing, Theodore E. (1996), 'Mitigating Social Impoverishment when People are Involuntarily Displaced', in Christopher McDowell (ed.), *Understanding Impoverishment: The*

Consequences of Development-Induced Displacement, Oxford: Berghahn Books.

Eckersley, Robyn (1996), 'Liberal Democracy and the Rights of Nature: The Struggle for Inclusion', in Freya Mathews (ed.), *Ecology and Democracy*, London: Frank Cass.

Freeden, Michael (1996), *Ideologies and Political Theory: A Conceptual Approach*, Oxford: Clarendon Press.

Gadgil, Madhav and Ramachandra Guha (1992), *This Fissured Land: An Ecological History of India*, Delhi: Oxford University Press.

Gadgil, Madhav and Ramachandra Guha (1993), *Ecology and Equity: The use and abuse of nature in contemporary India*, New Delhi: Penguin Books.

Ghimire, Krishna B. (1991), 'Parks and People: Livelihood Issues in National Parks Management in Thailand and Madagascar', Discussion Paper 29, United Nations Research Institute for Social Development, Geneva.

Ghimire, Krishna B. and Michel P. Pimbert (1997), 'Social Change and Conservation: An Overview of Issues and Concept?', in Ghimire and Pimbert (eds.) [*1997*].

Ghimire, Krishna B. and Michel P. Pimbert (eds.) (1997), *Social Change and Conservation: Environmental Politics and Impacts of National Parks and Protected Areas*, London: Earthscan/UNRISD.

Grove, Richard (1990), 'Colonial Conservation, Ecological Hegemony and Popular Resistance: Towards a Global Synthesis', in John M. MacKenzie (eds.), *Imperialism and the Natural World*, Manchester: Manchester University Press.

Guha, Ramachandra (1996), 'Radical Environmentalism: A Third-World Critique', in Merchant [*1996*].

Hayward, Tim (1998), *Political Theory and Ecological Values*, Cambridge: Polity Press.

International Bank for Reconstruction and Development (1998), Report on 'India Ecodevelopment Project: Rajiv Gandhi (Nagarahole) National Park', Washington, DC.

Khare, Arvind (1998), 'Community-Based Conservation in India', in Ashish Kothari, Neema Pathak, R.V. Anuradha and Bansuri Taneja (eds.), *Communities and Conservation: Natural Resource Management in South and Central Asia*, New Delhi: Sage Publications.

Kothari, Ashish (1997), *Understanding Biodiversity: Life, Sustainability and Equity*, Tracts for the Times/11. New Delhi: Orient Longman.

Kothari, Ashish, Singh, Neena and Saloni Sun (eds.) (1996), *People and Protected Areas: Towards Participatory Conservation in India*, New Delhi: Sage Publications.

Merchant, Carolyn (ed.) (1996), *Ecology* (Key Concepts in Critical Theory series), Jaipur: Rawat Publications.

Morrison, Roy (1995), *Ecological Democracy*, Boston, MA: South End Press.

O'Neill, John (1993), *Ecology, Policy and Politics: Human Well-Being and the Natural World*, London: Routledge.

Pushkarna, Vijaya (1998), 'Kiss of Life for Mother Earth', *The Week*, 27 Dec. 1998.

Rawls, John (1972), *A Theory of Justice*, Oxford: Clarendon Press.

Sarkar, Sarbani (2000), 'Settling Rights', in *Seminar*, 492: 'Protecting Nature: A Symposium on Some Legal Issues Concerning the Environment'.

Smith, Mick (1995), 'A Green Thought in a Green Shade: A Critique of the Rationalisation of Environmental Values', in Yvonne Guerrier, Nicholas Alexander, Jonathan Chase and Martin O'Brien (eds.), *Values and the Environment: A Social Science Perspective*, Chichester: John Wiley.

Society for Participatory Rçsearch in Asia and Rural Litigation and Entitlement Kendra (1993), 'Report on National Workshop on Declining Access to and Control Over Natural Resources in National Parks and Sanctuaries', New Delhi, mimeo.

Subramanian, K.S. and Michael Vlasoff (n.d.) *The Human Impact on the Environment: Population Pressure and Biodiversity: A Case-Study of Keoladeo National Park*, New Delhi: UNFPA.

Sukumar, R. (1994), 'Wildlife-Human Conflict in India: An Ecological and Social Perspective', in Ramachandra Guha (ed.), *Social Ecology*, Delhi: Oxford University Press.

Upadhyay, Sanjay (1999), *National Parks and Sanctuaries: A Guide to Legal Provisions*, Delhi: Enviro-Legal Defense Firm.

Judicial Proceedings

In the Supreme Court of India: Writ Petition (Civil) No. 337 of 1995, in the matter of Centre for *Environmental Law. WWF-India (Petitioner) vs. Union of India and Others* (Respondents) and in the matter *of Kalpavriksh and Others* (Applicants and Intervenors)

New Ethics for Old? Or, How (Not) to Think About Future Generations

TERENCE BALL

I. Introduction

There are a good many unresolved tensions within contemporary environmental ethics and political theory. Here I want to focus on one of these in particular: the current contests over the alleged unsuitability of our present moral and political vocabulary – roughly, the language of liberal individualism – for thinking critically, analytically and constructively about environmental questions generally, and about the fate of future generations in particular. The tension can be crudely described as follows. On the one side, one of the defining features of an emerging 'ecological' ethic is its emphasis on, and attention to, the health and well-being of future generations. But, on the other, the concepts constitutive of ethical and political discourse – rights, duties, obligations, justice, responsibility – sometimes appear to have been designed to deal with relations and conflicts between contemporaries; when applied to distant future generations they often seem stretched past the point of coherence and intelligibility. The invocation of such phrases as 'obligations to future generations' or 'the rights of distant posterity' or 'justice between generations' lead us very quickly into logical thickets and conceptual swamps. But this is not necessarily a bad thing. On the contrary, one of my purposes in this paper is to suggest that there is much to be learned about, and from, the philosophical life-forms inhabiting those thickets and swamps.

I propose to examine several key difficulties that arise when we try to think systematically about our relations with, and obligations to, future generations. Foremost among these are the problems of 'justice' and 'rights'. If justice and rights are based on the norm of reciprocity or exchange ('like for like', 'an eye for an eye', etc.), then we are, logically

---

This essay consists of a series of considerably compressed argument-sketches that will be expanded as chapters in a larger book-length study tentatively titled *Environmental Ethics and Political Theory*, one part of which deals with our obligations to future generations. An earlier version was very helpfully criticised by David Miller, Mathew Humphrey, Marc Stears, and other members of the Political Theory Workshop at Nuffield College, Oxford.

speaking, in no position to act justly toward, or to have obligations to respect the rights of, future generations. And this is simply because they are in no position to reciprocate. Some philosophers have accordingly argued that notions like 'the rights of future generations' and 'intergenerational justice' are incoherent and, consequently, future people have no rights and we have no duty to respect the (non-existent) rights of (non-existent) people. Radical environmentalists claim, on the contrary, that such arguments and conclusions are artifacts of Western liberal-individualist discourse. This discourse is said to be replete with subtle, systematic, and pervasive prejudices against the weak – women, minorities, non-human animals, and, weakest of all, generations yet unborn. We therefore need a radically new discourse, an entirely new non-Western ethic, if we are to respect and protect the health and well-being of future people.

The first view might variously be dubbed the ethic of exchange, the market model of moral and political discourse, or, if you prefer the language of the late C.B. Macpherson, the possessive individualist perspective. The second is almost invariably characterised by its adherents with the prefix 'post' and the suffix 'ism' – post-humanism, post-individualism, etc. – and has of late been taken up by many self-described radical environmentalists. The concepts and categories and frameworks that belong to 'Western culture' need to be obliterated and replaced root and branch by something at once new (or old and 'indigenous') and non-Western.

I shall argue that each of these opposing views is deficient insofar as each assumes or presupposes an unrealistic and untenable view of 'conceptual change', that is, the processes and mechanisms through which the meanings of concepts constitutive of ethical and political argument are altered, amended and extended. All social, political, and ethical concepts are, if not essentially contestable, then at least contingently contestable [*Ball, 1988: 12–14*]. Liberal-individualist understandings of rights and duties, justice and fairness, etc., are not forever fixed and frozen but are open to challenge, even from within the discourse of liberal individualism [*Ball, 1999*]. Introducing the idea of 'punctuated reciprocity' and related notions, I attempt to show how we can speak meaningfully and coherently of our obligation to act justly toward posterity by recognising and respecting their right to those two old liberal standbys, life and liberty. And against certain post-individualist claims I shall argue that, as a programme of radical conceptual change and innovation, theirs is a non-starter.

II. Some Background

Do we have obligations to future generations? If so, what are they, where do they come from, and on what are they based? And why have philosophers been asking these questions of late? The last of these questions is the easiest to answer. Not so long ago, biblical warnings about 'the sins of the fathers' – 'the fathers have eaten sour grapes and their children's teeth are set on edge' (Ezekiel 18:2) – seemed hopelesslesly old-fashioned and anachronistic. But with the advent of the environmental crisis – or crises – such warnings have acquired a new meaning and sense of urgency. This sense is variously expressed. The late Yehudi Menuhin, for one, opined that 'We are probably the worst ancestors that any people could possibly have'.[1] He was referring to our penchant for thinking only of ourselves and our needs and giving no thought to our descendants and their needs. We are living well, and leaving them with the bill for our follies and excesses.

The bill is not, of course, purely or even mainly monetary. The costs to be borne by future generations include ever-increasing health hazards from leaking toxic waste sites, a depleted ozone layer, decimated rain forests, disappearing farmland, the extinction of entire species, and polluted lakes, rivers and oceans. By these and other means future generations will be forced to pay for the folly of their fathers and mothers.

The idea that the present generation can with impunity take something away from their distant descendants represents a relatively new wrinkle in the history of human thought and action. Time was when members of one generation believed themselves to be under a divine obligation to benefit their descendants. The Bible is full of injunctions to act toward posterity as benefactors rather than predators. That was why old people planted trees whose shade and fruit they knew they would never enjoy.

Quite clearly, times have changed in several respects and for several reasons. One change is too obvious to be overlooked. Ours has become, by and large, a secular society. Most of us no longer think of ourselves as short-lived members of a longer-lived community of believers with whose past and future members we must keep faith. And even some 'born-again' Christians dismiss the idea that we owe anything to our distant descendants. This view was well expressed by the former US Secretary of the Interior James Watt, who once defended the Reagan administration's policy of unrestricted strip-mining, timber cutting, and other kinds of 'development' by saying that the imminent Second Coming of Our Lord made it unnecessary to conserve anything for future generations. Just why Jesus would wish to descend through toxic clouds on to a barren wasteland was not explained.

In a more psychoanalytic vein, the late Christopher Lasch [*1978*] diagnosed ours as a 'culture of narcissism'. In the technical clinical sense, of course, only individuals – and not entire cultures – can be narcissistic. A narcissist, strictly speaking, is one who is incapable of caring about anyone other than himself. But Lasch's point is that the values of modern consumer culture – living for the moment, seeking instant gratification for one's desires, buying now and paying later, and the hope of 'having it all' – encourage if they do not create the narcissist that presumably lurks within each of us. The only people who matter to the narcissist are those in whose presence he can prance and strut his stuff. Empty inside, he fills himself with the fleeting applause of others. Those who cannot see and applaud him will not be taken into any account. In the nature of the case, then, narcissists are constitutionally incapable of considering, much less worrying about, the well-being of future generations.

Although suggestive, such explanations lack historical depth. A more adequate explanation for our present predicament would take into account some of the deep-seated changes in Western culture over several centuries. Secularisation is certainly one of these changes. But this, by itself, hardly serves to explain why religious beliefs were not replaced with beliefs that give different but nonetheless due regard to questions of intergenerational equity and justice. By what route – ethical, economic, political, cultural – did we reach our present pass? And by what route might we yet escape? If we are to answer these questions, we need to turn to our past. As Burke remarked, 'People will not look forward to posterity, who never look backward to their ancestors' [*1973: 45*].

Earlier historians of ideas attempted to trace the root-system of the modern *mentalité*. Some traced it back to ancient Greece, others to the Judaeo-Christian tradition, and still others to the Renaissance, the Reformation, the Enlightenment, or some other monumental event or movement. But if we look less at an amorphous history of 'ideas' and more at a history of 'discourses' and the changing stock of concepts comprising them, we may be better placed to understand the subtle but signficant shifts that contributed to an identifiably modern way of talking and thinking about the world and our place in it [*Pocock, 1987*]. Modern German practitioners of *Begriffsgeschichte* ('conceptual history') have termed the late eighteenth and early nineteenth centuries a *Sattelzeit*, a turning-point or watershed, in which the European political and ethical vocabulary was radically transformed. In that period old concepts, such as 'revolution', took on new meanings; and altogether new terms – including 'ideology', 'industrialism', 'egoism', and 'altruism' – were coined. Conceptions of (historical) time – including 'past' and 'future' – were also radically altered.[2] Inquiries undertaken by Anglo-American conceptual historians have, on the whole, tended to support the claim that the late eighteenth and early nineteenth centuries comprised a period of profound conceptual change.[3]

But what does all this have to do with intergenerational relations? Just this: Until the late eighteenth century no one seriously questioned the idea that each generation should, as John Locke put it, 'leave as much and as good' to succeeding generations [*1988: paras 27, 33–4*]. Indeed posterity, as Kant later noted, derived considerable benefit from the labours and sacrifices of preceding generations [*1991: 44*]. Thus the relation of present to future generations was essentially that of benefactor to beneficiary. For example, land that was cleared and cultivated was passed on to posterity not in its original but in its 'improved' state. Jefferson's principle that 'the earth belongs in usufruct to the living' is the American (and agrarian-republican) articulation of a long-standing norm: 'the dead' (that is, earlier generations) may not act in ways that will impede or curtail the rights of later generations.[4]

The letter in which Jefferson stated this principle was written in 1789, the same year in which a new kind – indeed a new concept – of 'revolution' was in the making. Before the eighteenth century, the idea of revolutionary change was essentially conservative, a 'revolution' being a restoration of or a returning to an earlier state or condition [*Dunn, 1989*]. Just as a wheel turns 360 degrees to make one complete 'revolution', so do entire societies periodically return to and restore the rightful order of things. It was in this older sense that the Glorious Revolution of 1689 was 'revolutionary': it was a restoration of the rightful powers of Parliament that had been unjustly usurped by Charles II and his brother James II. And even the American Revolution of 1776 began as a revolution in this older sense: it aimed to restore the American colonists' rights as Englishmen. What began as an attempt to restore the old ended with the creation of something quite new and unprecedented, and thus was born the modern meaning of 'revolution' [*Arendt, 1963*].

Unlike the American Revolution, the French Revolution of 1789 aimed to overthrow the old and to create something entirely new and without precedent. It was Edmund Burke's horror at this hubris that led him to write *Reflections on the Revolution in France* (1790). And it was Burke's book that prompted Thomas Paine to reply with *The Rights of Man* in 1791. In this exchange we see the first self-conscious and systematic theoretical articulation of two quite different ethics – an older (and essentially religious) ethic of stewardship and a new (and essentially secular) ethic of individualism. The older ethic emphasises one generation's responsibility for, and obligations toward, other generations; the newer ethic claims that each generation is, or ought to be, autonomous and free to do as its individual members please, without regard to the wishes of earlier or the well-being of succeeding generations. To return to that exchange and its aftermath is to uncover an important part of the root-system of the modern *mentalité*, and most especially its views concerning the relations between generations.

Individuals in each generation ought, Burke believed, be caretakers, responsible to their ancestors and their distant descendants alike. The great danger – represented in its most insidious form in the thinking of the French revolutionaries – is that

> the temporary possessors and life-renters [in the world], unmindful of what they have received from their ancestors, or of what is due to their posterity, should act as if they were the entire masters; that they should think it [their right] to cut off the entail, or commit waste on the inheritance, by destroying at their pleasure the whole original fabric of their society, hazarding to leave to those who come after them, a ruin instead of a habitation.

Each of us belongs, Burke wrote, to an intergenerational community,

> a partnership in all science; a partnership in all art; a partnership in every virtue, and in all perfection. As the ends of such a partnership cannot be obtained in many generations, it becomes a partnership not only between those who are living, but between those who are living, those who are dead, and those who are to be born [*Burke, 1973: 108, 110*].

Paine found Burke's vision of an intergenerational partnership particularly galling. 'Every age and generation', Paine proclaimed, 'must be … free to act for itself'. The very idea of an intergenerational partnership he denounces as 'the most ridiculous and insolent of all tyrannies'. Individuals in the present generation must be free to live as they see fit, without regard to ancestors or descendants. 'Those who have quitted the world [i.e., died] and those who are not yet arrived in it, are as remote from each other, as the utmost stretch of moral imagination can conceive. What possible obligation can exist between them?' [*Paine, 1973: 277–9*]. Apparently none, according to Paine. The natural and inalienable 'rights of man' belong only to the living and cannot be limited or curtailed by the dead or by generations yet unborn.

Early in the nineteenth century the notion of 'rights' underwent a further modification. Whereas Burke spoke of the rights of Frenchmen and Englishmen, and Paine and Jefferson of 'natural rights', later liberals like Jeremy Bentham claimed that such rights derive from and are justified by utility and are merely matters of convenience and convention. Natural rights, Bentham huffed, are 'nonsense', and natural and inalienable rights, 'nonsense upon stilts' [*1843: 501*]. Rights come not from nature but from convention. Rights and duties are reciprocal. The idea that rights and duties rest on relations of reciprocity was itself part of an emerging ethic of exchange and self-interest – or, if you prefer, a market mentality and morality. On this view, it is rational to give up something only if one stands to gain something of equal or greater value in return. My having a right to property, for example, imposes upon you a duty to refrain from interfering in my use or enjoyment of my property, and vice-versa. Each of us gives up something in order to get something else in exchange. Bentham's disciple James Mill put the point succinctly when he said that 'We exchange burdens, called duties, for benefits, called rights' [*Mill, 1992: 49*].

Such a system might work well enough among contemporaries. But, as Alexis de Tocqueville asked, where does it leave future generations? Travelling through America in the 1830s, Tocqueville sought to trace the consequences of 'individualism' (a term, incidentally, of his own coining). On the brighter side he saw a spirit of exploration and innovation, a rapidly expanding economy, and a vital 'can-do' attitude toward the world and its myriad possibilities. But individualism also had its darker side. Individualism 'dams the spring of public virtues'. This damming, he added, 'is due more to inadequate understanding than to perversity of heart'. And yet the consequences of individualism, so far as future generations are concerned, are quite clearly perverse. In a society resting upon an individualist ethic of self-interested exchange, 'The woof of time is ever being broken and the trace of preceding generations effaced. Those who have gone before are easily forgotten, and no one gives a thought to those who will follow. All a man's interests are limited to those nearest himself.' Such an outlook 'not only [makes] men forget their ancestors, but also clouds their view of their descendants' [*Tocqueville, 1966: II, 477–8*].

In effect, Tocqueville restates Burke's point. The relationship that our (or any other) generation has with its distant descendants is not, and in the nature of the case cannot be, a relationship of reciprocity. Intergenerational relations are necessarily asymmetrical, inasmuch as what we do will affect our descendants; but nothing that they do can conceivably affect us. At least two important consequences follow from our recognising and reflecting upon this fact. The first, as articulated by philosophers from Jeremy Bentham through Robert Nozick, is that rights and duties derive from a norm of reciprocity. My having a right to be secure in my person and property imposes upon you the duty to refrain from harming me, all else being equal, and vice-versa. This reciprocity theory of rights holds that we have duties only toward those who are in a position to reciprocate by respecting our rights. And this in turn means that the members of one generation cannot – in a strictly logical sense – have a duty to respect the rights of future people. This, they hasten to add, does not necessarily imply that we therefore have a right to plunder the earth and deplete its resources; that would be to act carelessly and uncharitably, though *not unjustly*. To pass on to posterity a habitable planet would be very nice, though not morally obligatory [*Macklin, 1980; De George, 1980*].

In other words: to the degree that we act benevolently or justly toward our distant descendants, our relationship with them looks remarkably like a gift-giving or charitable relationship. For we freely and voluntarily give to them something that we are not morally required or obligated to give, expecting nothing in return for our largesse (save, perhaps, the gratitude of the recipients, even though we won't be around to receive and enjoy it). This is all very well, as far as it goes. But, morally speaking, the gift-giving view is weak in that it yields, at most, what we might (with apologies to Kant) call the Categorical Suggestion: Treat future people kindly, if you care to. And yet this looks like a pretty weak reed on which to hang the fate of future people. Protecting (or at any rate refraining from harming) their health, happiness, and welfare would accordingly appear to require an alternative to the charitable view of intergenerational relations. Charity being an insufficient basis, we need something that carries more moral weight – that has the heft of an obligation to act justly by respecting the rights of others.

Several contemporary philosophers have tried to amend and extend the liberal theory of rights and justice so as to provide grounding for, and to take into account, the rights of future persons. John Rawls's *A Theory of Justice* (1971) was among the first to raise, in a rigorous way, questions about intergenerational justice and obligations to posterity. That discussion, although suggestive, is quite brief. Most of Rawls's book is about the conditions and principles of justice among contemporaries. Rawls begins by updating the idea of a social contract among self-interested and risk-averse individuals. If such subjects are to choose in a distinterested way, they must be unaware of their own individual interests. Rawls accordingly imagines them choosing principles of justice from behind an imaginary 'veil of ignorance'. In this 'original position' they are unaware of their race, age, sex, economic class, social status, and so on. Thus the principles they choose would presumably be unsullied by considerations of power or privilege or particular interests [*Rawls 1971: 284–93*].

Rawls's argument is open to many objections, not the least of which is that it relies upon an imaginative but wholly imaginary construct. A more powerful objection, for my present purposes, is that Rawls' hypothetical choosers are all *contemporaries*; they belong to the same generation. Therefore the members of other (non-choosing) generations would not be accorded the protection that people of differing sexes, races or social classes would enjoy in a genuinely just society. If Rawls's principles of justice are to be truly timeless – applying, as Rawls famously puts it, *sub specie aeternitatis* – then one must add the further proviso that the choosers situated behind the veil of ignorance cannot know the generation to which they belong; they cannot, that is, know whether they are dead or alive or as yet unborn. Only then can we ensure that a person's place in the order of temporal succession has no bearing upon the rights he or she has, including the right to be treated justly [*Hubin, 1976*].

Other philosophers have made other attempts to amend liberal individualism's account of rights and duties so as to recognize and protect the rights of future persons [*Ackerman, 1980*]. Others, however, have suggested that liberalism, as a moral and political philosophy, is decrepit if not dead [*MacIntyre, 1981; Sandel, 1982*]. And still others have argued that our entire ethic of individualism, of the idea of the morally sovereign individual subject engaged in relations of reciprocity with other similarly situated subjects, is incoherent, if not indeed downright dangerous, and should now be discarded and replaced with an ethic that is either old and native-indigenous [*Salleh, 1997*] or radically new [*Jonas, 1984; Devall and Sessions, 1985; Naess, 1989*].

III. Toward a New 'Post-individualist' Ethic?

Exactly where this new ethic might come from and what it might look like is a subject of an increasingly intense debate that has too often tended to generate more heat than light. The most heated and least illuminating – though unfortunately quite influential – line of argument (or assertion) amounts to a case against a repressive monolith called 'Western culture'. The assertions are by now a familiar part of a certain sort of (mainly academic) discourse. Western culture is variously characterized and condemned as racist, sexist, homophobic – and antithetical to the preservation of the natural environment. And this is because Western culture is so – name your sin – 'individualistic', 'self-interested', 'anthropocentric', 'humanistic', etc. These charges are often accompanied by loud railings against rationality, science, logic, 'logocentrism', and the like. The upshot in all cases comes to this: The moral and intellectual resources of Western culture have been stretched to their limit and found wanting, if not worthless. The moral capital of Western culture has been exhausted. Western ethical and political thought is now morally and intellectually bankrupt, should be openly declared to be so, and abandoned forthwith.

Therefore, if future people are to be protected against the predation of the present generation – that is, us – we not only need to change what we think, but *how* we think, about nature, about non-human species, and about future generations of our own and other species. We need a wholly new, non-Western set of concepts and categories – a post-individualist 'planetary ethic' – to replace our outworn Western/liberal/individualist/humanist tradition of ethical and political thinking.

On this telling, then, the Western drama is being played out to its own self-destructive end. Now that its end is near, we can see it for what it is, or was – a tragedy. And it is a tragedy in the classical sense that a once-proud protagonist – in this case 'western man' – has in his *hubris* overstepped the bounds that bind and limit all earthly creatures. Pride must and most certainly will now be punished. Or, on another and closely related telling, white human males have exhausted an arrogant 'humanist' ethic that privileges human beings above all of creation, and must now choose an entirely new path or face richly deserved destruction, if not for ourselves, then for our unborn and innocent descendants.

This is, of course, a caricature, and a fairly crude one at that. And yet, like any caricature, it does contain a grain of truth. One might even profess a certain perverse sympathy with its redescription of, and prescriptions for, our present predicament. But at the same time, one is bound to have grave doubts as to whether the entire human species, or a substantial portion thereof, can create and learn an entirely new moral language within the ever-diminishing time available to them. Some few might effect a Nietzschian transvaluation of values. But as Nietzsche rightly recognized, many – perhaps most – lack the resources or the will to transvalue. We might then be in the paradoxical position described long ago by the Roman historian Livy. 'In our times', Livy lamented, 'we can neither endure our faults nor the means of correcting them' (quoted in Connolly [*1988: 1*]). One can acknowledge that our faults are evident and legion – as I certainly do – while doubting that the means of their correction can only come through arriving at and applying a radically new ethic with a concern for nature and future generations of humans and other species at its centre.

To pose my main question crudely and bluntly: What are the prospects for devising or arriving at a radically new ethic – an environmentally sensitive, earth-centred, post-humanist 'planetary' ethic? To answer it in equally blunt terms: Not very likely. If the fate of the earth and of future generations requires that most of us must abandon the familiar and become Buddhists or Deep Ecologists or Ecofeminists or indigenous earth-worshippers, then the earth and its future inhabitants are in very grave peril indeed.

The condemnation of 'individualism' (or 'Western individualism') that is the stock-in-trade of much radical environmental discourse does of course have a point. But it also seems to me to be both self-defeating and dangerous. It is certainly true that, as Clifford Geertz observes, 'The Western conception of the person as a bounded, unique, more or less integrated motivational and cognitive universe, a dynamic center of awareness, emotion, judgment and action organized into a distinctive whole [is] … a rather peculiar idea within the context of the world's cultures' [*Geertz, 1979: 229*]. Yet the peculiarity of this idea is hardly sufficient reason for discarding it. On the contrary, we have good reason to retain the idea of 'the individual' and see it for what it is – a unique and morally noteworthy evolutionary achievement deserving of recognition and respect and, of course, rational criticism. Individualism, like any idea, can of course be perverted and put to destructive uses, as Tocqueville and many modern ecologically minded writers rightly remind us. But we must not forget the destruction wrought earlier during the last century by anti-individualist ideologies which gave pride of place to race, *Volk*, nation and other such supra-individual and collective entities – and which professed to identify with, if not worship, 'the soil' and 'nature' [*Pois, 1987*]. We had best beware of being too ready to reject 'humanism' or 'individualism' in the name of some supra-individual or post-humanist ethic.

We should also beware of modeling our actions, institutions and practices on the animal kingdom or taking 'nature' as the standard or measure of value or right, or of merging ourselves into or 'identifying' with nature.[5] It is one thing to respect or to 'get along with' nature [*Berry, 1987*], and quite another – and more insidious – thing to somehow *identify* with nature. The naive and too-often unargued assertions of romantic nature-worshippers notwithstanding, nature's standard would appear to be that might makes right. When 'nature takes its course', the weak perish and the strong survive. Nature is indifferent to tyranny. Justice and fairness are unknown among non-human animals (although some among the higher primates are arguably a possible if perhaps doubtful exception); they are human inventions and achievements (albeit too often honoured in the breach). Lest we forget: there was at the turn of the last century a political perspective that purported to take its norms from 'nature'. It was called Social Darwinism. It viewed human life as a struggle for existence in which the 'fittest' survived and the 'unfit' did not [*Hawkins, 1997*]. As one of its American champions proclaimed,

> Nature's remedies against vice are terrible. She removes the victims without pity. A drunkard in the gutter is just where he ought to be, according to the fitness and tendency of things. Nature has set up on him the process of decline and dissolution by which she removes things which have survived their usefulness [*Sumner, 1883: 114*].

We had therefore best beware of a too-ready recourse to 'nature' as an alternative to, or antidote for, our 'humanism' or 'anthropocentrism'.

Having said that, however, it is clear that we cannot continue to live as we have, without regard to the rights and interests of generations yet unborn. The fate of future people hangs upon our ability and willingness to expand and enlarge our ethical universe so as to include them as members of our moral community. But how might we get there from here?

One cannot simply create moral codes or concepts, much less an entirely 'new ethic', *ex nihilo*. Modern conceptual historians who study the processes and mechanisms of 'conceptual change' are pretty much agreed on this point. If a conceptual innovation has any hope of succeeding, its proponents must satisfy two *desiderata*: intelligibility and legitimacy. In order to be intelligible to others, a would-be innovator must draw upon the ideas and idioms that are already available to her fellow citizens. She must practice what Walzer aptly calls 'connected social criticism' [*1987; 1988*]. These must, moreover, be invoked in ways that will legitimize new ways of speaking, thinking, and acting. As Quentin Skinner notes,

> however revolutionary the [innovating] ideologist ... he will nevertheless be committed, once he has accepted the need to legitimate his behaviour, to attempting to show that some of the *existing* range of favourable evaluative-descriptive terms can somehow be applied as apt descriptions of his own apparently untoward actions. Every revolutionary is to this extent obliged to march backward into battle [*Skinner, 1988: 112*].

And this, of course, is precisely what Deep Ecologists and other radical environmentalists have so signally failed to do. As innovating ideologists they have been singularly inept and unsuccessful. They have engaged in a kind of disconnected social criticism that is largely unintelligible to most of their fellow citizens. And this is why Anna Bramwell [*1994*] and other critics may well be correct, if perhaps a bit premature, in announcing 'the fading of the greens' and the demise of green politics, or at any rate its more radical variants.

If the greens – amongst whom I count myself – are to succeed politically, some way must be found to connect with, to use, and perchance to alter the dominant discourses, and particularly that of liberal individualism, *from within*. What is needed, then, is (in an older philosophical idiom) an immanent critique. Only through such a critique can conceptual innovation come about and succeed in reshaping the way we think and therefore act. Absent that, the greens are foredoomed to fail. And the failure of the green movement will not be due to its unimportance, but to the unintelligibility and thus the perceived illegitimacy of its discourse.

At or near the top of any green agenda or political programme is the need to pay conscious and articulate attention to the rights and interests of posterity and to the grounds and extent of our obligation to recognise, respect and protect them. What follows is not a systematic inquiry into what Brian Barry calls the 'mind-bending topic' of intergenerational justice [1989: 9], but a list of queries and concerns that would surely be central to such an inquiry.

IV. Thinking Clearly, Critically and Unsentimentally About Posterity

If we are to begin to think clearly and responsibly about our relations with and duties toward future generations, we need to keep several points in plain view. The first and most obvious is that the present generation has the power to affect the lives, health, happiness and well-being of our distant descendants, and this for two main reasons. One is technological: we have the means and machinery to alter the climate of the earth, to despoil the oceans, to move mountains, decimate forests, and to destroy entire ecosystems and species, not excluding our own. Such power is unprecedented in the history of the human species. The second reason is epistemological: we have this power *and we know that we have it*. We are also in a position to predict many of the longer-term consequences of the use and abuse of this unprecedented power. In both respects our generation is unique in the history of our species.

A second consideration is that our moral and political thinking has not kept pace with our power and our knowledge. Most of moral and political philosophy is concerned with relations within generations or between contiguous or overlapping generations. When we try to apply moral codes and concepts designed for dealings among contemporaries – the norm of reciprocity, for example – to relations between distant generations, our minds are bent and 'the light is fitful' [*Barry, 1989: 507*].

Do we then need, as some have claimed, a radically new ethic? Perhaps; but, as I noted earlier, such an ethic is as yet neither articulated nor, even if it were, is it likely to be widely shared for some time to come. But I do believe that we *can* – and arguably must – extend and amend codes and concepts already available to us, and in ways that will permit us to recognise the rights of distant descendants and acknowledge our duties toward them.

A third consideration follows from the first two. Every ethical code contains an implicit time-scale. In those codes in which the norm of reciprocity is paramount, the time-scale is considerably constricted, extending only to relations among contemporaries. But our technology has given us the power to produce – and we do daily produce – effects and by-products that will affect distant descendants 500 or 5,000 or even 50,000 years hence. This is perhaps most dramatically evident in the case of nuclear power, the by-products of which will remain radioactive and toxic for tens of thousands of years. Worse, we do not know how to store these wastes safely for the eons during which they pose a barely diminishing danger to humans, to other species, and to the environment that sustains them. The most commonly proposed 'solution' – storage in salt mines or deep caverns – cannot be counted on, since the earth's crust is sure to shift perceptibly over many thousands of years, thereby diminishing or destroying supposedly safe storage vaults and permitting radioactive wastes to seep through rock seams into underground rivers and aquifers. The moral and political point is simply this: For the first time ever, supposedly non-human or 'geological' time-scales have become morally relevant. No longer can we count in our moral calculations and reasonings on older constricted 'human' time-scales. Our moral and political thinking must now take into account the vastness of geological time.

This requirement is seldom recognised. But even when it is, we too often tend to project present codes, practices and institutions into the indefinite (or near-infinite) future. Consider, for example, the ruminations of Dr Alvin Weinberg, one of the 'founding fathers' of the nuclear power industry and a former director of the Oak Ridge National Laboratory:

> We seem to have struck a Faustian bargain. We are given the miraculous nuclear fire … as a means of producing very clean and … inexhaustible energy. The price that we must pay for this great boon is a vigilance that in many ways transcends what we have ever had to maintain: vigilance and care in operating these devices, and creation, and continuation into eternity, of a cadre or priesthood who understand the nuclear systems, and who are prepared to guard the wastes. To those of us whose business it is to supply power here and now, such speculations about 100,000 year priesthoods must strike an eerie and unreal sound … (quoted in Walker [*1983: ix–x*]).

This is not the stuff of science or even of science fiction; it is scientistic foolishness or, perhaps more accurately, madness posing as practical advice. Surely it is the sheerest madness to suppose – against every known or even conceivable human experience – that any human institution would or could be maintained intact and unbroken over non-human or 'geological' time. (Few rock formations are *that* permanent!) Madder still is the supposition that such a 'priesthood' of 'experts' would or could remain uncorrupted by their all-powerful status as a 'guardian' class, for even a few years, much less for the tens of thousands of years that this class would have to rule. (Even Plato at his most utopian recognized that the best, most just republic would not long withstand the ravages of time. All human creations are corruptible and liable to degeneration and decay.) Nor does Dr Weinberg flinch from the idea that we would or should happily trade our descendants' democratic birthright for a mess of nuclear pottage. His vision of a priesthood guarding the 'nuclear fire' is not at all utopian; it is dystopian – far more so, indeed, than the bleakly despairing dystopian visions of Orwell or Huxley. Moreover, to the dystopian and anti-democratic idea of an unbroken and uncorrupted 'priesthood' is added the even more fantastic idea of infallibility: These guardians must not make *any* mistakes, *ever*; they must, in short, be infallible. Which is to say that they must not be what they in fact are, namely human beings, with all the vanities, frailties, foibles and failures that characterise that species. But among our species' many shortcomings, one is clearly the most dangerous of all: *hubris*, or the pride that leads to, and legitimises, self-deception. This, more than anything, is the shortcoming that is so amply evident in Weinberg's vision of an intergenerational nuclear priesthood.

Unfortunately, Weinberg is not alone. His vision of a 'managerial' and deeply undemocratic future is all too typical of the 'public policy' genre, particularly as regards complex and dangerous technologies. 'If you open a public policy textbook, particularly one elaborating the rational decision approach to policy analysis', writes Douglas Bennett, 'you encounter almost complete silence about democracy' (quoted in Dahl [*1985: 101, n. 3*]). This silence should come as no surprise. One of the defining features of what I call 'epistemocratic' governance – rule by knowledgeable experts – is that the rulers claim to possess knowledge that is unavailable to others. Most decisions being beyond the ken or competence of the wider public, they must therefore be left to self-proclaimed experts. Democracy must therefore give way to epistemocracy [*Ball, 1988: 115–20*].

This brings me to my fourth point. Acting justly toward contemporaries requires that we act in ways that will respect, enhance, and perchance increase their freedom and autonomy, their capacity for self-rule. So also, by extension, acting justly toward our distant descendants requires that we refrain from acting in ways that will unduly limit their liberty or diminish their autonomy. If, for the sake of our own convenience and comfort, we opt for (say) Weinberg's '100,000 year priesthood' we are therefore clearly diminishing, if not destroying, our descendants' capacity for autonomy. To foreclose future people's opportunity to act freely and autonomously is *prima facie* to treat them unjustly.

From the foregoing a fifth and final point follows. All this talk about autonomy quite clearly presupposes an 'individualist' ethic which, as we have already seen, is regarded by certain radical environmentalists with deep suspicion if not outright hostility. If we are to save this planet and safeguard its myriad species – including future members of our own species – then (so the argument runs) we would do well to discard this tired and dangerous old ethic, replacing it with a new 'post-individualist' or 'post-humanist' ethic. I have already tried to show why such a move is mistaken and unrealistic. I now want to suggest that it is also unnecessary in that the already available discourse of liberal individualism – including the idea of reciprocity – may be open to significant conceptual innovation.

The concept of reciprocity might be amended so that reciprocity is serial rather than simultaneous. Lacking any better term, we might (with apologies to Stephen Jay Gould) call this practice 'punctuated reciprocity'. The idea underlying the practice of punctuated reciprocity is that each succeeding generation reciprocates what it had received from earlier generations, doing unto later generations what was (or at any rate should have been) done unto it. Punctuated reciprocity is the Golden Rule extended over time or, if you like, an intergenerational rendering of Kant's categorical imperative that we act as though legislating for all humankind – because, for better or worse, we are.

Let me give two rather homely examples of what I mean by punctuated reciprocity. The first is an altogether familiar one. It is rush hour and you are trying to get into the flow of traffic from a side street. Because there is no stop-light at the intersection you must wait for someone to let you in. To your left a car slows and stops; its driver waves her hand, inviting you to enter the thoroughfare. Once in the flow of traffic you are in a position to reciprocate – not to the driver who let you in, to be sure, but to some other hapless motorist stuck on a side street as you were moments ago. So when the opportunity arises, you take your turn at admitting another into the flow of traffic. When regularly and predictably practised, such courtesy is contagious. And when taught to young drivers, it can become a norm to which one adheres out of habit or custom..

My second example is more personal. Several years ago I was a Fellow at the Woodrow Wilson International Center for Scholars at the Smithsonian Institution in Washington, DC. My office overlooking the mall was cosy and equipped with the usual items – a desk, typewriter, bookshelves, and the like. But it had another and altogether unique feature, a white coffee cup with lavender cows on it. Nothing unusual about that – except that this cup contained a note from an earlier occupant of that office. It read: 'My daughter gave me this coffee cup as an office-warming present. Now I give it to you to welcome you into this office, and trust that you will welcome your successor in the same way.' I drank from this cup for four months. When the time came to vacate my office, I added a note of my own, placed the cup on the desk, and locked the door behind me. Returning to Washington several years later, I went to my old office and was delighted to find the lavender-cow coffee cup still in use by the present occupant, who assured me that she would follow the lead of her predecessors and mine. That is punctuated reciprocity.

Only the name, not the practice, is new. For when one thinks about it, punctuated reciprocity is among the practices that permit societies not only to exist through time, but to progress. Without it, every generation would have to begin again from scratch. It is only because we have received a rich inheritance – including scientific knowledge, educational institutions, art, music, literature, philosophy – that we have something to build on, and to pass along to our successors. As with any inheritance, we did nothing to earn it, nor can we repay our ancestors. But we can at least augment it, and pass it on to future generations.

Let me hasten to add that I do not make, nor do I wish to defend, the claim that the notion of punctuated reciprocity ensures intergenerational justice. Rather, I mean merely to suggest that punctuated reciprocity provides one illustration of the kind of thinking that can be done with the aid of moral codes and concepts that are already accessible and widely available.

Even so, I suspect, a sceptic will remain unconvinced. For, s/he might argue, the ethic of individualism and its constitutive concepts – individual rights, autonomy, freedom – tends to privilege presently existing individuals, favouring their freedom to act and thereby downplaying or discounting the health, happiness and well-being of future individuals and generations. And of course this does happen – witness, for example, the well-known practice of 'discounting' the future via 'the social rate of discount' [*Coase, 1960*]. Here again, however, the practice is open to telling criticisms that are themselves based on an identifiably 'individualist' ethic. Consider the following. Most of us do in fact 'discount' our own futures, in that, other things being equal, we would prefer present pleasures to future ones and future pains to present ones. I would, for example, prefer to have £10 now to receiving £10 ten years from now. If, however, I were offered a choice between £10 now and £100 ten years from now, I would probably opt for the latter. And why? Simply because my own personal rate of discount would be sufficiently offset by the latter option. Discounting one's own future is a perfectly rational and justifiable practice, and is widely recognised as such (that is why, for example, banks and building societies pay interest on savings accounts).

But it is quite a different matter with the so-called social rate of discount. Social discounting, as economists use the term, is the practice of discounting the utility or welfare of future people in favour of presently existing ones. In effect, social discounting treats a people, a society, or even our entire species as if it were a single super-individual existing over many generations of individuals (the latter being rather like cells that the larger organism sloughs off and replaces periodically). This super-individual then 'discounts' its own future utility, as ordinary individuals typically do, so as to favour the present over the further future. This in turn serves as a justification for such policies and practices as creating nuclear wastes that we do not know how to store safely for more than a generation or two [*Walker, 1983*]; to clear-cutting thousand year-old redwoods and not replanting hardwood trees [*Hardin, 1985*]; to whaling and driftnet fishing; to the unlimited extraction of metallic ores and fossil fuels and other finite and nonrenewable resources – to name only a few.

Such 'social discounting' can be, and has been, criticised on various grounds (see, for example Goodin [*1982*]; Cowen and Parfit [*1992*]). It might come as some surprise that the three most telling criticisms rely on readily recognisable 'individualist' premises and principles. First, the fictitious intergenerational 'individual' constructed by defenders of social discounting is just that – a fiction, and a 'collectivist' one to boot. Real individuals are entitled to discount; fictitious individuals are not. The so-called social rate of discount lends an aura of legitimacy to the selfish practices of some individuals, namely presently existing ones, at the expense of individuals yet unborn. It is therefore *prima facie* unjustifiable on 'individualist' grounds.

A second criticism of social discounting is that it clearly contravenes what is perhaps the preeminent principle of liberal individualism, namely Mill's 'harm principle'. In *On Liberty* (1859) Mill argues that any person's or group's liberty to act may be legitimately limited or forbidden only if it causes harm to some other person or persons. If that action produces consequences that are harmful to someone else, then their liberty to act may be legitimately limited to the extent required to prevent harm to other people [*Mill, 1989: 13*]. It is important to note that Mill nowhere stipulates that the people who stand to be harmed must be alive and present. The harm principle presumably applies to potential or future people, that is, to posterity as well as to the present generation. To discount the harm that we do to distant posterity is itself a violation of the harm principle.

Social discounting can also be criticised for a third reason: Might does not make right. The fact that the present generation has the power to help or to harm future generations, supplies no justification whatever for the former's riding roughshod over the rights and interests of the latter. Wendell Berry puts the point well, with particular reference to the 'progress' made possible by the present generation's unsustainable and hell-bent exploitation of oil and other nonrenewable fuels:

> fossil fuel energy ... could be made available to empower such unprecedented social change because it was 'cheap'. But we were able to consider it 'cheap' only by a kind of moral simplicity: the assumption that we had a 'right' to as much of it as we could use. This was a 'right' made solely by might. Because fossil fuels, however abundant they once were, were nevertheless limited in quantity and not renewable, they obviously did not 'belong' to one generation more than another. We ignored the claims of posterity simply because we could, the living being stronger than the unborn, and so worked the 'miracle' of industrial progress by the theft of energy from (among others) our children. That is the real foundation of our progress and our affluence. The reason that we are a rich nation is not that we have earned so much wealth – you cannot, by any honest means, earn or deserve so much. The reason is simply that we have learned, and have

> become willing, to market and use up in our own time the birthright and livelihood of posterity [*Berry, 1981: 127*].

Note that Berry is here, as elsewhere, speaking from a point well within Western culture. Berry's carefully chosen words – 'theft' and 'birthright' (and the concept of property or rightful ownership that both presuppose), of desert, and of course the denial that might makes right – do not derive from any 'new' ethic but belong instead to an old and once-familiar ethical code that has been eclipsed in a competitive, market-minded consumer society.

Eclipsed, but not yet forgotten. Our descendants' best hope may be that we will remember and revive what we have, to their peril and ours, come dangerously close to forgetting.

V. Conclusion

I have tried to suggest that the moral codes, concepts and traditions already available to us include at least some materials out of which an intergenerational ethic might yet be constructed. In making this attempt I have, of course, only barely scratched the surface of an enormously complex topic. I have also assumed – falsely and for the sake of simplicity – that ours is almost exclusively a liberal culture in which the discourse of individualism and self-interest is dominant. In fact, of course, 'Western culture' is not a monolith with one dominant discourse, but a chorus of many different discourses – religious, legal, civil, philosophical – which are off-key, often cacophonous, and sometimes contradictory. For example, it remains to be seen whether, or to what extent, some of the remnants of a religiously based ethic of stewardship might be revived and incorporated into a post-religious or secular system of ethics. My own view is that it would be surprising if this were not possible, since so many aspects of our ostensibly secular ethical precepts and principles have religious origins [*Siedentop, 1989*]. Our system of ethics is compounded out of many strands, some having religious roots and others having economic or legal origins. Ours being, as we so often remind ourselves, a society of law, our legal tradition – warts, flaws, and all – also remains a richly suggestive source upon which to draw. Let me conclude with an example of how we might do this.

Human societies are temporal entities existing not only in space but in and over time. And time, as poets and philosophers have often remarked, is like a river. It flows on relentlessly, and in one direction only. The very old metaphor of the river of time fits quite naturally with a concept long established in our legal tradition, that of riparian rights. Long before the eighteenth-century jurist William Blackstone systematised and committed them to paper, there were norms governing the conduct of people living along rivers and waterways. The rights of people living downstream imposed certain duties upon those living upstream. Justice required that those living upstream not disadvantage those living downstream by diverting, poisoning or otherwise impairing the flow of the river.

As with real rivers, so it may also be with the metaphorical river of time. Each generation occupies, as it were, a small village located along that river. As dwellers along the river of time each of us is accountable for what we do in and with our small stretch of the river. And we remain morally responsible for what we send to our descendants downstream.

NOTES

1. Yehudi Menuhin, in a conversation with Dr Jonas Salk, broadcast on PBS-TV, 27 Sept. 1982.
2. See Brunner, Conze and Koselleck [*1978–*]; Koselleck [*1985*]; Hoelscher [*1989*]; and, for a useful introduction, Richter [*1995*].
3. See Ball [*1988*]; Ball, Farr and Hanson [*1989*]; Ball and Pocock [*1988*]; Hampsher-Monk, Tilmans and van Vree [*1998*].
4. The following four paragraphs are a partial summary of Ball [*2000*]. My argument there is that although Burke and Paine were at odds over the value of inherited political institutions, their disagreement has implications that should be of interest to modern environmentalists.
5. See, for example, Salleh [*1997*] and the exchange between Humphrey [*2000*] and Salleh [*2000*].

REFERENCES

Ackerman, Bruce (1980), *Social Justice in the Liberal State*, New Haven, CT: Yale University Press.

Appleby, Joyce and Terence Ball (eds.), (1999), *Thomas Jefferson: Political Writings*, Cambridge: Cambridge University Press, 1999.

Arendt, Hannah (1963), *On Revolution*, New York: Viking.

Ball, Terence (1988), *Transforming Political Discourse: Political Theory and Critical Conceptual History*, Oxford: Blackwell.

Ball, Terence (1999), 'From "Core" to "Sore" Concepts: Ideological Innovation and Conceptual Change', *Journal of Political Ideologies*, Vol.4, No.3, pp.391–96.

Ball, Terence (2000), '"The Earth Belongs to the Living": Thomas Jefferson and the Problem of Intergenerational Relations', *Environmental Politics*, Vol.9, No.2, pp.61–77.

Ball, Terence and J.G.A. Pocock (eds.), (1988), *Conceptual Change and the Constitution*, Lawrence, KS: University Press of Kansas.

Ball, Terence, James Farr and R.L. Hanson (eds.), (1989), *Political Innovation and Conceptual Change*, Cambridge: Cambridge University Press, 1989.

Barry, Brian (1989), *Democracy, Power and Justice*, Oxford: Clarendon Press.

Bramwell, Anna (1994), *The Fading of the Greens: The Decline of Environmental Politics in the West*, New Haven, CT: Yale University Press.

Bentham, Jeremy (1843), 'Anarchical Fallacies', in J. Bowring (ed.), *Works of Jeremy Bentham* (Edinburgh), Vol.II.

Berry, Wendell (1981), *The Gift of Good Land*, San Francisco, CA: North Point Press.

Berry, Wendell (1987), 'Getting Along with Nature', in his *Home Economics: Fourteen Essays*, San Francisco, CA: North Point Press.

Burke, Edmund (1973), *Reflections on the Revolution in France*, Garden City, NY: Anchor Books.

Brunner, Otto, Werner Conze, and Reinhart Koselleck (eds.), (1978–), *Geschlichtliche Grundbegriffe: Historisches Lexikon juridisch-sozialen Sprache in Deutschland*, Stuttgart: Klett-Cottta, 6 vols. to date.

Coase, R.H. (1960), 'The Problem of Social Cost', *Journal of Law and Economics*, Vol.3, pp.1–44.

Connolly, William E. Connolly (1988), *Political Theory and Modernity*, Oxford: Blackwell.

Cowen, Tyler, and Derek Parfit (1992), 'Against the Social Discount Rate', in Peter Laslett and James Fishkin (eds.), *Justice Between Age Groups and Generations*, New Haven, CT: Yale University Press.

Dahl, Robert (1985), *Controlling Nuclear Weapons: Democracy vs. Guardianship*, Syracuse, NY: Syracuse University Press.

De George, Richard T. (1980), 'The Environment, Rights, and Future Generations', in Partridge [*1980: 157-66*].

Devall, Bill, and George Sessions, *Deep Ecology*, Layton, UT: Gibbs M. Smith.

Dunn, John (1989), 'Revolution', in Ball, Farr, and Hanson [*1989: Ch.16*].

Geertz, Clifford (1979), 'From the Native's Point of View: On the Nature of Anthropological Understanding', in Paul Rabinow and William M. Sullivan (eds.), *Interpretive Social Science*, Berkeley and Los Angeles, CA: University of California Press.

Goodin, R.E. (1982), 'Discounting Discounting', *Journal of Public Policy*, Vol.2, No.1, pp.53–72.

Hampsher-Monk, Iain, Karin Tilmans and Frank van Vree (eds.) (1998), *History of Concepts: Comparative Perspectives*, Amsterdam: Amsterdam University Press.

Hardin, Garrett (1985), 'The Binding of Time', in his *Filters Against Folly*, New York: Penguin Books, Ch.8.

Hawkins, Mike (1997), *Social Darwinism in European and American Thought, 1860–1945: Nature as Model and Nature as Threat*, Cambridge: Cambridge University Press.

Hoelscher, Lucien (1989), *Weltgericht oder Revolution*, Stuttgart: Klett-Cotta.

Hubin, D. Clayton (1976), 'Justice and Future Generations', *Philosophy and Public Affairs*, 6, pp.70–83.

Humphrey, Mathew (2000), 'Ontological Determinism and Deep Ecology: Evading the Moral Questions?' in Katz, Light and Rothenberg [*2000: 85–106*].

Jonas, Hans (1984), *The Imperative of Responsibility: In Search of An Ethics for the Technological Age* , Chicago, IL: University of Chicago Press.

Kant, Immanuel (1991), 'Idea for a Universal History with a Cosmopolitan Purpose', in Hans Reiss (ed.), *Kant: Political Writings*, Cambridge: Cambridge University Press, 1970.

Katz, Eric, Andrew Light and David Rothenberg (eds.) (2000), *Beneath the Surface: Critical Essays in the Philosophy of Deep Ecology*, Cambridge, MA: MIT Press.

Koselleck, Reinhart (1985), *Futures Past: On the Semantics of Historical Time* (transl. K. Tribe), Cambridge, MA: MIT Press.

Lasch, Christopher (1978), *The Culture of Narcissism*, New York: Norton.

Locke, John (1988 [1690]), *Second Treatise of Government* (ed. P. Laslett), Cambridge: Cambridge University Press.

MacIntyre, Alasdair (1981), *After Virtue*, Notre Dame, IN: University of Notre Dame Press, 1981.

Macklin, Ruth (1980), 'Can Future Generations Correctly be said to Have Rights?' in Partridge [*1980: 151–6*].

Mill, James (1992 [1823]), 'Jurisprudence', in Terence Ball (ed.), *James Mill: Political Writings*, Cambridge: Cambridge University Press, 1992.

Mill, John Stuart (1989 [1859]), *On Liberty* (ed. Stefan Collini), Cambridge: Cambridge University Press.

Naess, Arne (1989), *Ecology, Community, and Lifestyle*, Cambridge: Cambridge University Press.

Paine, Thomas (1973 [*1792*]), *The Rights of Man*, Garden City, NY: Anchor Books, 1973.

Partridge, Ernest (ed.), (1980), *Responsibilities to Future Generations*, Buffalo, NY: Prometheus Books, 1980.

Pocock, J.G.A. (1987), 'The Concept of a Language and the *Métier d'historien*: Some Considerations on Practice', in A. Pagden (ed.), *The Languages of Political Theory in Early-Modern Europe*, Cambridge: Cambridge University Press.

Pois, Robert A. (1987), *National Socialism and the Religion of Nature*, London: Croom Helm.

Rawls, John (1971), *A Theory of Justice*, Cambridge, MA: Harvard University Press.
Richter, Melvin (1995), *The History of Social and Political Concepts: A Critical Introduction*, New York: Oxford University Press.
Salleh, Ariel (1997), *Ecofeminism as Politics*, London: Zed Books.
Salleh, Ariel (2000), 'In Defence of Deep Ecology: An Ecofeminist Response to a Liberal Critique', in Katz, Light and Rothenberg [*2000: 107–24*].
Sandel, Michael J. (1982), *Liberalism and the Limits of Justice*, Cambridge: Cambridge University Press.
Siedentop, L.A. (1989), 'Liberalism: The Christian Connection', *Times Literary Supplement*, 24–30 March.
Skinner, Quentin (1988), 'Some Problems in the Analysis of Political Thought and Action', in James Tully (ed.), *Meaning and Context: Quentin Skinner and his Critics*, Princeton, NJ: Princeton University Press.
Sumner, William Graham (1883), *What Social Classes Owe to Each Other*, New York: Harper & Brothers.
Tocqueville, Alexis de (1966), *Democracy in America* (trans. G. Lawrence), New York: Harper & Row.
Walker, Charles A. (ed.), (1983), *Too Hot to Handle? Social and Policy Issues in the Management of Radioactive Wastes*, New Haven, CT: Yale University Press.
Walzer, Michael (1987), *Interpretation and Social Criticism*, Cambridge, MA: Harvard University Press.
Walzer, Michael (1988), *The Company of Critics: Social Criticism and Political Commitment in the Twentieth Century*, New York: Basic Books.

Ten Commandments of How to Fail in an Environmental Campaign

AVNER DE-SHALIT

Introduction

The question this essay asks is 'Why, and when, do environmentalists fail in environmental campaigns'. Before answering, we first need to define what such failure is. The answer is fairly straightforward: failure is when a group campaigns to have a policy introduced and fails to convince the relevant decision-makers, *or*, when a group campaigns against a policy and fails to prevent its implementation. This constitutes failure. However, I would first like to note that sometimes when a group fails it nevertheless makes gains in other spheres; for example, it might become more cohesive, or its public profile might improve. However, rather than seeing such a gain as an additional campaign goal, I would call this a competing goal, that is, a goal which attracts activists away from their original, environmental goal.

Many activists tend to regard each campaign attempted as a link of a chain. The goal is not so much to win the battle – they might even lose it – the aim is to win the war.[1] They often claim that campaigns make an indirect impact – by direct means. The means, or action itself is seen by the public as direct, timely, spontaneous, courageous and thus impressive. This impression is meant to shift public opinion and put a stop to or bring about an amendment in government policies. This account, however, assumes that the question of *whether* indeed these activities exert an indirect impact still remains to be examined. Moreover, scholars writing on direct environmental action define it as 'protest action where protestors engage in forms of action designed not principally to change government policy or to shift the climate of public opinion through the media, but to change

---

An earlier version of this essay was presented as a paper to the annual conference of Environmental NGOs in Israel. The author learnt a lot from activists in this meeting, and thanks the participants for their helpful comments and suggestions. While writing this account he tried to find a balance between academic jargon and original style. His wish is that this account be accessible to a wide audience. Special thanks are due to Mathew Humphrey for his careful reading and comments. Thanks also to Meira Hanson for challenging his views. The opinions presented here are, however, his own, and if those reading this account suddenly feel that they want to play darts, he should be the target.

environmental conditions around them *directly*'. [*Doherty, 2000*]. Thus the definition of failure in this account describes the attempt to remove or prevent the actual environmental bad.

The research described here was mainly conducted in Israel and there are comparisons of cases in England and the USA. Ten reasons for environmental campaign failure have been identified. In what follows, these are presented in the form of '*Ten Commandments for How to Fail in an Environmental Campaign*'. There is no cynicism in this title or in what follows. Being an activist myself, the question of how to win this campaign, or, to be more precise, how to refrain from losing it, seems to me too serious to be locked behind the walls of false beliefs, prejudice, and theories that have never been examined. I hope that this analysis, as well as the other contributions in this volume, will contribute to the debate about activists' success and failures.

First Commandment: *Always Struggle For Total Change; Never Accept Reform or Compromise*

Two arguments that are made by many activists are at stake here. The first is that only an all-out – hence radical – fight brings results. The second is that the main point is to win the war, not the battles, and that since this is an all out war,[2] there can be no room for compromise. I would now like to examine both these claims critically.

Stephen Young distinguishes between two models of campaigning. One is the 'radical/populist'; the other is the 'moderate/conventional' [*Young, 1993: 23*]. The former employs unconventional political action, is never ready to compromise, and is confrontational in character and approach. The moderate/conventional approach uses established consultation procedures, dialogue with the authorities, is prepared to compromise, and is democratic in reaching decisions regarding whether to accept the authorities' decisions. The dispute between groups using the different models is not so much about what is wrong and who the enemies are, but about optimal solutions and about how to achieve them. In general terms, some groups regard themselves as 'insider groups', because they are accorded special consultative status, and others as 'outsider groups' which are denied access by the authorities to decision-making processes [*Young, 19–20*]. Young concludes that groups that develop a regular form of dialogue with local councils ... have better prospects of influencing policies relating to statutory plans [*ibid*].

And yet, many activists see radical activism as the only effective measure, convinced that the 'system' will never react to moderate pressure. This is often claimed without adequate empirical proof. For example, Derek

Wall writes: 'The direct action anti-roads movements of the 1990s was given a kick-start by green activists frustrated and dismayed by the ineffectiveness of conventional environmental groups and traditional lobbying techniques. There is *some evidence* to suggest that such radical campaigning has shifted the balance of power between pro- and anti-road advocates' [*Wall, 1999: 187,* my emphasis]. But what does Wall mean by 'some' evidence? How is this measured? Indeed, McLeod [*1998*] argues that the violent protest against the export of live animals (in 1995) had only partial success in transforming of general public opinion.

Let me elaborate here by examining the activities of the anti-roads activist, 'Swampy' (real name – Daniel Hooper). In 1997, the then 24-year-old eco-warrior discovered a new way to fight the construction of new roads, starting with the A30 project near Exeter. He dug a tunnel and holed up there for several days, so that construction had to stop. There were those who assumed that Swampy's action changed other people's minds,[3] but it is very difficult to sustain this thesis. Swampy was mentor to 20 eco-warrior trainees from Europe (*The Guardian,* 15 Sept. 1998], but this does not imply that he had any widespread, positive impact on the thinking of large numbers of people about the environment. Several writers have suggested that Swampy — who was described as 'David cocking-a-snook at developers' Goliath excavators [*Ridley, 1998: 309*] – actually triumphed (Hugo Young, *The Guardian,* 21 July 1998). Young's proof for this is that even such organisations as the RAC have admitted that road building is not a solution. But why should we assume that the RAC and other previously pro-road organisations, reached this conclusion as a result of Swampy's acts? Perhaps these people tired of rush hour traffic snarl ups, and decided there had to be an alternative to road travel? Also, isn't it possible that a number of MPs changed their minds about building roads for all kinds of reasons?

Indeed, as Anna Murphy candidly writes (*The Observer,* 12 July 1998) 'Swampy might have got his cause noticed but, for many, he was never anything more than a bit of a joke'. In any case, now, some time after Swampy's activities, new roads are still being planned and opened. One year following his activism, Swampy's legacy appears to have faded: the only reference we find to him in the press after his 1997 protest was a story in August 1998 that Swampy had been fined £100 for admitting possession of magic mushrooms. When it comes to real politics, when it comes to making decisions, Swampy – and many like him – have still not made an impact. George Monbiot has admitted (*The Guardian,* 10 Sept. 1998) that John Prescott's anti-car positions were not very popular in the government. His plans were potentially offensive to the two constituencies that most scared Blair, wrote Monbiot: Big Business and Middle England. The government did not adopt Prescott's policies. In fact, wrote Monbiot, car ownership in Britain would actually be encouraged. If this was so in 1998, how can we claim that Swampy triumphed in 1997?

Israel provides another example. In 1985, Kibbutz Kfar Hanasi, which is situated a mile from the River Jordan, one of Israel's main water resources, suggested diverting the river along a 1300 foot open canal into an artificial lake. From there, the water would be channelled into a 100 foot high artificial waterfall, at the bottom of which would lie turbines. Thence the water would be returned to the river [*de-Shalit and Talias, 1994*]. Although the scheme meant damaging the River Jordan in the only place where it still ran its original course, for economic reasons, several environmental bodies supported the plan. This was a bad starting point for environmentalists opposing the plan. However, the Society for the Protection of Nature in Israel (SPNI), Israel's largest NGO, steadfastly contested even the slightest alteration to the river course. They argued that the ecological damage would be incalculable. When, in 1990, the regional committee for planning dismissed all objections to the scheme, scenes of great violence erupted. Two weeks later, 20,000 people – the largest demonstration held in Israel that year – marched on the area in protest against the project. In June 1991, several activists chained themselves to tractors and threw the keys into the river. This proved effective in so far as several politicians decided to side with the protestors. However, the outcome was that the kibbutz decided to end all negotiation with the environmentalists. This marked the demise of the protest: the protestors failed in court, because there was nothing illegal about the kibbutz plans. In fact, it is quite likely that the court found it difficult to comprehend why the protestors had not agreed to a compromise in the first place. So, by rejecting all compromise, the protestors lost their entire case.

Let us now explore the second aspect of this mistake. Various organisations have argued that, while they might have lost their battles against the roads, they ultimately win the war. To support this argument they point, for example, to the fact that the number of road construction plans in Britain has dropped since 1992. Doherty also supports this assertion when he claims that 'by 1997 the original plans for the roads programme were in disarray' [*Doherty, 1999: 276*], however, he himself admits that a need to cut public spending and a 'more sceptical attitude to road transport from within sections of the government also played a role' [*ibid.*; also *Doherty, 2000*]. It may be argued that the anti-roads campaigns increased the political and economic cost of road building, and that this, in turn, constructed the more sceptical attitude to road transport within sections of the government. But this remains to be proved (I elaborate below on other reasons for this re-thinking within the government). Moreover, as Wolfgang Rudig claims 'as on many occasions before, government action has been used to limit the mobilization potential of protest groups' [*Rudig, 1995: 238*]. Thus, in fact, we find that the government curtailed motorway construction schemes as a means of disarming the environmental organisations.

It seems that many activists are quite aware that they lose many battles through their choice of extravagant strategies, and yet justify this with the argument that they ultimately win their wars. As indicated above, this paper means to focus on winning the interim battles. At the end of the day, activists want to prevent things from happening. If that is their goal, then they must win battles, not just wars. Moreover, their claim that the choice of extravagant tactics helps them in winning wars is questionable. Let me refer here to Paul Wapner's thesis [*1995: 307–8*]. He writes:

> In 1989 Greenpeace activists infiltrated a DuPont manufacturing plant in Deepwater, New Jersey. Activists climbed the plant's 180 feet water tower and hung a huge, blue ribbon banner awarding DuPont a prize for being the world's number one ozone destroyer.[4] The following day, Greenpeace bolted a steel box – with two people inside – onto the plant's railroad tracks and blocked the export of CFCs from the plant.

However, as Wapner admits, 'within minutes of removing the blockade, business proceeded as usual'. Wapner claims that although Greenpeace lost this case, they won in the propaganda stakes. But the success he ascribes to Greenpeace seems groundless. He claims that DuPont's workers continued to manufacture CFCs, but 'now they did so knowing that others knew about it and were *concerned*' (my emphasis). One may ask: so what? So people knew about it. They thought about it for briefly, and forgot it after. Or, even if they didn't forget about it later, did these people do anything about it? *Was the manufacture of CFC's stopped?*

Wapner goes on to claim that because Greenpeace captured its actions on film and distributed video news spots to TV stations throughout the world, vast numbers of people were able to understand the connection between the production of CFCs and ozone depletion [*Wapner, 1995: 308*]. This seems to be out of touch with reality. It is well known that many people do not understand what they see on the TV news.[5] While this is true for any news item, it is so *a fortiori* for ecology. Most people do not have a clue about the relationship between CFCs and the ozone layer or other similar issues,[6] not to mention when they learn about it in a 30-second TV news item. People often forget about these new items after several days. In the summer of 1999, the New Israel Fund decided to support a campaign against a huge new motorway in Israel. They advertised their campaign and there were reports about it. They then conducted a poll to see whether this had any impact. While they were campaigning ten per cent of the population declared they knew about this campaign and the NIF's activities. Several days later only one per cent said so.[7] In Israel 50 per cent watch the main TV news show and above 80 per cent of the adults read a daily (real, not tabloid) newspaper. And yet, only one per cent knew about the NIF and its activities.

Furthermore, activities of the kind described by Wapner often alienate the public to Greenpeace and similar organisations: people interpret activists' activities as a proof of the environmentalists' hatred of, or at least indifference towards, workers. They regard such acts as an attack on the workers – not on the company's owners and board of directors – in this case DuPont. Thus people who watch the news are likely to conclude that environmentalists are rich people with plenty of free time (unlike the workers of DuPont) – who can afford to engage in such weird activities, and who don't care about the workers or their source of income.[8] Does this sound like winning a war or losing respect?[9]

Why does this mistake happen? Naturally activists involved with environmental NGOs are idealistic; they are willing to sacrifice time and energy for animal welfare, ecosystem integrity or the preservation of beauty spots. This is particularly so with regard to the younger, more radical activists [*Doherty, 1998: 277*]. Obviously, without such devoted people it is almost impossible to oppose the power of bureaucracy and capital, not to mention change reality. But, as Shakespeare queried, 'Hath not this rose a canker?' People like this do not give up easily – even when a small retreat might pay dividends. In their dogged efforts to achieve all or nothing they might fumble a potential victory without even noticing it.

The psychology of these activists is simple:[10] they feel that they know what is right, and they want to pursue justice. That is fine, but it is also a misconception of the political environment in which they live and operate, that is, democracy. Democracy is the best regime around, but it is incapable of accomplishing everything. Basically, it is a regime of compromise. It is not a regime in which justice triumphs absolutely. It cannot totally eradicate evil. In short, democracy is not a system through which ideals and values can be realised. Instead it is a mechanism – perhaps a dull one – which allows people who hold different ideals and values to find a way of living together. Not only *cannot* democracy totally realise all values and ideals, it is also *not supposed* to. This may be a pity, and indeed, as I will show below, many activists conclude that for this reason democracy is redundant. But it is also the magic of democracy: never have democracies fought against each other, and rarely have democracies witnessed violent domestic clashes. This is no small achievement. In fact, quite the contrary – not only because sparing bloodshed is a good thing in itself, but also for environmental reasons. Wars cause the worst ecological disasters human beings have managed to create. But alas, we often find activists who would hastily do away with democracy in order to protect a forest, without understanding that relinquishing democracy might result in wars that would destroy dozens of such forests.

Second Commandment: *Always Use the Terminology of Despair*

The question of what terminology to use when trying to persuade the public of the rightness of a particular environmental position is important since the public is generally unenlightened about ecology, and will find it difficult to judge the relevant issues. Thus many people rely on their 'gut feelings' when deciding whether or not to support a position. In these situations, developers can usually spend more on advertising and publicity campaigns than environmental organisations, and have better access to politicians and decision-makers. Thus environmental NGOs need to stir up public outcry for truth, but lacking the means to do so, must fall back on their only weapon – trustworthiness. They should therefore be extremely accurate about depicting the future, analysing consequences and conceivable scenarios resulting from different policies, and so on.

However, there is a problem: environmental organisations also need to sustain their membership. They do this by, among other things, relying on ideological commitment. To earn this, they try to show how desperate a situation is [*Taylor, 1992: 36*]. Furthermore, perhaps due to their frustration at their inability to convince others, and due to the perceived blindness to the truth in others, environmentalists often tend to exaggerate the despondency of their scenarios. Consequently, people often start off with doubts in their mind. Moreover, many developers can point to cases in which scenarios predicted by environmentalists have failed to materialise. One good example of this concerns the water policy for the Sea of Galilee in Israel. This lake is one of the most important sources of water for irrigation in Israel. Environmentalists have long argued that political pressure from farmers has caused over-pumping of the water, and warn that the system will eventually collapse when brackish underground water penetrates the lake. They drew what was meant to be a very strict minimum water level (the 'red line'), but after two years of serious drought, the government proceeded to pump below the red line. When nothing happened in terms of water quality, the environmentalists' credibility was lost.

Also, people generally react in a very basic way to the threat of dire consequences and horrific scenarios. They simply repress and doubt what they hear – a common strategy when faced with alarming prognostications. Thus while environmentalists try to force an impression on the general public with their somewhat exaggerated predictions, the eventual outcome is counter-productive: many people simply disbelieve, do not want to believe, or even refuse to listen.

Environmentalists have to remember that words have power, and that often people are carried away with words. Sometimes this applies to the activists themselves. In Israel, for example, many of the public believed a group of activists which claimed that the damage to the few rivers left flowing in Israel was 'irreversible'. They took the activists at their word, and concluded that since things were irreversible, nothing could be done. And Dave Foreman (formerly of *Earth First!*) surely forgets who his potential allies are when he asserts that 'it is the hardy swain, the sturdy yeoman from the bumpkin proletariat ... who holds the most violent and destructive attitudes towards the natural world' [*Chase, 1991: 51–2*]. If activists use such terminology, they will of course never manage to persuade the working classes or the 'sturdy yeoman' to support their environmental campaigns. (I elaborate about this below.)

Until now I have discussed the use of the language of despair as a means of manipulating public opinion. Often, however, the language of despair simply reflects honesty and sincerity. People become so worried and so tired of trying to change things, or feel frustrated with struggling against bureaucrats' obduracy time and time again, that they really do become desperate. However, when presenting their analysis of the situation as they see it, they must avoid using such language if they really want to win. Thus activists must carefully distinguish between exaggerating the gravity of a situation for rhetorical reasons, and presenting responsible scientific description of the state of affairs. They must not employ exaggerations when they are expected to use accurate descriptions.

Third Commandment: *Always Use Biocentric Arguments*

Many environmental activists have internalised the moral standpoint and language of environmental ethics. In other words, they have internalised 'biocentric' or 'ecocentric' arguments. Therefore, they reject anthropocentrism, that is, the placing of human beings in the centre of things – as a speceisist attitude. These activists often discuss animal rights, ecosystem integrity, etc.[11] My argument here is that regardless of whether biocentric theories are true or not, the radical language of biocentrism is, politically speaking, unwise.

Let me be clear: by arguing that environmentalists should leave aside biocentric arguments I do not mean they should also change their positions.[12] Rather I relate to the language used outside of the environmental circles. As Andrew Dobson argues [*1990: 20*], among environmentalists, ecocentrism and biocentrism are like an internal language, whereas anthropocentrism, or what Hayward [*1994*] might have termed 'enlightened anthropocentrism', should be used outside the environmental circles, where people are not very likely to understand the meaning of biocentrism. I would therefore argue that while these activists may hold their ideological positions, they should, nevertheless, revise the terminology they use. Their language can still be confrontational, but it must also be understood.

Although sometimes biocentric arguments seem more dramatic and therefore more appealing, the use of biocentric arguments may still be counterproductive. For example, between 1988 and 1991, there was a campaign in Israel to prevent Voice of America's transmitters being installed in an area of desert traversed by millions of migrating birds each year [*de-Shalit and Talias: 1994*]. All biocentric arguments (for example, that electromagnetic radiation from the antennae would damage the birds' navigational systems) failed, because they seemed irrelevant to American and Israeli decision-makers.[13]

I would like to suggest that successful campaigns are campaigns that employ concepts and terminology which large numbers of people can relate to. A good example is when the WWF (World Wildlife Fund) declares that 'it is the responsibility of all who are alive today to accept the trusteeship of wildlife ... to hand [it] on to posterity as a source of wonder and interest, knowledge and enjoyment. ... This generation has no right, by selfishness ... to rob future generations of this great heritage.' [*Evans, 1992: 126*]. Note the language: they speak of '*trusteeship*' – a concept having religious connotations; '*source*' – a concept greatly disliked by environmentalists, but known to the public; '*selfishness*' and '*rob*' – no one wants to appear selfish or to rob; and '*heritage*' – a very familiar term in Britain.

The use of novel language (or jargon) could be the reason why, despite the fact that minorities and poorer populations do care about the environment, many among them do not support environmental NGOs. Dorcetta Taylor [*1992: 29*] claims that environmental organisations fail to address these minorities and their needs by 'continuing to place high priorities on wildlife and preservation issues' instead of combining these with social issues. It can thus be suggested that environmentalists often regard radicalism as inherent in the shift from anthropocentrism to biocentrism, rather than in standing at the side of the poor and the least advantaged who are exploited by polluting firms [*Benton, 1988, 1993; de-Shalit, 2000: Ch.6*]. However, by adopting this view, even if they manage to shift public attention to biocentrism, they will lose crucial support for their case.[14]

Fourth Commandment: *Don't Initiate; Just React!*

According to Brian Doherty [*1999*], activists in the new social and environmental movements, especially those in Britain which are oriented toward more direct action, are young and often unemployed.[15] However, many small-scale, *local*, organisations consist of non-professional activists – working people in their thirties or forties, often at the peak of their careers.[16] They usually have little spare time, being very caught up with their work, families, children's education, caring for elderly parents, etc. They therefore tend to join NGOs and become more active post-factum, that is, after a pollution threat has materialised as a hazard, or when a local municipality decides to convert a small park into an industrial zone. Then they decide to react 'forcefully'.

Reaction, however, is by its very nature often too late, too weak, and most of the time too desperate. Action takes place under pressure of time, and the chances of persuading the authorities to re-think their policies are rather slim. As Shaw [*1996: 2*] has argued, 'activists must develop an agenda and then focus their resources on realizing it. Unfortunately, many activists have failed to establish and implement their own agendas and instead have focused on issues framed by their opponents.' The notion of 'framing' here is crucial. The first side to define the terms and boundaries of the battle is more likely to win since the terms and boundaries are defined according to the field or argument in which that side is the strongest. Indeed, activists are often dragged into defensive battles on issues they did not intend to fight, rather than being called on to define issues and promote productive campaigns. As Shaw [*1996: Ch.8*] writes, the meetings in which activists decide upon goals, tactics and strategies are long and tiring. It is a shame if after all the meetings and waste of energy, the NGOs find themselves fighting a totally different set of issues, or responding to campaigns and agendas set and framed by developers. In other words, activists must realise that contemporary politics often starts with setting the agenda.[17]

Moreover, if activists respond rather than initiate, they appear to be acting against those who are 'trying to get something done here'.[18] Often the public sees development as an effort to better the plight of the worse off, as in the case, say, of a new factory or a road cutting travel time from the periphery to the centre. If environmentalists later pop up and start opposing these projects, they appear to be interfering with a decent project proposed by kind-hearted people. Environmentalists who use the language of 'us and them', are seen as selfish people obsessing about marginal matters.

Fifth Commandment: *Always Declare That You Are Not Doing Anything Political*

One of the main mistakes made by environmental activists is to present their campaign as a-political.[19] Sometimes they believe that this is the way to gain increased support from the left and the right. They are making three mistakes however: first, by thinking that a non-political cause will garner more support; second, by confusing 'political' with 'party oriented', and third, by failing to see just how political their campaign is.

So first, why do environmental activists assume that if they present their campaign as non-political it will gain more support? Through interviews that I conducted with activists in Israel and other countries, I learned that many of them think of politics as 'ugly', 'nasty', 'dirty', 'power games and nothing else', 'corrupt', 'career-oriented', or just 'another of the affluent bourgeoisie's games'. They believe that if they present their campaign as non-political, more people will be happy to support them; people who tend usually to keep politics at arm's length.

This seems, however, to contradict research observations regarding who joins public activism. People decide whether or not to support a case or campaign depending on whether they believe the case to be just or not, not according to whether it is political or not. Thus the more people see a case as just, the more they will join and support the activists. A very good example is the mass student strike organised in Israel between October and December 1998. The strike, for lower tuition fees, was launched with an announcement that it was not a political campaign. This, naturally, seemed very odd to many people, including students. Moreover, many people from the inner cities and poorer neighbourhoods refused to join forces with the students as long as the students failed to recognise the close linkage between lowering the costs of higher education and raising the chances of the less well-off for social mobility. However, once the students dared to admit their opposition to the government, and declared their campaign political, many unemployed people and social organisations came out in public support of the students and even joined a hunger strike by student leaders.[20]

The second mistake occurs when many environmentalists, including Green activists and politicians, declare themselves to be 'neither left nor right'. They claim instead to be 'ahead' [*Porritt, 1984: 14, 224–35;* also *Kitschelt and Helleman, 1990*]. This may be an excellent piece of copy editing, but it is far from the truth. The very author of this slogan, Mr. Porritt, who is without doubt one of Europe's leading Green politicians and activists, quite often raises the issue of 'rights' in his books, article, and essays [*Porritt, 1984: 115–17*], describing the minimum criteria for a green society as 'open, participatory democracy', 'harmony between people of every race', and so on [*Porritt, 1984: 10–11*]. This is clearly leftist terminology and rhetoric. It hails, perhaps from the revisionist left, but is far from part of right wing ideology. It is equally far from being apolitical. While it is true that not every issue that is political can be squeezed under the positions of existing parties, and that environmental NGOs do usually conduct non-party campaigns [*Maor and Smith, 1993*], these are still political campaigns, by any definition of the word 'political'.

The third mistake is that many activists dislike being political so much that they shift the emphasis of their campaigns from political matters to issues more likely to be seen as non-political. Hence many concentrate on consumer habits and the number of babies born. But, as John Bellamy Foster argues, in doing this, such environmentalists misinterpret reality: they think that the general public, as consumers, is the enemy of the environment [*Foster, 1998: 188*]. But then, they overlook the complexity underlying environmental degradation.

> An ecological movement that stands for the Earth alone and ignores class and other social inequalities will succeed at best in displacing environmental problems, meanwhile reinforcing the dominant relations of power in global capitalism, with their bias towards the unlimited commodification of human productive energy, land and the built environment, and the ecology of the planet itself [*Foster, 1998: 188*].

Sixth Commandment: *Emphasise Legislation – Not Politics*[21]

Activists often pin their hopes on legislation. They assume that where there is a law there is no way developers or anti-environmental forces can harm the environment. There are, however, two problems with this: first, it is often counter-productive to legislate on the environment, and second, it is very easy to legislate; the question is are the laws enforceable?

To begin with, laws are rigid, whereas ecosystems change. It is difficult to revise laws in synch with changes in ecosystems. Sometimes therefore a law may be counter-productive. Take the case of deer protection in the UK: growing concern for the declining number of deer and deer species led to a series of acts.[22] These acts proved so effective that after 25 years 'deer are posing a significant threat to woodland management'. [*Evans, 1992: 118*]. But then, who would dare to re-legislate and limit the ban on deer hunting?

At the same time, efforts to force legislated protection for other types of wildlife have often failed due to the impossibility of enforcing the laws without becoming a police state. For example, a series of laws introduced in the 1960s to protect British flora [*Evans, 1992: 124*] failed for this reason. It thus seems that environmentalists need to work hard to change attitudes, rather than impose threats. Indeed, such was the case when the National Trust campaigned against the destruction of coastal areas which were being threatened by increased leisure time and rising numbers of holiday-makers. On this occasion, people listened, and enough money was donated to the NT to allow it to acquire 160 kilometres of coastline [*Evans, 1992: 125*]. In Israel a similar case involved a campaign organised by the SPNI (Society for the Protection of Natured in Israel) during the 1960s to save wild flora. The campaign was based solely on education and public relations, and was highly successful. However, a law introduced to protect nature reserves in general has not been enforced because in many cases this would mean putting to trial so many people.[23] Environmentalists now realise they should have educated the public instead of campaigning for legislation.

Laws in themselves are often meaningless: in Britain, the 1968 Countryside Act extended the definition of national parks to cover woodlands, rivers and canals. However, the last area to be declared a national park was the Brecon Beacons in 1957 [*Evans, 1992: 82*]. Section 37 of this act also required all ministers to address agricultural, forestry, economic and social interests. [*Evans, 1992: 123*]. Notice, however, that some of these interests may contradict each other, for example, forestry interests may clash with agriculture, or social interests might conflict with economic ones. Thus ministers can dodge their obligation to address environmental issues on economic grounds.

After a comprehensive survey of 735 key sites in the UK conducted between the mid 1960s and 1977, efforts to introduce legislation that would protect sites of special scientific interest, mostly came to naught. Farmers owned most of the lands in question and would need to be compensated. However, the farmers either refused to accept compensation (in which case there was nothing to do), or began planning potentially damaging land usage, which, they declared they would abandon in return for 'appropriate compensation'. The Environment ministry had no funds to compensate farmers for their 'theoretical losses' [*Evans, 1992: 189*] and consequently as many as 255 SSSIs were irrevocably damaged before anything could be done.

According to Randy Shaw [*1996: 58–9*], environmentalists are the victims of 'random lawlessness' when a government itself refuses to enforce its own environmental regulations. He quotes American writer William Greider, who states that eighty percent of the Environmental Protection Agency's hazardous waste enforcement regulations are ignored. Moreover, says Greider, during the 1980s, 92,500 people earned their living by arguing over the content of federal regulations. This might indicate that the legislator was not serious when legislating environmental laws.

It is interesting to explore why this happens. Two reasons can be suggested. First, many MPs depend on their constituencies for their careers. If they are to win reelection, they must convince their constituents that they have worked hard in their interests. Thus when pressured to legislate, they do legislate, even if they consider the law to be unenforceable or illogical.

They would rather legislate and show that they made the effort, even if the effort is useless, than explain to their constituents that their legislative proposals are flawed. As a result, dozens of laws are passed each year without any intention of enforcing them. Environmental laws comprise a vast proportion of these laws, since citizens often approach their MP with environmental, often local, problems. Randy Shaw, an attorney, calls them 'hollow laws'. He writes: 'Such laws allow legislators to war a false pro-environmental mantle while creating the potentially dangerous illusion that Congress has addressed a critical problem' [*Shaw, 1996: 70*]. Shaw calls upon environmentalists to attack such legislation early enough in the process of legislation.

Second, there is so much pressure on legislators to legislate and regulate environmental laws and regulations, that even if their motives were genuine and did take the environment seriously, they could not possibly acquire enough information to know a good law from a bad one. Environmental matters are complicated matters, and it takes time to study them. Legislators lack the time to do this thoroughly, and therefore legislate without giving due consideration to the implementation or enforcement of these laws. Their primary aim is to appear environmentally friendly.

Seventh Commandment: *Do Your Very Best to Attract Media Attention*

Many organisations think that at least some of their members must be experts at 'capturing media attention' [*Adams, introduction*].[24] They believe this since they tend to take the view that 'MP + TV = Success' [*Young, 1993: 26*]. They are so eager to gain a press review or an item on TV that they focus on protest gimmicks instead of real change. 'Silence is death', they say, and they will go out of their way to make as much noise as they can.

However, we find a recurring pattern of media and press coverage emerging for such protest acts. Journalists arrive on site, and make their report. But then, after given it roughly 20–30 seconds on TV, they move on. The first question that springs to mind is: What can environmentalists achieve in 30 second reports? It is usually very difficult to explain ecological issues to begin with, let alone in such a short time. Thus activists focus on other goals. They give up trying to convince the public through information and enlightenment – and that is their first mistake. The activists play by the rules of the game set by capitalism and its obsession with TV ratings: no serious discussion, no information to help the public make decisions.

Then the activists become frustrated. It dawns on them that 20 seconds on TV will not change anything. They infer that what they need to do is hold the media's attention longer. They undertake even weirder things. Out trots the media once more. This time presenting the activists as people who do 'odd' things. Next time these people climb trees or tie themselves to sundry objects, the media beings to lose patience. Their reporting takes on a negative slant. Consider, for example, the report on Israeli TV about a group of students, members of the '*Peula Yeruka*' (Green Action) organisation, who in the spring of 1999, climbed up and tied themselves to cranes, to demonstrate against the construction of mega-hotels on the actual sea shore. The media's immediate response was to report them, though for less than a minute. They interviewed one of the activists for roughly 15 seconds. The next day more students joined them. This time the TV report was shorter. Next thing the students did was threaten that if they did not receive a promise that the hotels would not be built they would remain on the cranes 'for ever'. The journalists took it literally and thought this was rather stupid: 'Can a person *really* live on a crane forever?' they queried. The report discussed a strange group of people, who did not really know what they wanted. The students did not budge. The TV news editor decided it was all a non-issue. No more reporting. Several days later one article newspaper grumbled about those people who can afford the time to do such things … Needless to say, the students have dispersed and the hotels are fast going up. What is worse, the general public did not know whether to like them or laugh at them. Eventually people decided they were 'pathetic'.[25]

If this was the only problem, fine. But those activists who chase the media put all their eggs in one basket – the wrong one. They forget that their goal is to end pollution, end damage to an ecosystem, etc. But they must never forget that the world out there is real. What we see on TV is not. Thus not only do they achieve a negative image in the public eye, they fail to solve the real problem they were fighting for in the first place. Thus, in 1993, one of Greenpeace's leading environmental campaigners, Chris Rose, wrote in all sincerity that a wrong approach was being taken in media-driven campaigning [*1993: 292*]. Greenpeace, he explained, had focused on capturing media attention, but since the organisation's target was 'packaging the messages to fit media opportunities and prejudices and paradigms of what is environmental news', it had failed in only managing to create a formulaic 'sameness' in its messages. This not only limited its members' imagination and creativity, but also gave TV viewers a sense of 'O.K. So this is serious. But haven't we heard it all before?' [*Rose, 1993*]. Moreover, since Greenpeace focused on how things would look on TV, reality and solving real problems had given way to virtual reality. The public felt that 'it was all on TV' and that therefore had nothing to do with them, argues Rose.

This approach not only serves to distance activists from problem solving, but might alienate many potential activists by encouraging them to believe that only campaigning of this kind works. Knowing that they themselves are not the sort of people who climb trees and tie themselves to tractors, many of them might conclude they have nothing to offer.

Moreover, when action is directed deliberately toward to capturing media attention, the wrong message is sent to the public. A good example of this is Greenpeace's campaign against genetically modified crops. Greenpeace decided to 'go violent' in the case of genetically modified maize being grown in Norfolk. Some days before their action, the village in which the GM maize was being grown, assembled and resolved to oppose the raising of GM crop in their village – through non-violent means (*The Observer,* 1 Aug. 1999). Greenpeace, however, led by Lord Melchett, went storming over the field, destroying all the crops (*The Guardian,* 22 July 1999). Following violent clashes between Greenpeace activists and farmers (the Brigham brothers), a number of activists, among them Lord Melchett, were arrested. The story then changed tack: instead of focusing on GM trials on a farm-level scale, Lord Melchett and his arrest became the story. And, rather than the farmers and their risky crops being targeted for criticism, Greenpeace was condemned for its violence. Instead of the farmers being portrayed as anti-democratic and growing crops (against the will of the rest of the village) that might threaten local organic farming – Greenpeace was portrayed as anti-democratic. As the report ends, quoting one of the Brigham brothers: 'This has nothing to do with genetically modified organisms – it's whether we want democratic government or anarchy' (*The Guardian,* 22 July 1999). This was the message sent to anyone who read this report to its end.

Indeed, we see from the press reporting on the Newbury bypass campaign that it is not always so important to capture media attention: often what is important is what the media writes – not *if* it writes. Let us consider what the more environmentally sympathetic newspapers – *The Guardian* and *The Observer* – had to say on the bypass campaign: for example, on 25 October 1999 we read about the security guard who suffered a ruptured chest muscle when he was struck by a rock thrown from a catapult. This could well seem excessively violent to readers, whose sympathy would then go out to the innocent guard now in the hospital instead of at home with his family. This same journalist (Alex Bellos) had been far more supportive of the environmental campaign only a few months earlier. On 18 March 1996 he had written: 'Anger against the Newbury pass has united old and young, rich and poor, left and right'. On 19 February 1996 he reported that the bypass would only save two minutes of driving. *The Guardian's* John Vidal described the road builders as being engaged in a 'battle' against the protestors (15 Feb. 1996). But soon afterwards, as protestors started to prove their capacity for violence, Melanie Phillips claimed that (*The Guardian,* 24 March 1996) 'Greens are not Always Good for You', a critical reference to Charless Secrett, then director of FoE, who had argued that the environmentalists were above the democratic process since they 'possessed unchallengeable truths.'

As already noted, one of the most radical activists in the anti-road campaign was Swampy. The initial coverage of his actions was very colourful and supportive. Alex Bellos wrote about 'Swampy Fever' (*The Guardian,* 12 May 1997). Swampy's first public appearance after his long stay in the tunnel was described in heroic terms: 'When Swampy came out of the tunnel he and his friends dug a journalist shouted across the melee of security guards and police officers: "why did you risk your life?"' 'The answer' writes Bellows, 'was eloquent, well spoken and on television. "It was the only way to get a voice these days. If I wrote a letter to my MP, would I have achieved all this? Would you lot be here now?"'

But in reply dare I ask, what exactly did Swampy achieve? What long-run popular support did he gain? Would not a mass, silent demonstration have achieved the same? Admittedly certain newspapers, normally condemnatory of law breaking activists, had 'fallen in love with him', but they still didn't take any notice of the real issue. Swampy gave the magazines and newspapers a touching human interest story. But did we not lose the environment somewhere? Was this a story about whether Britain needed the A30 and other roads? Or was it about a boy who was willing to sacrifice himself. Or was it to do with the 'thrill' at finally having a peacetime hero? Indeed, it is interesting to note that Swampy went on to appear on a TV celebrity show, on "Have I got News for You" show, and that he was interviewed for a teenage magazine and earned the doubtful distinction of being compared to the 'Spice Girls'. He was actually asked by a record company to record a version of 'I am a mole and I live in a hole' under the name of 'Swampy and the Swampy Girls' (*The Guardian, 18 May* 1997, p.3). Swampy became an overnight celebrity (for a short time), while the car culture remained.[26]

Eighth Commandment: *Promote the Organisation Itself*

It is commonly known, from studies of organisations, that they are often established for an ad-hoc purpose, but having solved whatever problem they wished to solve, they remain active, although their function does change. It is often the case that organisation members so enjoy belonging to this type of organisation that sustaining and fostering the organisation becomes paramount for many members and activists. Orly Peled [*1994*] studied the socio-economic and motivational background of the membership of Israel's largest environmental NGO, the Society for the Protection of Nature in Israel (SPNI). She found that a high percentage of those who were active and received actual payment for their involvement, had joined, or remained within the SPNI for social reasons. People reported feeling wanted and needed, that they had made good friends, or had experienced enhanced self-esteem since joining the organisation. People often join an NGO for reasons of this nature and only later adopt its environmental position.

Members and activists often ascribe far more to the organisation and to the experience of being active in a campaign than they had hoped to find when they joined. A good example is the list of 'lessons' which Merrick says he learned through being involved in the Newbury bypass campaign:

> How to get on with people, about western politics, commitment, passion, making chapatties, when to accept someone's word, when to step in and when to step back, my body, my capacity to learn, trusting myself, getting along with whoever crosses your path, hope, love, defiance in the face of power, corruption and ridicule, the politics, fucking quietly so as not to wake up those around you, grand gestures, fruity porridge, loyalty to old friends, the joy of new ones, violence, truth, perception of beauty, the strength of collective will, determination, the way of the exceptional can become mundane, the way the mundane can become exceptional, empowerment, resolve, having visions, seeing the facts, acting responsibly in the midst of enormity and crassness, being a responsible ancestor, history, about the future, never giving up [*Merrick, 1997: 6*].

Often activists become so involved and committed that a sense of belonging to a very intimate community develops. In such cases, activists are likely to be trapped by the 'having fun' mentality. If 'enjoying it' is a serious component of the protest, the activists will continue with their existing protest strategy even if it fails and needs to be revised. Merrick's testimony is so honest and naive that it is revealing. He devotes much space to describe in details his sexual experiences during the campaign [*Merrick, 1997: 84*]. Merrick goes on to describe the music tapes they had and how they enjoyed listening to them while up in the trees. However, as one reads this fascinating document one has the feeling that the saving the trees was gradually forgotten. It could have been any objective: the original, environmental goal becomes instrumental to having fun, fostering the group, forming a community, and so on.

However, not only do members try to foster the organisation for personal reasons, the organisation finds itself in the position of having to promote itself. Because people join up not so much because their support is in 'demand', but because they are attracted to what the organisation can 'supply' [*Jordan and Maloney, 1997: Chs.4–6*], organisations thus feel they must market themselves to potential members. This means that much of their energy and time is spent on persuading those who are already in to stay in, and in convincing potential members to join, instead of persuading developers and politicians that their projects are unfriendly to the environment and should therefore be abandoned.

Ninth Commandment: *Never Be Benevolent To Other Organisations*

Many activists report tensions between organisations and their activists. These tensions, they claim, prevent the organisations from presenting a united front. There is rivalry between organisations for similar financial and human sources, donations, media attention, and social kudos. They even compete for membership. Several organisations, usually the more radical ones, were established by people who had been frustrated with the way their previous organisations led their campaigns. For example, the first *Earth First! UK* group was founded by two students in Hastings, East Sussex. The students and those who joined them from local peace and anti-nuclear networks, had participated in other green groups and ended up disillusioned with them [*Doherty, 2000*].[27] In fact, many activists are members of more than one organisation. For example, 65.8 per cent of *FoE* members belong to other environmental organisations [*Jordan and Maloney, 1997: 79*]. This means that these groups find themselves in competition for members.[28]

It is important to note that often the tensions derive from the more 'genuine' environmentalists, but work against them. Often environmentalists throw mud at those more established organisations, claiming that they are not radical enough, picturing those who have more access to decision making centres as 'not genuine environmentalists' (see below). Thus, the public learns to identify those who succeed, who get to be listened, as not genuinely environmentalists. However, consequently, when a more radical organisation does achieve something, it ceases to be genuinely environmental in the eyes of the public. Similarly, as Jordan [*1998: 315*] claims, among academics there is a tendency to relabel any group using non-conventional strategies as 'social movements', but once the groups begins to succeed, it ceases to be a movement.

I now want to explore the four sources of these tension: tension between local and national organisations, tension between grass-roots activists and the professional echelon, personal differences and ideological divergences among activists.

The first source of tension, then, emerges from the clash between the local and the national – or even the international – organisation. These clashes are about what is really important, how a specific case fits the broader picture of environmental campaigning, which values should be emphasised and when. The local, often *ad-hoc*, organisations tend to suspect the national ones for not paying them sufficient attention and for 'having a different agenda', while the national organisations tend often to underestimate the local organisations' potential. Moreover, national and international organisations wish to be involved in all campaigns, but also, at the same time, to distribute their energy and money wisely and invest more of their resources in cases in which the odds of winning are more favorable. They want also to feel they have mastered the relevant subject matter.

We find a good example of this in the Twyford Down anti-roads campaign in the UK. In February 1992, the British government decided to construct a road in Twyford Down in Hampshire to shorten the travelling time between Southampton and London. *Friends of the Earth (FoE)* entered the town and established its protest camp on 13 March 1992. However, when warned by their lawyers that they would be liable to fines of £250,000, they packed up and left. A well-established organisation like the *FoE* cannot afford the sort of bad press and publicity that a court case would bring – or for that matter the economic damage [*Lamb, 1996: 6*]. Local organisations interpreted their action as betrayal and defeatism. Not long after, *FoE* was back to work, fighting assorted road development schemes on several fronts. For them, the Twyford Down affair, and the M25 campaign were 'two battles in the same war' [*Lamb, 1996: 10*]. However, many of the people and organisations that stayed on at Twyford Down did not see things this way. They had believed that the Twyford Down protest was to be the 'launching ground for the direct action road protest' [*Wall, 1999: 65*]. Thus relations between the *FoE* and other groups such as *Road Alert* 'turned sour' [*Lamb, 1996: 10*].[29] Roger Higman of *Friends of the Earth* complained that there were 'elements of jealousy' on both sides [*Lamb, 1996: 202*]. While local organisations indeed accept that in certain cases the national organisation knows too little about the issue at stake, the locals nevertheless claim that national inaction derogates the issue at stake, which, in turn, can have negative repercussions on the locals' chances of success.[30]

Tensions between smaller and larger environmental organisations might also be due to the greater power of the larger organisations and their dominance over access to decision-makers. This is very frustrating for many small, local, or minor organisations, which feel they have failed to put their message across. For example, there have been many complaints about the larger organisations from an environmental justice perspective, by many activists [*Shlosberg, 1999: 143, fn. 3; Dowie, 1995*].

The second source of tension is when one organisation tends to work with professionals, while the other works on the grass roots level. Each claims to know how best to make an impact. Both may be right and wrong at the same time. When I discussed this matter with media representatives in Israel, many of them claimed that the 'local' arena is more attractive to them: they would rather present local, non-professional, under-dog activists fighting for a cause than interviewing professors or technicians who claim to know it all. The local is more interesting in terms of ratings, they admit. However research demonstrates that it is not necessarily the local people who solve the problems. Often local people play a 'discovery role' [*Rootes, 1999: 5*], but 'once an issue is securely on the national agenda, the baton of protest passes to the bigger battalions of better resourced environmental movements organisations' [*Rootes, 1999*]. As Schlosberg [*1999*] explains, in the USA, while many small, local organisations regard the national and larger organisations as being too paternalistic and disempowering, replacing these organisations with a spontaneous, egalitarian network does not always solve the problem of being able to sustain long term protest.

At this point Randy Shaw takes sides, blaming the Washington based, main stream national environmental groups (the 'Big Ten') for being more concerned with maintaining their status within the establishment than changing reality [*Shaw, 1996: 59*]. In fact, thousands of people make a living working for these organisations, and do not want to kiss good bye to their livelihood. They fear that this will happen if the organisation becomes antagonistic to the establishment and therefore loses its political status. Shaw suspects that they therefore spend a great deal of energy and time confronting grass-roots environmental organisations instead of solving problems,[31] and even if this is not objectively the case, the suspicion is there, overshadowing relations between the national and the smaller, local organisations.

Naturally, some tensions between organisations result from personality differences among the people involved in them. However, to students of environmental politics, it often seems that every conceivable tension of this kind exists among environmentalists. For example, Merrick [*1997 51*] describes his frequent debates with people representing other organisations and other approaches – mainly those opposed to the protestors' 'direct action' approach. Looking disdainfully down at his opponents, his parting shot to them is: 'Ideas without action are called bullshit, If you can't walk it like you talk it, shut up till you learn how.' Derek Wall quotes an interview with Charles Secret, director of *FoE UK* in the mid-1990s, about the relationships between *FoE* and *Earth First!*: 'One of the things which pissed me off when I came back into *FoE* was these 20-somethings, who told me I had it all wrong and theirs was the only way of contributing, "Who the xxxx are you?"' [*Wall, 1999: 112*].[32]

However, this is also an ideological type of tension deriving from different organisations interpretations of the social causes of environmental problems. The differences relate to the question of whether the root social cause of environmental problems is the 'system' or the 'structure' (in Marxian terms). Those who see it as the latter conclude that the situation can only be partially improved by changing people's views; in fact, since people's views reflect their socio-economic status, they will only change their political behaviour if the structure changes. As a result, the activists who take this view do not engage in heroic, self-sacrificing acts, but in consistent and, indeed, dull efforts to change the structure of society: to change production relations, to make institutions more environment friendly, and so on. However, those who accuse the 'system' of being the root of all evil, blame it on mentality, on crookedness, on corruption. But the problem with corruption is that it conceals itself from public sight – by corrupt means. So, these people claim, the way to fight the 'system' is to expose, *corum populo*, those misdemeanours. This of course, calls for courageous men and women and personal devotion. You cannot beat a 'system' which has been described as 'hierarchy, bureaucracy and compromised strategies' [*Wapner, 1995:: 300*] using huge, cumbersome, complicated multi-million-dollar corporations[33] with thousands of employees, or indeed by political parties. Instead, these people argue, what we need is direct action by dedicated individuals against actual instances of ecological abuse.[34]

Some activists believe that an authoritative, national 'convention' would solve the problem of the distrust and enmity dividing the organisations. Randy Shaw, for example, writes:

> A national convention could accomplish several goals. First, it could help create a specific national environmental agenda. Most of the public does not really understand what environmentalists want at the national level. Confusion over the specifics of environmentalists' demands weakens political accountability; it is not always clear to the public when a betrayal has occurred. For example, even people sympathetic to the environmentalist position on the spotted owl would have had a difficult time learning the 'true' pro-environment position (if one existed). Such a position could have become widely known through adoption by a convention. If the convention voted that the only pro-environment position on the spotted owl was a total ban on harvesting in the owl's habitat, politicians who supported weaker restrictions would be seen as opposing rather than supporting environmentalists. This clarity would still not prevent groups like the Wilderness Society from hailing weaker restrictions as a great environmental victory, but the public would know that the weaker restrictions violate the national environmental platform [*Shaw, 1996: 269–70*].

This paragraph seems to me rather frightening. What is described here is the end of debate, the narrowing of freedom of opinion, the death of pluralism.

Rather than open and free debate on what constitutes the right solution, this is a vision of despotic and irreversible decisions, together with a threat to those who do not conform with the national convention, or, in fact, the majorities. As was argued by J.S. Mill over 150 years ago, an open, never ending debate is crucial if we are to know better, or at least to know why we think what we think. We should never believe that a solution is right because the majority, or the national convention, says so. We should understand *why* it is the right solution, and if we have doubts we should be able to raise them. Thus the relationships between the national conventions and larger NGOs, and the local groups should be founded on mutual respect and reciprocal consultation rather than hierarchy and authority. Tensions are destructive, but we also need to be very cautious regarding the solutions.

Tenth Commandment: *Do* Not *Trust This Research: It is the Advice of a 'Softie'!*

There are very few who would dare deny that many, if not most, academics who study environmental politics, philosophy, or economics, also support the environmental movement, at least to some degree. They may also be committed to a particular environmentalist school of thought, whether ecocentrism or ecofeminism, etc. Therefore this account could be read as a manifesto of the more 'square', or perhaps more conservative (*not* with a capital C) environmentalists. Indeed, I might be suspected of being precisely such a 'boring environmentalist' and indeed have been 'accused' of this by more radical environmentalists on the basis of some of my academic works [*1995, 1997, 2000*]. And yet, it is important to note that in my own case, I reached the position of a 'moderate' following research and continuing exploration of the conclusions of my research. Thus this account is *not* a 'softy' manifesto, though I suspect many would like to claim it is and ignore it.

Current environmental activism is very promising. In many countries environmental problems have become legitimate issues on the political agenda, and no doubt environmental activists were responsible for this. However, it is my fear that when environmental campaigns succeed they are anlaysed and studied carefully, and many claim to be liable for them, whereas failures remain orphans. It has been my aim here to analyse these failures without disheartening anybody. Indeed, I believe that if activists learn from failures, especially when there appears to be a pattern in those failures, they can improve their chances of success tremendously.

NOTES

1. See, for example, the statement by Merrick, the road activist (*Merrick, 1997: 66*).
2. Many activists present the situation as a moral debate, rather than as a political one. The fight is on values and ideas, not on distributive shares. Rudolf Bahro, for example, complains about the give and take culture of politics [*1986: 196–210*], and therefore thinks that politics only leads to self-extermination [*1994: 79–150*]. Only an all-out war, with no compromise, will win, he claims.
3. George Monbiot's essays in the *The Guardian* suggest so.
4. DuPont were responsible for 25 per cent of the world annual production of CFCs.
5. During the Gulf War of 1991, tourism from the USA to Britain dropped significantly because many Americans had seen on TV how the Iraqis were bombing neighbouring countries, and were afraid to travel to Britain, being unable to distinguish the UK from the Middle East.
6. A group of my students examined this in neighbourhoods of different social-economic backgrounds and found very little evidence of understanding the issues at stake. For example, during the Gulf War, Iraq bombed Israel with conventional missiles. Israelis were very concerned about the possibility of chemical weapons being used. A month later my students interviewed supermarket customers about whether they were checking for chemicals in the products they were purchasing, referring, of course, to different kinds of additives. However, many people were surprised and answered that they could not see why they should check, given that it was known that Iraq had not fired chemical warheads.
7. I thank Mr Eli'ezer Y'aari of the NIF.
8. For such attitudes see Morrison and Dunlap [*1986*]. For a critique of these positions see Eckersley [*1989*].
9. Moreover, what does a total change campaign imply? It in fact implies distrust and despair with democratic politics. Swampy claims that he did what he did because regular politics does not work. Hugo Young writes that the lesson learned from Swampy's activities is that parliamentary democracy is counter-productive (*The Guardian*, 13 March 1997). Or consider, for example, Rudolf Bahro's speech of resignation from the Greens, in which he claims that parliamentary democracy and parties are "counter productive tools" [*Bahro, 1986: 210–11*]. I have elaborated on this point in de-Shalit [*2000: Ch. 5*].
10. This is based on interviews and discussions with activists. But see also Rose [*1993: 291*] where he discusses environmental activists' commitment to protecting the natural world, and their favour of the 'optimism of the action over the pessimism of the thought'.
11. At other times, the language used by many activists is not necessarily biocentric, but is nevertheless so radical or odd that it may seem totally alien to large numbers of potential supporters. Merrick, an activist in the Newbury bypass campaign quotes a flyposter from January 1996: "We, the road protesters … in the true spirit of England, in the true spirit of our mythical heroes, King Arthur and Robyn Hood, we are prepared to stand up for truth and justice." [*Merrick, 1997: 1*] He then goes on to compare himself to the heroes and heroines that England has always produced while 'in great need' [*Merrick, 1997: 1*], and calls himself 'the Great Mighty Eco-Warrior' [*Merrick, 1997, 6*, capitals in original].
12. Often environmentalists complain that they are asked to be 'reasonable'. For such a complaint regarding the Big Ten's attitude to grass-roots activists see Shaw [*1996: 60–61*].
13. However, arguments raised by an epidemiological expert concerning the impact of the transmitters on local inhabitants did hit the spot, and the programme was abandoned. Perhaps the most famous case involving the use of a biocentric argument was when Christopher Stone, a nature loving lawyer from California suggested that trees had a right of standing before the Supreme Court. Stone however lost the case. [*Stone, 1979*: 'A Personal Preface'].
14. What language will people understand and be most likely to internalise? This question demands a separate paper. Here I shall just remark that I subscribe to the view that it is the language of environmental justice [*Schlosberg, 1999*]. Activists should show, time and time again, that the environment has to be protected as a matter of social justice, and that environmental nuisance is more likely to harm the elderly, the poor and the weaker segments of society. At a time when garbage and waste are being transported from one country to another, it is the weaker elements in society who end up with it buried next door.

15. Although according to McLeod [*1998*], 73 per cent of the demonstrators in Brightlingsea against live animal transport were between the age of 41 and 70, 38 per cent were retired and 80 per cent had never protested before.
16. Findings of a survey I conducted in Israel
17. Zaller [*1992*], for example, argues that voters, or the general public, have a variety of interests and other considerations, most of which do not tie in with each other. Hence the first party to set up the agenda is more likely to have an impact on these voters or potential supporters than the party that responds, simply by virtue of being the first to address their reservations.
18. In 1997–99, when the mayor of Haifa in Israel, Mr Amram Mitzna confronted resistance to his programmes to build several marinas on the beautiful, open and wild seashore south of the city, he used this argument against environmentalists.
19. This is also done by academics. Ridley characterises these campaigns as standing 'outside the run of established politics, involving people who would be offended if described as politicians' [*Ridley, 1998: 309*].
20. For more details: www.haaretz.co.il/arch/index.asp/students
21. This title might be misleading. I do not mean that the two – legislation and politics – are mutually exclusive. Legislation is, of course, part of politics. However, the core of politics, in its democratic and participatory meaning, is the bargaining, public deliberation, and agreements that are reached between activists, organisations, often with the help of politicians. Many students of politics today consider legislation to be the target of most political actions, but this is not how politics has always been seen. See Crick [*1993*] and Cunningham [*1994*].
22. For example, in the 1966 Scotland Deer Act: the Protection of Deer Act (1959) was extended to all deer species in Scotland; in 1963 the Deer Act was extended and provision made to protect red, fallow, roe and silka deer in England and Wales [*Evans, 1992: 118*].
23. In several cases the law could not be enforced for political reasons. The Arab minorities in Israel regard many of the nature reserves, especially those bordering with their villages as another mechanism of the Israeli government to limit the Arabs in Israel. Demands by the SPNI and other environmentalists to enforce the law in one of Israel's largest nature reserves, in Mount Miron, ended up with the local Arab villagers campaigning with slogan such as 'environmental fascists'. The environmentalists withdrew, realising that education would be a much better way to prevent damages.
24. However, Wolfgang Rüdig writes that 'there are signs that the media stunts performed by Greenpeace have lost much of their novelty value' [*Rüdig, 1995: 231*].
25. This is based on interviews that I conducted during these events. For more details see www.haaretz.co.il/arch
26. Admittedly, some cuts in road programmes were done, but often due to the Treasury's desire to cut public expenditure [*Doherty, 1998: 383*].
27. See also the tables of membership trends among UK environmental campaigning organisations in Jordan and Maloney [*1997: 13*]. It is clear that while some groups gain more members others lose theirs, and the total number remains more or less stable. This prompts the suspicion that new members are actually the former members of other organisations.
28. Jordan and Maloney [*1997: 118–19*] argue that participation is a function of mobilization and of groups persuading people to become members. Since potential members have more or less the same class, education, income and occupational background [*1997: 106–7*], groups compete over members.
29. Notice that Lamb wrote this book in collaboration with the FoE. Other sources simply blame the FoE for abandoning the battlefield. See Wall [*1999: 67–8*].
30. Randy Shaw describes such a case when Clinton and Gore promised the inhabitants of East Liverpool, Ohio, to protect them against the interest of the Waste Technology Industry before the elections of 1992, but turned their backs on the local people after the elections. See Shaw [*1996: 59–66*].
31. In Israel, the Society for the Protection of Nature employs thousands of staff. The Society competes for grants against smaller organisations. According to a recent report, if a minor NGO competes against the SPNI for grants, its chances are slim [*de Hartouch, 2000*].

32. See also the description of such personal tensions between *FoE* campaign coordinator, Andrew Lees, and other organisations [*Wall, 1999: 122*].
33. For example, by 1990, the revenue of Britain's National Trust was some £56 million per annum [*Young, 1993: 18*].
34. Hence, Earth First! UK would like to be called a 'disorganisation' rather than 'organisation' [*Lamb, 1996: 4*].

REFERENCES

Adams, W.M. (1986), *Nature's Place: Conservation Sites and Countryside Change*, London: Allen & Unwin.

Bahro, Rodulf (1986), *Building the Green Movement* (trans. Mary Tyler), London: GMP Books.

Bahro, Rudolf (1994), *Avoiding Social and Ecological Disaster* (trans. David Clarke), Bath: Gateway Books.

Bennie, Lynn G. (1998), 'Brendt Spar, Atlantic oil and Greenpeace', *Parliamentary Affairs*, Vol.5, pp.397–410.

Benton, Ted (1988), 'Humanism = Speciesism?', *Radical Philosophy*, Vol.50, pp.4–18.

Benton, Ted (1993), *Natural Relations: Ecology, Animal Rights and Social Justice*, London: Verso Press.

Carmin, Joann (1999), 'Voluntary Associations, Professional Organisations and the Environmental Movement in the United Sates', *Environmental Politics*, Vol.8, No.1, pp.101–21.

Chase Steve (ed.) (1991), *Defending the Earth: A Dialogue between Murray Bookchin and Dave Foreman*, Boston, MA: South End Press.

Crick, Bernard (1993 [1962]), *In Defence of Politics*, London: Penguin.

Cunningham, Frank (1994), *The Real World of Democracy Revisited*, Atlantic Highlands, NJ: Humanities Press.

de Hartouch, Amnon (2000), *State support for public organisations*, Jerusalem: The Florsheimer Research Institute for Policy Analysis (in Hebrew).

de-Shalit, Avner (1995), *Why Posterity Matters*, London: Routledge.

de-Shalit, Avner (1997), 'Down to Earth Environmentalism', in Fotion Nick and Jan Heller (eds.), *Contingent Future Persons*, Boston, MA: Kluwer Academics.

de-Shalit, Avner (2000), *The Environment: Between Theory and Practice*, Oxford: Oxford University Press.

de-Shalit, Avner and Moti Talias (1994), 'Green or Blue and White? Environmental Controversies in Israel', *Environmental Politics*, Vol.3, No.2, pp.273–95.

Dickson, Lisa and Alistair McCulloch (1996), 'Shell, the Brendt Spar, and Greenpeace: A Doomed Tryst', *Environmental Politics*, Vol.5, No.1, pp.122–30.

Dobson, Andrew (1990), *Green Political Thought*, Hammersmith: Harper & Collins Academics.

Doherty, Brian (1998), 'Opposition to Road Building'. *Parliamentary Affairs*, Vol.5, pp.370–84.

Doherty, Brian (1999), 'Paving the Way: The Rise of Direct Action Against Road-Building and the Changing Character of British Environmentalism', *Political Studies*, Vol.XLVII, pp.275–91.

Doherty, Brian (2000), 'Direct Action in British Environmentalism' (unpublished).

Dowie, Mark (1995), *Losing Ground: American Environmentalism at the Close of the Twentieth Century*, Boston, MA: MIT Press.

Eckersley, Robyn (1989), 'Green Politics and the New Class: Selfishness or Virtue?' *Political Studies*, Vol.37, pp.205–23.

Evans, David (1992), *A History of Nature Conservation*, London: Routledge.

Foster, John Bellamy (1998), 'The Limits of Environmentalism Without Class: Lessons from the Ancient Forest Struggle in the Pacific Northwest', in Daniel Faber (ed.), *The Struggle for Ecological Democracy*, New York: The Guildford Press, pp.188–217.

Hayward, Tim (1994), *Ecological Thought*, Cambridge: Polity Press.

Jordan, Grant (1998), 'Politics Without Parties; a Growing Trend?' *Parliamentary Affairs*, Vol.5, pp.314–29.

Jordan, Grant and William Maloney (1997), *The Protest Business*, Manchester: Manchester University Press.
Kitschelt, H. and S. Helleman (1990), 'The Left-Right Semantics and the New Politics of Cleavage', *Comparative Politics*, Vol.23, pp.210–38.
Lamb, Robert (1996), *Promising the Earth*, London: Routledge.
McLeod, Rhoda (1998), 'Calf Exports at Brightlingsea', *Parliamentary Affairs*, Vol.5, pp.345–57.
Maor, Moshe and Gordon Smith (1993), 'On the Structuring of Party Competition: The Impact of Maverick Issues', in T. Bryder (ed.), *Party Systems, Party Behaviour and Democracy*, Copenhagen: University of Copenhagen Press, pp.40–51.
Merrick (1997), *Battle for the Trees*, London: Godhaven Ink.
Morrison D. and R. Dunlap (1986), 'Environmentalism and Elitism', *Environmental Management*, Vol.10, pp.581–9.
Peled, Orli (1994), 'Environmental Positions and Environmental Activism' (in Hebrew; unpublished seminar paper).
Porritt, Jonathan (1984), *Seeing Green*, Oxford: Basil Blackwell.
Porritt, Jonathon and David Winner (1988), *The Coming of the Greens*, London: Fontana.
Ridley, F.R. (1998), 'Crusaders and Politicians', *Parliamentary Affairs*, Vol.5, pp.309–14.
Rose, Chris (1993), 'Beyond the Struggle for Proof: Factors Changing the Environmental Movement', *Environmental Values*, Vol.2, No.4, pp.285–99.
Rootes, Christopher (1999), 'Environmental Movements: From Local to the Global', *Environmental Politics*, Vol.8, No.1, pp.1–13.
Rüdig, Wolfgang (1995), 'Between Moderation and Marginalization: Environmental Radicalism in Britain', in Taylor [*1995: 219–40*].
Schlosberg, David (1999), 'Networks and Mobile Arrangements: Organisation Innovation in the US Environmental Justice Movement', *Environmental Politics*, Vol.8, pp.122–48.
Shaw, Randy (1996), *The Activist's Handbook*, Berkeley, CA: University of California Press.
Stone, Christopher (1979), *Earth and Other Ethics*, New York: Harper & Row Publishers.
Taylor, Bron (ed.) (1995), *Ecological Resistance Movements*, Albany, NY: SUNY Press.
Taylor Dorcetta (1992), 'Can the Environment Movement Attract and Maintain the Support of Minorities?, in Bunyan Bryant and Paul Mohail (eds.), *Race and the Incidence of Environmental Hazards*, Boulder, CO: Westview Press, pp.28–55.
Wall, Derek (1994), *Weaving a Bower Against Endless Nights: An Illustrated History of the UK Green Party*, Aberyswyth, Wales: The Green Party.
Wall, Derek (1999), *Earth First! And the Anti-Roads Movement*, London: Routledge.
Wapner, Paul (1995), 'In Defence of Banner Hangers: The Dark Green Politics of Greenpeace', in Taylor [*1995: 300–14*].
Young, Stephen (1993), *The Politics of the Environment*, Manchester: Baseline Books.
Zaller , J.R. (1992), *The Nature of Mass Opinion*, Cambridge and New York: Cambridge University Press.

Three Conceptions of Irreversibility and Environmental Ethics: Some Problems

MATHEW HUMPHREY

A significant amount of weight is placed, in some branches if environmental philosophy and ecological economics, on the 'irreversibility' of some types of deleterious environmental change. Typically, examples of this would include habitat destruction, radioactive contamination, global warming, and species loss.[1] This variety of examples already suggests that 'irreversibility' might be a matter of degree rather than an absolute value. Furthermore, the notion of what constitutes an irreversible change is to some extent dependent upon the various ontological and axiological assumptions being made. For example, environmental habitats such as rivers or rain forests can be restored after damage has been done, and might plausibly include the same variety and population numbers of species of flora and fauna post-restoration as they did prior to the infliction of environmental damage. Such restoration will satisfy a reversibility criterion for some people, but not those for whom the historical coming-to-be of an entity is constitutive of that entity's very nature. There is already a significant literature on the ethics of restoration revolving around the question of authenticity, to which this essay has little to add.[2] By contrast it is effectively impossible, under current technology, to 'restore' a species to the planet once it has been exterminated, and thus such a change seems to impose a 'stronger' form of irreversibility than habitat loss.

Indeed species loss is where, I would suggest, the irreversibility problem strikes most forcefully in environmental ethics. Species[3] of flora and fauna have evolved through millennia, and (subject to future developments in genetic science) when they are rendered extinct, sometimes as a result of human activity, they remain extinct at all future points within our comprehension. Species loss captures the notion of irreversibility at the heart of the concerns of much environmental ethics, regardless of the question of historical authenticity.[4] Such irreversibility is seen, especially, as a factor that should weigh heavily in planning decisions that trade economic development against human-induced change to the natural environment. Andrew Dobson, for example, in his recent book on justice and the environment, notes a particular conception of sustainability that seeks to the protection of 'irreversible nature'. While a call to prevent all irreversible change would not be feasible, 'the point here is, rather, that the notion of irreversibility needs to be taken into account when calculations of this sort are made' [*Dobson, 1998: 48*].

Dobson goes on to note that species (as types) rather than individual species-members (as tokens) constitute the object of concern here, citing Goodin: '[T]he protection of endangered species is so much more important to greens than the protection of individual specimens … what is crucial is that there be some blue whales, not that there be any particular number of them' [*Goodin, 1992: 61*]. As it stands that statement by Goodin is not strictly accurate, numbers *do* matter, but only as a function of species viability. Greens will be concerned that the numbers of blue whales is sufficient to maintain a viable population. None the less, it is true that in environmental ethics 'types' normally trump 'tokens'.

I want in this account to interrogate the notion of irreversibility as employed in environmental discourse in terms of the amount of work that it is able to perform in support of species-preservation arguments. I will do this, first, through an exploration of different ways in which irreversibility has been conceptualised. We will see that there are at least three different conceptions of irreversibility, and each has its own implications with regard to environmental problems. This will lead on to the second part of the essay, where some of the problems involved in reliance upon the invocation of an irreversibility effect in environmental decision-making are discussed. An alternative conception of irreversibility to that most commonly used in environmental literature is used to highlight some difficulties with using the concept of irreversibility for environmental purposes. Irreversibility is not a constraint unique to the environmental side of the environment-development dilemma.[5] The implications of this are explored in relation to a supposed trade-off between species-loss and development with distributional implications for human welfare. Finally it is suggested that this conception shows that irreversibility is an inappropriate conceptual framework for thinking about the ethical implications of the loss of environmental goods.

Reversibility and Irreversibility

The first point to make is in regard of the idea that 'irreversibility' is a property only of a special class of entities known as 'environmental goods' (or if not them only, then it is taken to attach to those goods especially).[6] There are, to both generalise and represent schematically, three literatures on the nature of irreversibility and its importance to various entities in the universe. The literatures in environmental ethics and environmental economics employ a similar notion of irreversibility, although in general they are enquiring into different problems. Economists are concerned, broadly, with optimising investment decisions and levels of risk-taking under conditions of uncertainty and irreversibility. Environmental ethicists are concerned with whether an irreversibility constraint has any moral implications for human decisions regarding the legitimate use of environmental features. The main focus of this paper is environmental ethics, but despite their differing emphases, these literatures are also inter-related, as can be seen in the work of writers such as John O'Neill [*1993, 1997*], Alan Holland [*1997, 1998*], David Stern [*1997*] and Olof Johansson-Stenman [*1998*] and are clearly capable of informing each other. A third literature, in (broadly) the philosophy of science, tends to view the properties of reversibility and irreversibility rather differently, and also to apply these notions to a far broader category of phenomena, than do the first two literatures [*Denbigh, 1989; Landsberg, 1996; Palti, 1997*]. This third perspective tends to portray the universe as either completely reversible, in the sense that time has no relevant bearing, or as generally irreversible, due to problems of complexity and path-dependency. This gives us three conceptions of irreversibility, what I will call the 'experiential' version generally employed in environmental economics and environmental ethics; an 'illusory' conception in some of the philosophy of science literature, and a 'comprehensive' conception in a second understanding related to the philosophy of science. In the following section I will outline each of these conceptions, and then enquire as to whether the experiential conception, and the ethical consequences that are taken to flow from it, can stand up to a challenge from the other conceptions, particularly the latter.

The Experiential Conception

The 'experiential' conception of irreversibility implies, as the name is intended to suggest, that irreversibility relates to something that human beings actually experience. A defence of the employment of this conception of irreversibility rather than another is given by Krutilla and Fisher, who try to foreclose the very kind of critique of this conception to be offered in this analysis. They say:

> We recognize that for some of our readers, everything is irreversible in the sense that time does not move backward. For others, perhaps including many of our fellow economists, the consequences of any decision (e.g. to develop a natural environment) are reversible given sufficient application of technique and conventional resource inputs. We suggest that neither of these views is particularly helpful in

determining how best to use the resources of a natural environment [*1978: 40*].

Krutilla and Fisher consider either the view that everything is reversible, or the view that all is irreversible, as, even if strictly true, *unhelpful* for the enquiries of ecological economics, which relate to choices that have to be made in the real, sensory world. Instead, (the useful conception of) irreversibility is taken as involving two considerations, both the 'time during which the adverse consequences of an investment decision must be suffered', and the degree to which any restoration and reproduction can be faithful to the original [*Krutilla and Fisher, 1978: 43*]. Clearly, if the answer to the first consideration is 'over a long run' and/or the second is that faithful restoration is impossible, then we are dealing with irreversibility. Alternatively but in very similar vein, irreversibility is said to exist when 'it would cost virtually infinite sums to correct the damage … [or when] we have to tolerate whatever the irreversible damage is for a very long time, perhaps forever' [*Pearce et al., 1989: 9*]. Both of these accounts of irreversibility have an intuitive plausibility – an irreversible change has occurred when something cannot be restored to its previous condition – it is also (unlike the perfectly reversible universe described below) something we actually experience, thus the 'experiential' label.

The 'Illusory' and 'Comprehensive' Conceptions

A second view of irreversibility is that it is an illusion (or at least a partial and misleading perspective), which follows from the ineluctably limited intelligence and subjective experiences of creatures such as human beings. We *experience* time's arrow, we have memories of the past, but not the future. One possible explanation for this is that as 'memory traces laid down in the brain are biochemical, this arrow determines that (1) the biological, (2) the psychological, and (3) the thermodynamic arrows all point in the same direction' [*Landsberg, 1996: 253*]. The determination means that the biological arrow entails that the other arrows appear to go in the same direction to us, but the 'appear' and 'to us' are both important here. Laplace's famous demon (1812) was used to demonstrate that on the assumption of perfect knowledge of all movements, collisions, and velocities at the atomic level, past and future disappear and all events become completely reversible. A being with this information holds the past and the future completely within its view, and the existence of a 'past' and a 'future', an arrow of time, is seen as a function only of a coarse-grained view of the universe and limited information. Einstein expressed a similar view when he wrote to his friend's widow that 'For us convinced physicists the distinction between past, present, and future is an illusion' [*Landsberg, 1996, 252; Palti, 1997: 47*].

Although this view of irreversibility (or rather the lack thereof) makes a distinction between human experience of the universe and that of a being with a peculiarly distinct kind of knowledge, it has come under theoretical challenge from proponents of systems theory and chaos theory [e.g., *Capra, 1997; Gleick, 1996*]. Chaos theory posits non-linear physical developments though time and therefore unknowable past and future states (even to Laplace's demon). Furthermore, Boltzmann's work on understanding future states in terms of probabilities showed that, although there were no physical laws that make reversibility an impossibility, the *probability* of reversal taking place – on the assumption of large numbers of molecules and random motion – is infinitesimally small.[7] Thus we have both an explanation as to why we never *experience* the spontaneous reversal of physical processes such as diffusion and heat transfer, but also an acknowledgement that, strictly speaking, reversibility is never impossible, just improbable to a vast order of magnitude.

There are two reasons why it is not worth pursuing this understanding of irreversibility within environmental ethics, even if we were to assume that it is strictly correct. Firstly, both economic and ethical decision-making is done by and for human beings, who experience time's arrow and possess very limited information about the state of the universe at any particular point. Thus irreversibility exists *for them*. Secondly, because under nearly all conditions the possibilities for the kind of reversibility discussed by Boltzmann are so low that they are not worth considering on a human timescale. On this, I believe that Krutilla and Fisher are right – the view that all decisions are reversible is, even if strictly true, unhelpful to human beings trying to make decisions about how to use, or what attitude to take towards, natural objects.

Boltzmann's work suggests another, indeed opposite, view of irreversibility. This is that we should consider irreversibility as the norm. To put this another way, 'Complete reversibility is not actually attainable in the real world. Irreversibility is the natural state of affairs' [*Denbigh, 1989: 507*]. With regard to the notion of irreversibility used by environmentalists and referred to above, this may well seem as counter-intuitive as the 'all things are reversible' view. The whole point about favouring species preservation over development is that once a species is lost it is lost for good, whereas a development good (a bypass or factory, say) could still be built at a particular spot at any point in the foreseeable future, should society so decide. We still live in a world without the dodo, but we also live in a world *with* a tunnel under the English Channel, despite the fact that this tunnel-building project was commenced and then abandoned at least two times before the tunnel was finally built. Species exterminations are irreversible, whereas non-development decisions are not.

This experiential notion of irreversibility has an understandable appeal. I want in this analysis, however, to employ the more comprehensive notion of irreversibility, which has wider applicability precisely because it treats irreversibility as the normal state of the world. It also, I suggest, shows that the language of irreversibility is inappropriate for helping us to making moral judgements about the use that we should make of natural objects. I take the following description of the conditions necessary for reversibility from Denbigh [*1989: 506*].

> A process[8] is said to be reversible if, and only if, the system which undergoes that process, together with *all parts of its environment which are affected*, can be restored reproducibly to their original states. For example, let the system go from an initial state A, through states B, C etc., to a final state X. The corresponding simultaneous states of the affected environment are α, β, γ etc., up to a final state ω. There is reversibility if it is possible not only for the system to be restored from X to A, but for this reversal to be accomplished by a simultaneous reversal of the affected parts of the environment from ω to α. In short all relevant parts of the universe must be capable of being put back to how they were.

Outside of a set of processes involving infinitesimal changes to both object and environment [*Denbigh, 1989: 507*], which at least approximate reversibility, no physical processes are practicably reversible. Some of these irreversible changes are entropic, some not, but they are sufficiently general that examples are not difficult to imagine. These would include not only the 'usual candidates' for irreversibility – the transfer of heat from warmer object to cooler object; the development of knowledge in the human mind; the release of a concentration of gas into the atmosphere, and the evolutionary process of speciation – but much more besides. It is important to note that it is not a counter-argument to irreversibility in these contexts to point out that, for example, human minds can be robbed of accumulated knowledge through diseases such as Alzheimer's, or that natural species can be exterminated en masse. These events can of course occur, and concern about the latter is a prime motivational element in environmentalism. The point is rather that such 'reverses' can never satisfy the criterion that not only the object but also the object's complete environment have to return from X to A/ω to α. A belief that speciation was truly reversible involves a commitment to the idea that a species can exist without leaving a trace upon the environment in which it has evolved. Absent that assumption, the world in condition X is a substantively different world from the world that existed at W. The elimination of an element, the creation of which resulted in the movement from W to X, results in a further move to Y, not a reversal to W.[9]

The Implications of Comprehensive Irreversibility

Does this comprehensive conception of irreversibility impact upon the attempts made by political ecologists and those engaged in ecological economics to employ the concept in support of environmental policies such as species preservation? What one might call the preservationist 'argument from irreversibility' normally runs along the following lines. If we engage in a process that results, as a foreseeable consequence (intended or unintended) in the destruction of environmental good A (for example, a species), that environmental good can never be recovered once that process has removed it. The process thus results in an irreversible change. If development good B is foregone, and the process does not take place, there is a cost in terms of unrealised development but the non-performance of the process is not irreversible. The process could take place at a future time, or there may be alternative development strategies that can substitute, at least partially, for good B. The irreversible nature of the former type of environmental change should, at least, carry an appropriately heavy weighting in development decisions because (at the very least) it involves the destruction of option-value. According to the axioms of welfare economics, fewer choices (as brought about through this destruction) entails lower levels of welfare.

This consideration is taken as particularly germane not only with regard to the future options of the present generation, but also with respect to the current generation's dealings with generations to come. The assumption of irreversibility in the case of development decisions as against the reversibility of legislation taken to protect the natural environment leads Krutilla and Fisher to suggest that 'Legislative classification of wilderness areas, perhaps with provision to make reclassification more difficult, could then be viewed as partial compensation for the asymmetry [between present and future generations]' [*1978: 69*]. Arguments of this type rely upon the experiential conception of irreversibility outlined above.

Employing the comprehensive conception of irreversibility, however, things appear rather different. The process resulting in extinction will remain the same, but foregoing development good B at time *t* now also has irreversible consequences. The world in which development good B is brought into existence at time *t* will be a *different* world to that in which it is not, that much is merely a commonplace observation. The world either remains in state α or moves to condition β. If development is foregone it remains in α. However, if the society decides at time $t+1$ to undergo the development previously foregone, the world will not then move from α to β, because that is the world in which development occurred at time *t*, instead the world now moves from α to γ, a world where development has taken place at time $t+1$. The time period that elapses between *t* and $t+1$ can (by assumption) occur in either of two states – with-development or without-development. The point is that world γ is not world β. It never could be because the account of the universe necessary to describe world β completely will never offer a complete description of world γ.

An environmentalist might still want to respond to this with a shrug of the shoulders and a 'so what?' A world where an oil-field is developed in ten years' time will look pretty indistinguishable from a world with the same oil-field developed ten years ago, whereas a world without a species remains a world without that species, period. This comprehensive notion of irreversibility carries no moral weight, it might be suggested, against the experiential version used by environmentalists. Before we can accept such an argument, however, we need to think about the distribution of costs and benefits involved in development decision, and the way they impact upon individuals. This will lead us to a discussion of substitutability, compensatability, and justice in the distribution of non-basic goods.[10]

Irreversibility, Justice and Environmental Goods

There is an important distinction to be made here between basic and non-basic goods, and this across two dimensions. First, even those who claim that some environmental goods such as the preservation of species (assuming that such a thing is a good) are *not* a matter of justice [*Miller, 1999a: 196; Miller, 1999b*], allow that this is because such goods are not basic in the Rawlsian sense [*Rawls, 1971*]. By contrast, there are taken to be a list of environmental goods that *are* considered to be basic and thus part of the metric of justice. So, any environmentalist claim that justice demands goods such as preservation of natural objects will have to confront this distinction.

Secondly, the distinction between basic and non-basic goods has important implications for the relationship between substitutability and compensatability. David Pearce et al. note that 'irreversibility is an extreme form of non-substitutability. Once lost, no man-made capital can recreate a species, for example' [*1989: 38*]. Dobson draws a connection between substitutability and compensatability, thus 'the organizing point behind this [irreversible nature] conception of sustainability is precisely that some forms and features of irreversible nature are not substitutable, and *therefore* not compensable in anything more than an attenuated sense' [*1999: 50*, emphasis added]. Here we need, however, to be careful not to confuse substitutability, as a functional concept, with compensatability, as a welfare concept. It is true that, with regard to basic goods, non-substitutability often implies non-compensatability. This is most famously illustrated in the bread and water example.[11] If I am starving, no amount of water will compensate me for a lack of bread, precisely because bread and water are not functionally substitutable. Similarly a lorry-load of bread will not compensate me the lack of a glass of water when I have a raging thirst. Thus for such basic goods Dobson's 'therefore' holds. Things look rather different, however, when we come to non-basic goods and the relationship between substitutability and compensatability, and this is because of the distinction between a functional and a welfare concept.

Take, for an example, someone with Miller's tiger-preserving preferences. This person values the existence of tigers in the wild, just knowing that they are there is sufficient to increase this person's sense of well-being, s/he does not actually have to see them. If tigers were to be exterminated as a species, this person would suffer the concomitant welfare loss. However, unlike with the bread-and-water example, this person is perfectly capable of functioning absent the tigers, s/he merely functions at a lower level of welfare. Now, even if we assume that it is true that nothing can *substitute* for a tiger in a functional sense, as long as *some* other good is capable of increasing this person's welfare, then it is false to say that *because* tigers are non-substitutable their loss cannot be compensated for. If this person also gains welfare from a greater stock of wealth, s/he will have an indifference curve between wealth and tigers, such that we can (assuming the indifference curve is 'normal') supply him or her with wealth to the point where s/he is indifferent between gaining this increased stock of wealth and knowing that tigers still exist. It is possible under this scenario to compensate the welfare loss for tiger extinction with the provision of wealth – even though it is also true that functionally, for this person, wealth and tigers could never substitute one for the other. Thus for non-basic goods it is not true to claim, without a confusion of functional substitution and welfare compensation, that good x has no substitute and *therefore* it is not compensatable.

The above is by way of a preamble to a consideration of the role of irreversibility in the question of justice and environmental goods. I want to accept for the sake of argument (and also because I believe it to be the case) that there is a class of basic environmental goods, the distribution of which is a matter for principles of justice. The less certain and thus more interesting question is whether the possession of the character of irreversibility can render a demand for a non-basic environmental good such as species-preservation a demand of justice, either between members of an existing generation or intergenerationally.

To take the present generation problem first,[13] if nature-preserving preferences are not taken to have a claim in justice on the grounds that the goods they concern are non-basic, absent irreversibility, can the invocation of irreversibility add anything to the demand? In Miller's treatment of this topic the idea that preservation preferences can make demands grounded in justice is dismissed, instead these preferences have to be fed into the democratic political process along any other preferences, including those for development. Irreversibility does not enter the picture [*Miller, 1999b*]. If we introduce the experiential version of irreversibility, it might well make a difference to the weighting given to the various preferences for non-basic goods. Irreversibility might, for example, amplify the loss of welfare that accompanies the loss of the preferred good. Tiger-lovers are denied their preferred good, and furthermore know that, even if they could persuade the rest of society to hold tiger-loving preferences also, their preferred good will never be restored to them. Those with development preferences know that if they can persuade the rest of society to hold their preferences, development can still go ahead. We might say that, if they lose out, the tiger preferrers are placed in a position that is, strictly speaking, hopeless with regard to their preferred good, whereas the development preferrers are not. Thus the condition of hopelessness should add some weight to preferences when development decisions are taken, otherwise tiger-lovers are being treated unjustly.

According to the 'comprehensive' conception of irreversibility a decision either for development or for preservation is irreversible. The question is, does this matter, or should we, along with Krutilla and Fisher just dismiss it as an unreasonable conception? We can begin to address this question by asking ourselves what the implications of the comprehensive conception are. One aspect of decision-making that this conception highlights is path-dependency. The corollary of the insight that the 'relevant pieces of the universe' cannot be put back together is that outcomes are path-dependent. Particular decision points come around because they have a particular history, and alternative histories that we can imagine but have not experienced would be highly unlikely to result in the same decision point. Path-dependency in turn highlights how the problem of irreversibility can do work on both sides of the development/preservation equation. The insight that irreversibility is not a property only of natural objects is not new [*Holland, 1999: 54, contra Turner and Pearce, 1993*]. Holland's insight that a Norman church is no easier to *replace* than an ancient forest is true, (although it may be easier to replicate). The comprehensive notion of irreversibility, along with path-dependency clarifies the implications of this. Once we accept that the destruction of a Norman church is as impossible to reverse as the destruction of a nature habitat or a species, we begin to see the logic of the comprehensive conception. Irreversibility is not true only of the Norman church, but of *any* particular human development. This just has to be true unless a category difference can be demonstrated between a Norman church and (say) a Bauhaus building or the Mona Lisa and, therefore, less beloved developments such as a chemical factory or motorway.

There is, I suspect, a tendency for environmentalists to think of developments such as these latter as reversible because they are not valued – why should we care any more for a motorway built in 1970 than one built in 2000? But value cannot determine reversibility or lack thereof in this way. We can not replace a Norman church because a church that looked in every respect the same but was built in 1990 would not be a Norman church. It is logically no different to argue that only a motorway built in 1970 can *be* that particular motorway. Holland's Norman church example highlights the importance of the difference between development at time t and development at time t+1, because the gap between the two time periods is large in terms of human experience. Once that principle is established, however, it *has* to be generalised if one is to avoid imposing arbitrary distinctions based upon the lapse of time since development.

So, all we have established so far is that irreversibility is not a property of only those things that environmentalists happen to value, be they old buildings or ancient forests. How does that impact upon the decision as to whether to develop or preserve? It shows that the both sides of this dilemma are path-dependent and irreversible in two different but related senses. First, we are faced at the decision point with (at least) two possible futures, and (because the relevant parts of the universe will be rearranged and never return to where they were), *both* (or all) of those futures are irreversible. The condition of the world in (say) ten years time will be path-dependent upon the result of the development decision. Secondly, the arrival at a particular development/preservation decision is itself path dependent. For example, because national economies have certain functional dependencies that are a result of the way they have developed, non-development in one area will often entail compensating development elsewhere, the impact of which also needs to be taken into account. The USA is an oil-dependent economy because of its development history. It may be better in the long-run if it changes its patterns of energy dependency, but oil dependency cannot just be reversed. As Stern notes, there is a significant body of economic literature in which 'Economic development is seen as an evolutionary process that is by its nature irreversible … system history is relevant to current and future possibilities' [*1997: 199*]. If resistance to the opening up of the Arctic National Wildlife Refuge in Alaska to oil companies is successful, for example (*The Observer,* 20 Aug. 2000, pp.10–11), then alternative oil development will take place elsewhere. That development will impose its own set of costs and benefits, and for those people affected these will be non-reversible. This needs to be taken into account when this decision is made. A world where the Alaskan field is opened up at time *t* is different to a world at which it is opened up at *t+1* is different to a world where it is never opened up. On this view there is no reversibility in any of these cases. It is not clear, then, that irreversibility adds any weight to the preservationist case on this account.

The story is similar with regard to tiger-preservation story in India (see Jayal, this volume). The political decision to protect tiger habitats from agricultural development has led to particular patterns of behaviour and socio-economic developments in the park areas. The people who live around the parks live with the results of a history in which tiger-protection measures have been undertaken, and nothing about this history can ever be 'reversed' even if the parks were opened up tomorrow for agriculture. Again it needs to be stressed that this is not intended as a circuitous argument against such preservationist measures. It is merely to point out that the highly visible non-reversibility of their extinction is not in and of itself something that distinguishes tiger-preservation from tiger-destruction. There may well be, none the less, very good reasons for preserving tigers in the wild.

In the intergenerational case it should be apparent that similar considerations apply. On the experiential notion of irreversibility there are certain choices we can make as the present generation that close down options for future generations in a 'hard' way [*Barry, 1977*]. For example if we completely consume a fossil-fuel resource, leave radioactive contamination, or exterminate species, it inevitably closes down options for future generation as these processes are irreversible, and this irreversibility is taken to have moral significance. On the comprehensive conception of irreversibility, this is no less true of decisions to preserve species and not to develop, or to conserve fossil fuels and switch to renewable energy resources. Whatever reasons there may be to engage or otherwise in particular actions and processes, *irreversibility* is not a concept that can be used to make a moral distinction between one and another. It should be noted that this does not entail that we should be uncaring about leaving future generations with a world in which we would expect them to have very low levels of welfare. What it does mean is that, as the conclusion to this paper points out, we should discuss the fate of future generations in terms of the appropriateness of different irreversible options.

Irreversibility and the Precautionary Principle

Even if irreversibility can add nothing to the moral calculus involved in making development decisions, can it not help decide what it is prudent to do, what levels of investment, production, pollution and so on are sustainable on a long term basis? There is of course a large literature on sustainability, and a significant amount of it does invoke the notion of irreversibility as a relevant factor in decision making. There are disagreements amongst environmental economists as to the point at which an 'irreversibility constraint' should actually affect decisions about investment and consumption [*Arrow and Fisher, 1974; Gollier et al., 2000; Henry, 1974; Ulph and Ulph, 1997*]. Ulph and Ulph in particular are sceptical as to the magnitude of an irreversibility constraint and even its direction, finding that at times an expectation of increasing information would actually lead to more exploitation of a resource now. By contrast Gollier, Jullien and Treich [*2000*] find that, on the Bayesian assumption that changing information can alter beliefs about risk, irreversibility and scientific uncertainty should lead to stronger prevention measures being taken now (under a set of 'restrictive but plausible' conditions). A more typical line from environmental writers comes from John O'Neill, who notes that 'There are good principles that govern our dealings with the future – that we minimize resource depletion, that we avoid irreversible changes' [*1993: 59*] and 'two old fashioned strategies – "mini-max", and "avoid irreversible changes" – provide principles that apply ... to conditions of epistemological uncertainty' [*1993: 148*]. In similar vein Robin Attfield says that the precautionary principle 'conveys that action to prevent irreversible or serious damage should be undertaken even in the absence of scientific consensus' [*1999: 186*]. Bulte and van Kooten refer to the 'safe minimum standard', which 'dictates that where irreversibilities exist (loss of a species), the irreversibility should be avoided unless the cost is prohibitively high' [*2000: 118*].

The point, however, is that 'avoiding all irreversible losses is an impossible objective' [*Dobson, 1999: 48*], and that this insight needs to be taken seriously. Once we accept that avoiding irreversible *change* (whether it be 'damage', 'loss', or 'benefit') is impossible, the question we have to ask ourselves is different: we now have to ask, what *sort* of irreversible change do we want to engage in? This may be no bad thing, if it forces environmentalists to stop using irreversibility as a kind of 'thou shalt not pass' line in the sand ('avoid irreversible change') and instead we ask ourselves on what grounds some forms of irreversible change might be preferable to others. As Holland suggests, the call to prevent irreversible change is on a par with a call to bring a halt to evolution, natural extinctions have been an integral part of the process of the history of life on earth [*Holland, 1999: 54*]. Furthermore, 'since it is of the essence of natural processes that they are dynamic, no freeze-framing programme of any particular state of the natural world could possibly be construed as the conservation of nature' [*Holland, 1997: 128*]. The call to avoid irreversible change is a call to freeze-frame nature, as all evolutionary change is by its nature irreversible. Again, such an insight is not intended to dispel the idea that at times a precautionary principle in development may be appropriate (nor should it have that result). It does suggest that 'irreversibility' is not the appropriate driver for the application of such a principle.

Conclusion

This analysis set out to enquire whether a conception of irreversibility taken from a literature in the philosophy of science could shed light on the problem of irreversibility as applied, from time to time, in environmental ethics. Although the 'comprehensive irreversibility' conception is dismissed by Krutilla and Fisher, I believe it does serve to throw some light upon problems in environmental ethics associated with irreversibility. Two points in particular stand out: (1) irreversibility is not a unique feature of the type of objects in the world environmentalists tend to favour such as species and ancient monuments, and (2) any demand to 'prevent irreversible change', (or even to prevent irreversible change 'where feasible') is a demand for the impossible, as well as a demand for the petrification of evolutionary development at a single point. The comprehensive conception of irreversibility entails that most changes are effectively irreversible, and this has obvious implications for decisions to forego development as well as to develop. That certain types of irreversibility change are more visible to us than others is not in itself a reason to give them privileged status. What we need to look for instead are reasons to prefer one sort of irreversible change to another

Does the contention of comprehensive irreversibility completely destroy the applicability of the experiential notion to environmental problems? It does demonstrate that a comprehensive understanding of irreversibility entails that it is a mistake to discuss a phenomenon such as species loss as if it were irreversible in a way that other processes were not. That is, it is unhelpful to discuss these environmental processes in terms of irreversibility. The non-reversibility of decisions taken not to develop at a particular time, and the non-reversibility of the destruction of human-made objects should not be treated more lightly merely because they are less visible.

None of this, however, alters the observation earlier in this paper that we live in a world without a dodo but with a channel tunnel, or that if we all develop dodo-preferring preferences tomorrow there would be little we could do about it. Nor does it entail that an investment decision is not legitimately affected by the degree of difficulty involved in switching that investment into something else. In this regard 'irreversibility' is probably a more appropriate language for discussing the optimisation of investment decisions, the retention of option value, or risk-taking, than for an investigation of the ethical implications of environmental change. Economic decision-making of this kind is more amenable to a merely technical language, such that 'irreversibility' can have a particular meaning for economists. But for environmental ethics these phenomena need to be articulated in a different vocabulary than that of irreversibility, which can be misleading with regard to the *morality* of environmental decision-making. There are reasons applicable to the question of whether we should prefer one type of irreversible change to another, and our inability to re-create a particular entity, such as a species, can of course be a very important example of such a reason. However, to discuss this in terms of our inability to 'create again' more accurately brings out the difference between the dodo and the channel tunnel than the language of irreversibility, in that it does not suggest that creating an entity anew is equivalent to a return to a prior state of affairs. The language in which we choose to fight the ethical battles about conservation and development is important, and the language of irreversibility is unfortunately inappropriate for this task.

NOTES

1. For example 'for the problem of global warming, the irreversibility constraint is our inability to emit a negative quantity of greenhouse gas, i.e. to use energy to remove the excess gas' [*Gollier et al., 2000;* also *Chevé, 2000*]. Also, for Pearce *et al.*, 'once lost, no man-made capital can recreate a species'[*1989: 38*].
2. An extensive treatment is given in Elliot [*1997*]. Questions of authenticity inevitably arise in discussions such as the one engaged with in this analysis.
3. There are of course controversies over the ontological status of species, see Sheryl Breen's contribution in this volume. There are many books and papers that cover the need to prevent species loss. [e.g., *Bilderbeek, 1993; Ehrlich, 1990; Myers, 1999; Peters and Myers, 1991; Wilson, 1992*]. For a more sceptical view of the signiflcance.and magnitude of species loss see Simon [*1995*].
4. This distinction is however contingent rather than universal. Were it to become possible for genetic scientists to recreate extinct species, then the grounds for an anti-extinction argument would have to rest on authenticity rather than (experiential) irreversibility. Indeed, as I make the very final revisions of this essay news comes on the radio this morning that the very first attempt is to be made to clone an officially extinct species (a type of goat found in Spain), the last specimen of which (a female) died in 2000. If this is successful, it strengthens the argument of this analysis that 'irreversibility' is not an appropriate criterion for drawing ethical distinctions. What is or is not 'reversible', in the experiential sense, is contingent upon human technology. If extinction becomes reversible in this sense then environmentalists will have to employ an argument from authenticity instead to press for the preservation of species.
5. Holland [*1999*], does note this quality of irreversibility, and draws out some of its implications. It is my contention that his insight has more significant implications for an irreversibility defence of natural objects than he suggests.
6. As claimed by Pearce *et al.* [*1989: 43*], Turner and Pearce [*1993: 181*], Krutilla and Fisher [*1978: 39*].

7. A good example of how (even moderately large) numbers impact upon the possibility of reversibility is given by Landsberg (who takes the example in turn from Shallis). 'We take a pack of 52 cards, which is a tiny number compared with the millions of molecules even in a cubic centimetre of typical gas. The probability of regaining the original arrangement of the cards after a proper shuffle is nevertheless tiny ... If every person on earth were to shuffle a pack once every second, it would still take statistically much longer than the age of the universe to come to the original arrangement (10^{50} as against 10^{11} years)' [*1996: 249*].
8. It is important to be clear that irreversibility is a property of processes, not 'things'. The process we are most concerned with in this case is that of extinction.
9. Holland suggests, interestingly, that species extinction (often taken as the paradigmatic case of irreversibility) in fact demonstrates the *reversibility* of the processes of evolution and speciation. This demonstrates how a change of perspective can change how the world appears. However, on this conception of irreversibility Holland's conjecture would be incorrect because speclation is not understood as a reversible process. The cloning of extinct species (see note 4) is also most accurately seen as a new development, rather than a reversal to a previous order.
10. Some account needs to be given here with regard to the presentation of the problem in this way. I am making a distinction between 'basic' and 'non-basic' goods in the Rawlsian sense. That is, basic goods are those goods (referred to in Rawls as 'primary') that could reasonably be expected to form part of the 'thin' conception of the good. That is, are likely to be desired by individuals even when they are placed behind the veil of ignorance and therefore absent knowledge of their comprehensive conception of the good. It seems to me that whilst some environmental goods (breathable air, potable water) would certainly count as basic in this sense, but demands for the preservation of particular species would not. I could not know I had tiger-preserving preferences until I emerge from behind the veil. Should I emerge as an indigenous subsistence farmer in India I may well have quite the opposite preference. The interesting question is whether the constraint of Irreversibility can add weight to the tiger-preservers demands even though tiger preservation is a non-basic good. I leave aside here the question of whether we have direct obligations to tigers in the manner set out by, for example, Taylor [*1986*], and focus instead on an implicit understanding that the demands of justice concern human welfare.
11. See, for example, Stern [*1997: 207*].
12. This would not be true of lexicographic preferences. These entail that beyond a certain point a supply of tigers in the wild would always be preferred to wealth. For a discussion of lexicographic preferences see Stem [*1997: 203–5*].
13. The question of justice between members of the present generation is taken by Miller to be logically prior to the question of intergenerational justice [*1999b: 153*]. If, however, the structural differences in the relationships between members of the present generation on the one band, and those between the present and future generations on the other (most famously with regard to the possibility of reciprocity) make a significant difference, then Miller's claim is almost certainly false.

REFERENCES

Arrow, K.J. and A.C. Fisher (1974), 'Environmental Preservation, Uncertainty, and Irreversibility', *Quarterly Journal Of Economics*, Vol.88, pp.312–19.

Attfield, Robin (1999) *The Ethics of the Global Environment*, Edinburgh: Edinburgh University Press.

Barry, Brian (1977), 'Justice Between Generations', in P.M.S. Hacker and J. Raz (eds.) *Law, Morality, and Society*, Oxford: Clarendon Press, pp.268–84.

Bilderbeek, Simone (1993), 'Biodiversity as Political Game', *Politics and the Life Sciences*, Vol.12, No.2, pp.265–72.

Bulte, Erwin and G.C. van Kooten, (2000), 'Economic Science, Endangered Species, and Biodiversity Loss', *Conservation Biology*, Vol.14, No.1, pp.113–19.

Capra, Fritjof (1997), *The Web of Life*, London: Flamingo.

Chevé, Morgane (2000), 'Irreversibility of Pollution Accumulation: New Implications for Sustainable Endogenous Growth', *Environmental and Resource Economics*, Vol.16, pp.93–104.

Denbigh, K.O. (1989), 'The Many Faces of Irreversibility', *The British Journal for the Philosophy of Science*, Vol.40, pp.501–18.

Dobson, Andrew (1998), *Justice and the Environment*, Oxford: Oxford University Press.

Dobson, Andrew (ed.) (1999), *Fairness and Futurity*, Oxford: Oxford University Press.

Ehrlich, Paul (1990), 'Habitats in Crisis: Why We Should Care About the Loss of Species', *Forest Ecology and Management*, Vol.35, pp.5–11.

Elliot, Robert (1997), *Faking Nature*, London: Routledge.

Foster, John (ed.) (1997), *Valuing Nature?*, London: Routledge.

Gleick, James (1997), *Chaos*, London: Minerva.

Gollier, Christian, Jullien, Bruno, and Nicolas Treich (2000), 'Scientific Progress and Irreversibility: an Economic Interpretation of the "Precautionary Principle"', *Journal of Public Economics*, Vol.75, pp.229–53.

Goodin, Robert (1992), *Green Political Theory*, Cambridge: Polity.

Henry, C. (1974), 'Investment Decisions Under Uncertainty: the Irreversibility Effect', *American Economic Review*, Vol.64, pp.1006–12.

Holland, Alan (1997), 'Substitutability: Or Why Strong Sustainability is Weak and Absurdly Strong Sustainability is not Absurd', in Foster [*1997: 119–34*].

Holland, Alan (1999), 'Sustainability: Should We Start From Here?' in Dobson [*1999: 46–68*].

Johansson-Stenman, Olof (1998), 'The Importance of Ethics in Environmental Economics with a Focus on Existence Values', *Environmental and Resource Economics*, Vol.11, Nos.3–4, pp.429–42.

Krutilla, John V. and Anthony C. Fisher (1978), *The Economics of Natural Environment*, Baltimore, MD: Johns Hopkins University Press.

Landsberg, Peter T. (1996), 'Irreversibility and Time's Arrow', *Dialectica*, Vol.50, No.4, pp.247–58.

Miller, David (1999a), *Principles of Social Justice*, Cambridge, MA: Harvard University Press.

Miller, David (1999b), 'Social Justice and Environmental Goods', in Dobson (ed.) [*1999*].

Myers, Norman (1999), 'What We Must Do to Counter the Biotic Holocaust', *International Wildlife*, March/April, pp.31–9.

O'Neill, John (1993), *Ecology, Policy, and Politics*, London: Routledge.

O'Neill, John (1997), 'Value Pluralism, Incommensurability and Institutions', in Foster [*1997: 75–88*].

Palti, Elías José (1997), 'Time, Modernity, and Time Irreversibility', *Philosophy & Social Criticism*, Vol.23, No.5, pp.27–62.

Pearce, David, Markandya, Anil and Edward Barbier (1989), *Blueprint for a Green Economy*, London: Earthscan.

Peters, Robert L. and LP. Myers (1991), 'Preserving Biodiversity in a Changing Climate', *Issues in Science and Technology*, Winter, 1991/2, pp.66–72.

Rawls, John (1971), *A Theory of Justice*, Oxford: Oxford University Press.

Simon, Julian L. (1995), 'Species Loss Could be a Statistical Shell Game', *Forum for Applied Research and Public Policy*, Spring, pp.106–10.

Stern, David I. (1997), 'Limits to Substitution and Irreversibility in Production and Consumption: A Neoclassical Interpretation of Ecological Economics', *Ecological Economics*, Vol.21, pp.197–215.

Taylor, Paul (1986), *Respect for Nature*. Princeton; Princeton University Press.

Turner, R.K. and D. Pearce, 'Sustainable Economic Development: Economic and Ethical Principles', in E. Barbier (ed.), *Economics and Ecology*, London: Chapman & Hall.

Ulph, Alistair and David Ulph (1997), 'Global Warming, Irreversibility and Learning', *The Economic Journal*, Vol.107, pp.636–50.

Wilson, E.O. (1992) 'Living with Nature', *US News and World Report*, 30 Nov. 1992, pp.61–7.

Abstracts

The Urban Blind Spot in Environmental Ethics
ANDREW LIGHT

In the past 30 years environmental ethics and political ecology have emerged as two of the most vibrant and exciting areas of applied philosophy. Several journals and hundreds of books testify to their growing importance inside and outside philosophical circles. But surprisingly very little has ever been said, in particular, by environmental ethicists about cities, and what has been written is largely negative. This contribution offers an explanation for why the urban environment has been ignored in environmental ethics; second, provides a series of ecological and social arguments for why urban issues cannot be overlooked in a complete environmental ethic; and finally, offers an example of the sorts of issues that an expanded environmental ethic, inclusive of urban environments, would need to focus on.

Ecocentrism, Weighted Interests and Property Theory
SHERYL D. BREEN

As a political and ecological philosophy, ecocentrism argues that nature in systemic terms exists for its own sake, not for the benefit of humans. The core environmental value at risk is the holistic wellness of ecosystems. Ecocentrists have demanded an ideological revolution based on dynamic ecosystem relations, not incremental policy reforms. In this regard they have been vigorous in their rejection of dominant Western ideas of property. Unfortunately they have been less devoted to the development of an alternative ecocentric theory of property. This paper clarifies ecocentrism's theoretical foundations and argues for an ecocentric theory of property based on the concept of interests.

What's Wrong with Ecofeminism?
LUCY SARGISSON

This essay aims to establish that feminism and ecologism, when linked, have a potential that exceeds the sum of its parts. Feminism and ecologism as bodies of thought meet most frequently in the field of ecofeminism. This is not the most exciting or profitable terrain on which they can address each other. Rather, feminism and ecologism can meet on two coexisting levels. The first concerns matters of content - specifically, their shared concern with certain issues and concepts. The second is their respective natures: both have emancipatory and utopian potential.

Balancing Political and Ecological Values
NIRAJA GOPAL JAYAL

This account makes the case for a closer examination of the view that the anthropocentric ethic is adequately accommodative of human interests and the assumption, following from this, that it is capable of accommodating specifically political values such as justice and rights. Some contradictions between ecological values and political values are identified, and ways of reconciling these are explored. The third world provides the most obvious exemplar of how environmental impacts are often inequitably distributed. The case of official conservationist policy in India illustrates this. Human specificities need to be worked into any adequate anthropocentric ethic.

New Ethics for Old? Or, How (Not) to Think About Future Generations
TERENCE BALL

Radical environmentalists often decry and dismiss as outmoded and dangerous the 'western' ethic of individualism, of freedom and autonomy, of individual rights. They hope to replace this ethic with one that is post-individualist and non-Western, and either radically new or old and native-indigenous. Only then, they say, will the well-being of the planet and its present and future inhabitants be protected from the predation of the present generation. I argue that this view is unrealistic as well as unnecessary, in as much as western liberal-individualist discourse contains at least some of the moral and conceptual resources out of which a responsible environmental ethic can be constructed.

Ten Commandments of How to Fail in an Environmental Campaign
AVNER DE-SHALIT

When environmentalists fail political scientists often relate these failures to structural difficulties or to the 'system'. But are these activists responsible for these failures as well? Analysing several cases in which environmental activists failed to persuade the public or the government (most cases from Israel, but some from the UK as well) this paper asks: what is common to all these cases? I find ten 'rules', which are transcribed as the 'ten commandments of how to fail as an environmental activist'.

Three Conceptions of Irreversibility and Environmental Ethics: Some Problems
MATHEW HUMPHREY

One objection to certain environmental changes such as species loss is that, unlike many other changes, they are irreversible and so should be avoided, where feasible. This paper examines three ways of conceptualising irreversibility, and suggests that the 'experiential' version favoured by environmental ethicists is misleading on a number of grounds. A 'comprehensive' conception of irreversibility demonstrates that irreversible change is a far more general phenomenon than has been acknowledged in environmental ethics. Irreversibility is shown to be an inappropriate conceptual language for discussing the ethics of environmental decisions. We require a set of principles for decisions involving different forms of irreversible change.

Notes on Contributors

Terence Ball is Professor of Political Science at Arizona State University, USA. He is the author of *Rousseau's Ghost: a Novel* (1998) and *Reappraising Political Theory* (1998). He is also co-editor (with Joyce Appleby) of *Thomas Jefferson: Political Writings* (1999) and (with Richard Bellamy) of *The Cambridge History of Twentieth Century Political Thought* (2001).

Sheryl Breen is Instructor in the Department of Political Science, St. Olaf College, Northfield, Minnesota, USA. She is also a small-acreage farmer and former journalist who remains active in environmental, agricultural and land-use issues.

Mathew Humphrey is a Lecturer in Political Theory at the University of Nottingham, UK. He has published various papers on environmental political philosophy, and has a forthcoming book on the philosophy and politics of nature preservation (Oxford University Press, 2001).

Niraja Jayal is Associate Professor at the Centre for Political Studies, Jawaharlal Nehru University, New Delhi, India. Her chief area of academic interest is the intersection of political theory and Indian politics. Her most recent book is *Democracy and the State: Welfare, Secularism and Development* (Oxford University Press, 1999).

Andrew Light is Assistant Professor of Environmental Philosophy, and Director, Environmental Conservation Education Program at New York University, USA. He is editor of *Social Ecology after Bookchin* (Guilford, 2000), and co-editor (with Eric Katz) of *Environmental Pragmatism* (Routledge, 1996), and (with Eric Katz and David Rothenberg) of *Beneath the Surface: Critical Essays in the Philosophy of Deep Ecology* (MIT Press, 2000).

Lucy Sargisson is a Lecturer in Politics at the University of Nottingham, UK. She works on utopias and is the author of *Contemporary Feminist Utopianism* (Routledge, 1996) and *Utopian Bodies and the Politics of Transgression* (Routledge, 2000).

Avner de-Shalit is Professor of Political Theory at the Hebrew University of Jerusalem, Israel, and an Associate Fellow of the Oxford Centre for Environment, Ethics, and Society, Mansfield College, Oxford, UK. He is the author of *Why Posterity Matters* (Routledge, 1995) and *The Environment: Between Theory and Practice* (Oxford University Press, 2000).

Index